BUSINESS IN THE CONTEMPORARY WORLD

Edited by

Herbert L. Sawyer
Bentley College

UNIVERSITY
PRESS OF
AMERICA

Lanham • New York • London

Business
in the
Contemporary
World

To the Memory of my Parents

ACKNOWLEDGEMENTS

I am grateful to Dr. Tony H. Bonaparte, Vice President for Academic Affairs at Bentley College, for having asked me to undertake this project, which involves both the current volume and a forthcoming journal. The relationship between the book and the journal is described by Dr. Gregory H. Adamian, President of Bentley College, in his Foreword to this collection. President Adamian has been a source of encouragement and support for the project since its inception, and I deeply appreciate his commitment to the endeavor.

My colleague at Bentley, Professor David Honick, read the entire manuscript with the greatest attention to detail, and made numerous suggestions, almost all of which have been incorporated. I must also add that his efforts were made with such a generosity of spirit that I take great pleasure in thanking him for his help. A second Bentley colleague, Professor Tony Buono, read both the introduction and conclusion, and improved them markedly through his suggestions. Scotty Gibson pored over all of the contributions and helped to bring to the collection an appropriate consistency, without doing violence to the preferences of individual authors. Finally, I owe much to Mary Trimble, a superb secretary, who has been a partner in earlier projects. As in the past, she has put up with my mistakes and last minute changes with grace and good will as she has sheparded the manuscript through its several phases. I am in her debt.

CONTENTS

FOREWORD

Bentley College is privileged to sponsor this book, a probing exploration of an important subject by distinguished authors. The purpose of this collection of articles is to present fresh insights into ways in which business activity influences other sectors of society and vice versa, thereby effecting significant change. Given the cardinal importance of the corporation in society and the accelerating rate at which change is occurring in the contemporary world, it is imperative to expand and deepen understanding of reciprocal influences between the corporation and other institutions. Many would argue that currently this is not being done in as comprehensive, profound and systematic a way as it should be.

The present volume approaches that task by focusing on the corporation in the context of several specific issues: business and education; management-labor relations; business and the American constitutional system; business, democratic values and their projection abroad; the global competitiveness of American business; the relationship between U.S. commercial and national security interests; business and global communications; business and the phenomenal development of technology; and business and leadership. Prominent authors from the academic, governmental and religious communities, some of whom are, or have been, closely involved with the corporate world, analyze these issues from the perspectives of public policy, business administration, sociology, technology, and international affairs (political, economic and military). The editor, in stepping back from the specific issues, and in integrating the authors' analyses, provides, in his conclusion, a sense of the intricate nature and magnitude of the challenge confronting us as we attempt to give direction to powerful, interconnected forces shaping the present and the future.

The foregoing alone would justify the current project. But such an endeavor, by its very nature, is an ongoing one. This book, therefore, has the additional purpose of introducing a new, multidisciplinary journal to be published by Bentley College, beginning in October 1988. That journal, under the editorship of Professor H. L. Sawyer, will regularly explore the kinds of issues so perceptively analyzed in this volume, as well as other reciprocal relationships. The new publication, because it will carry on what has been initiated here, will also be entitled "Business in the Contemporary World." The importance of the undertaking and the broad support that it enjoys are reflected in the stature and diversity of the journal's editorial board, listed below.

It is most appropriate that an institution such as Bentley, a college of business, provide a home for a journal of this kind. Business schools

ix

have a special obligation to be concerned with broad societal values that should, ideally, guide behavior.   "Business in the Contemporary World" is one of the ways in which Bentley College will be fulfilling its obligation in this regard.

Gregory H. Adamian, President
Bentley College
Waltham, Massachusetts

April 1988

BUSINESS IN THE CONTEMPORARY WORLD

Editorial Board

CONTRIBUTORS

JOHN B. ANDERSON was the Independent candidate for President of the United States in 1980 and a member of the U.S. House of Representatives, 1961-1978. Among his publications are <u>Between Two Worlds: A Congressman's Choice</u> and <u>Vision and Betrayal in America</u>.

CHARLES H. FERGUSON is Research Associate at the M.I.T. Center for Technology, Policy, and Industrial Development. He is author of "High Technology Entrepreneurialism and U.S. Competitiveness: A Reply to George Gilder," <u>Harvard Business Review</u> (forthcoming).

ALEX INKELES is Professor of Sociology and Professor of Education, Stanford University; and Senior Fellow, Hoover Institution. Among his books are <u>Exploring Individual Modernity</u> and <u>Becoming Modern: Individual Change in Six Developing Countries</u>.

ROSABETH MOSS KANTER, Class of 1960 Professor of Business Administration, Harvard University, is author of <u>Creating the Future: The Massachusetts Comeback and Its Promise for America</u> (with Michael Dukakis), <u>Men and Women of the Corporation</u>, and other works.

LAWRENCE J. KORB is Director, Center for Public Policy and Education at the Brookings Institution, and has held senior positions in government, academe and business. Included among his numerous books is <u>The Joint Chiefs of Staff: The First Twenty-Five Years</u>.

DONALD E. NUECHTERLEIN is Professor of International Relations at the Federal Executive Institute. His publications include <u>America Overcommitted: U.S. National Interests in the 1980s</u> and <u>Thailand and the Struggle for Southeast Asia</u>.

DAVID RIESMAN, Professor of Sociology emeritus at Harvard, has been elected to, among other organizations, the American Academy of Arts and Sciences. His many works include <u>The Lonely Crowd</u> and <u>The Academic Enterprise in an Era of Rising Student Consumerism</u>.

LEON H. SULLIVAN, Pastor, Zion Baptist Church in Philadelphia, has been active over the past four decades in community affairs from the local to the international level. Among his numerous writings are <u>Build Brother Build</u> and <u>Alternatives to Despair</u>.

EDWARD WENK, JR. was on the science policy staffs of Presidents Kennedy, Johnson and Nixon, and has held a joint appointment in Engineering and Public Affairs at the University of Washington. His latest work is <u>Tradeoffs: Imperatives of Choice in a High-Tech World</u>.

ROBERT S. WOOD is the Dean of the Center for Naval Warfare Studies and the Nimitz Professor of National Security and Foreign Affairs at the Naval War College. Among his several books are <u>The Process of International Organization</u> and <u>France in the World Community</u>.

INTRODUCTION

The centrality of business corporations in capitalist societies is far more than an ideological concept. It is also a powerful reality. That reality manifests itself in the ways in which corporations influence other sectors of society, and vice versa, thereby effecting or frustrating significant societal change.

Several sets of relationships in this regard are obvious: business and government; business, education, labor and management; business and technology; and business and foreign affairs. Many other relationships--some bilateral, some much more complex--can and should be identified, but this collection of essays addresses only those aforementioned. The book, thus, does not pretend to be a comprehensive exploration of the enormously intricate network of linkages between corporations, other institutions, forces, change (positive and negative), and stagnation. Moreover, it is self-evident that no single book could analyze exhaustively even the relationships herein addressed.

Nonetheless, this collection does represent a beginning towards the development of what ideally would be a holistic understanding of the ways in which business and other sectors of society are dependent upon each other and how these dependencies and reciprocal influences affect the whole. Such an understanding is sorely needed, and even if the goal is not fully attainable, we must attempt to move towards that understanding.

The task is to stimulate thought that ranges over a variety of disciplines and levels of analysis (regional, national and international), thereby contributing to the integration of separate strands of inquiry. The need to integrate ideas from different perspectives--geographic and disciplinary--has long existed, but it is growing exponentially because of increasingly powerful, global interdependencies. A general awareness of these reciprocal influences is not new. However, their intricate nature and their causes deserve deeper exploration from more viewpoints than thus far has been undertaken.

In our first article, John Anderson writes about the much discussed issue of global competitiveness and the challenge it poses for the United States. A major part of that challenge involves: Japanese exports, Japan's coming domination in the development of capital systems, and competition from an expanding Japanese banking system based on financing the export of those capital systems. The Japanese challenge threatens not only our historic global economic position, but also our ability to maintain a high standard of living and to help others around the world.

The response of the U.S. political system, Anderson claims, has been halfhearted and characterized by inadequate proposals from the entire political spectrum. He argues that we need a completely new conceptual approach to government-business relations. Two major departures, he says, are required. Both involve some form of planning, although emphatically not production planning in the traditional sense. Rather, the government needs to help develop a societal infrastructure that will make the following available to the business sector: capital, resources, trained labor, newly developed technological knowledge, better opportunities for entrepreneurship, and better approaches to training managers. The second departure, Anderson says, is to develop attitudes of greater cooperation between business and government.

While Anderson draws attention to the competitive aspect of U.S.-Japanese relations, Robert Wood points to the need for greater cooperation between the two countries in the interest of maintaining the credibility of deterrence in Europe. That cooperation is essential because, as Wood reports, U.S. corporations have become increasingly dependent upon Japan and other Asian countries for components of military items needed by the conventional forces of the North Atlantic Treaty Organization (NATO). Factors that have led to America's dependency on foreign suppliers include strategic decisions by corporate business, policies of the U.S. Government, and socioeconomic changes in the American polity.

Wood identifies three possible solutions to the problem: do nothing; attempt to become self-sufficient; reduce significantly America's dependency on foreign suppliers. He rejects the first option because the degree of vulnerability associated with it represents too great a danger to U.S. national interests. The second option, even if it were feasible, would have heavy economic and political costs in terms of relations with our allies. Hence, Wood identifies ways to mitigate, not eliminate, the "foreign dependencies."

Given our continuing dependence on them, a number of Asian countries, Japan especially, represent "arsenals of democracy." As such, their cooperation will be critical to the maintenance of Europe's conventional deterrent posture and war-fighting capability. Therefore, in the interests of a robust deterrence, the United States should strengthen political ties between itself and Asian suppliers. For the same purpose, Wood argues, America and Japan should undertake highly visible joint military exercises demonstrating our capability to protect supply lines between Asia, the United States and Europe.

The issue of military production brings us to Lawrence Korb's article. Korb explores a major problem in the Department of Defense (DOD) procurement process that manifests itself in two basic ways. First, there are tensions between DOD, the purchaser of billions of dollars worth of weapons and equipment, and the defense industry, the vendor of those weapons and that equipment. The tensions stem from: (1) distorted, deeply negative images of each other held by officials of DOD and the defense industry; (2) the desire of each side to take credit for positive results and to blame the other for negative ones; and (3) conflicting aims --DOD wants to hold down costs, while industry wants to increase profits. The second, and potentially far more pernicious, weakness of the

DOD procurement process is the disregard for the Congress of the United States and the mass media held by some officials of both the defense industry and DOD. These officials regard as frustrating, and maybe even unnecessary, their responsibility to testify publicly before Congressional committees regarding procurement.

Korb argues that the defense industry and DOD must change their attitudes. Each has to realize that its image of the other is oversimplified. At the same time, each has to recognize that the complaints of one about the practices of the other are sometimes justified. Korb also contends that substantial attention to the liberal arts in the education of future leaders of both sectors would result in a deeper understanding of and commitment to the procedures of our constitutional system. He is, however, somewhat pessimistic about the prospects for positive change.

While taking account of Korb's pessimism, David Riesman would argue that private liberal arts colleges are the institutions best able to develop in people the qualities our leaders must possess. The private liberal arts college, Riesman claims, imparts the attitudes and develops the strengths that lead to "unconventional wisdom," and therefore are best able to educate for leadership roles. By "unconventional wisdom," he means an eagerness to accomplish something beyond financial success and personal career enhancement. Such wisdom, he says, involves a longer-run, more inventive ambition, based on one's ability to develop oneself, and one's hope to leave an institutional as well as a personal legacy. That kind of legacy is possible only in the context of loyalties broader than exclusively personal ones, and, we might add, loyalties beyond narrow institutional interests as well.

However, many of the very institutions most capable of imparting such values, and which therefore represent a national resource, are facing increasing competition and fiscal constraints to the point that their existence is threatened. Riesman suggests that the corporate world, in an era of decreasing public assistance to these institutions, can and should help, both by continuing to recruit employees from, and increasing financial assistance to, private liberal arts colleges.

It is probably not far off the mark to suggest that the managers and labor leaders discussed by Rosabeth Moss Kanter most likely have the "uncommon wisdom" described by Riesman. Those managers and labor leaders recognize the increasing degree to which management and stakeholders (suppliers, customers, employees) of the corporation are becoming dependent upon each other. According to Kanter, this growing interdependence results from the corporation's need to cut costs and to facilitate technological innovation in order to be competitive in an era of accelerating change. Some corporations are responding to the increasing interdependence by establishing strategic partnerships with vendors, customers and labor unions. One form of these new partnerships is the "complementary alliance"--for example, a strategic partnership between management and labor. Such alliances have brought about substantial, if sometimes wrenching, changes in relationships between management and labor as well as within these institutions. One notable innovation has been the establishment of Local Common Information Forums in which presidents of local labor unions and upper-level management for the first time are participating together in the making of important corporate decisions. Although the process has produced stress at many levels, both in the union and the corporation, it also has produced mutual benefits for management and labor. Indeed, Kanter suggests that the complementary alliance could become the model for corporate success.

The corporation's need to facilitate technological innovation is also an issue of concern for Charles Ferguson. While Kanter explores implications of that need for management-labor relations, Ferguson focuses attention on that same need in the context of U.S.-Japanese competition in the semiconductor industry. He points to a severe erosion over the past decade of America's technological and competitive position in a number of areas critical to future economic growth and military power, for example, robotics, microelectronics, and advanced materials. One symptom of and contributor to that erosion, he says, has been the decline of the U.S. semiconductor industry in the face of Japanese competition.

The Japanese industry succeeded, Ferguson claims, because its strategy encouraged external predation and rewarded investments in future productivity while simultaneously restraining consumption and unproductive distributional conflict. Conversely, the American practice encouraged short-term calculations, distributional conflict, and consumption relative to investment. Moreover, in the presence of external challenges, U.S. firms, in Ferguson's view, practiced lifeboat diplomacy, betraying each other, their customers and their suppliers, rather than improving collective, long-run productivity.

Ferguson is not certain whether American practice can be changed sufficiently to preserve a competitive industry. However, he is certain that policy measures which do not recognize the strategic deadlocks facing the industry will be ineffective or even detrimental. Policy interventions must lengthen the time horizons of U.S. actors, encourage vertical integration, and ensure that assistance yields enduring productivity gains rather than short-term profits. Otherwise, he predicts, the industry will waste government support just as it has wasted the superiority it once enjoyed.

Edward Wenk also focuses on technology, but not on winning the competition it elicits and exacerbates. Rather, his concern is with the ethical and functional relationships between technology, business and government. He explores the potential dangers to democratic values inherent in those relationships. Wenk asserts that technology concentrates wealth and power, and claims that whoever controls technology will control the future.

Regarding that technologically-dominated future, he discusses a "hidden partnership" between business and government--hidden because American ideology views as evil any close collaboration between the two sectors. In spite of ideology, such collaboration already exists in a variety of ways, notwithstanding the oft-repeated rhetoric about "getting government off the back of business." Given the increasingly complementary roles that government and business will play regarding technology, moreover, that collaboration is destined to grow in the future.

If present trends continue, then, the already firm linkages between technology, government and business will evolve into what Wenk calls the "corporate state." Such a state will result from a merger between industry and government regarding "goals, creed, commitment to similar management strategies and interchangeable managers." And technology will play a dominant role in that state.

Wenk argues, therefore, that a future in which democratic values can be protected will require "an open acknowledgement of the partnership between government and industry, integrity, . . . [more accurate and generally available] information, reform in education and foresight." He also argues that "American business has a responsibility to take initiatives in all of these areas, and to nurture them to fruition."

Alex Inkeles' concern with global communications is simultaneously both more narrow than Wenk's general treatment of technology and broader than his focus on the United States. Inkeles asserts that a "single worldwide social system is emerging." A key factor in this development, he says, is global electronic communications, which is increasing at a phenomenal rate. That growth has resulted chiefly from dramatic reductions in the cost of communications and the speed with which new technologies can transmit messages. Inkeles discusses various instruments of communication, and he assesses the extent to which each of these facilitates the transmission of ideas, habits, attire, and so forth across national borders.

The business corporation is a major participant in this rapidly evolving drama, and the relationship between the corporation and technology provides a striking example of mutual influence. The business sector figures so prominently in international affairs that INTELSAT launched, in 1983, a special International Business Service, "specifically designed to serve the needs of the international business community." Just as business has stimulated technology, the reciprocal is also true. Communications, broadly defined, accounts for 10-15 percent of any modern economy, according to Inkeles.

In his view, the importance of the communications revolution is seven-fold. The first point concerns its scope and immediacy. We all are now part of a world audience. Second, change is occurring at a dizzying pace. Third, this is so largely because of technological breakthroughs and the associated dramatic decrease in communications costs. Fourth, although we all participate in the communications revolution as recipients of information, the means of communication and the wealth generated are not evenly distributed throughout the world. Nevertheless--and this is Inkeles' fifth point--as global communication further develops the interdependencies that bind nations together, mutual vulnerabilities will increase. Sixth, these vulnerabilities are to a degree effecting a homogenization of cultures. Finally, Inkeles is concerned with the potential inherent in such a culture for global cooperation, on the one hand, and fear and hostility, on the other.

Leon Sullivan shares both Inkeles' attention to affairs beyond America's borders and Wenk's concern with democratic values. Sullivan writes about those values primarily in the context of South Africa. But he also says that apartheid must be abolished in the interest of peace in the southern region of the African continent and the world in general, as well as in South Africa.

He describes the origins of the Sullivan Principles (his code of ethics for corporate behavior); their evolution; some positive changes in South Africa since their appearance; the responses of the South African government to those changes; his own call in 1987 for the disengagement of U.S. companies and for the economic and political isolation of South Africa by the United States Government until apartheid ends; and guidelines for that disengagement.

Sullivan asserts that the ethical and moral influence of multinational companies is being tested in South Africa as never before. He poses the basic question as to what role American companies and companies of other nations should play in ameliorating deep social problems facing the poor and disadvantaged. He believes that the actions companies take in this regard will be critical for human justice; he also believes that those actions will be critical for the survival of free enterprise in general. Indeed, Sullivan sees the potential for a race war in South Africa, a war into which the superpowers would be drawn, unless apartheid is abolished.

Donald Neuchterlein is interested in the same linkages that are evident in Sullivan's article: those between America's private sector, the U.S. Government and American foreign policy. Neuchterlein's compass, however, is broader than Sullivan's focus on a single country. Neuchterlein's general proposition is that the foreign policy interests of the United States and the foreign commercial interests of American business corporations are complementary. Therefore, he calls for increased consultation and cooperation between the public and private sectors in America in order to develop strategies for pursuing those interests.

Nuechterlein offers to decision makers in both sectors a systematic approach to (a) deciding how important any given interest is by establishing its nature and intensity; (b) identifying benefits, costs and risks associated with pursuing that interest; and (c) determining instruments available and appropriate for its pursuit. He applies his system to both governmental and corporate policies regarding several issues, including economic sanctions against South Africa and U.S. political-economic relations with the Peoples Republic of China. His approach, if it were adopted by decision makers, would force them to think through--in a systematic way, and in the context of a judgment about the importance and intensity of any given issue--the potential benefits, costs and feasibility of any policy proposed to address that issue. The presumed result would be wiser policies. Also, Nuechterlein's system, if it were applied to both governmental and corporate strategies over a range of issues, could help to identify interests common to American foreign policy and American corporations. It is those common interests that lead Nuechterlein to conclude that governmental and corporate leaders should increasingly consult and cooperate in the formulation of their respective policies and strategies.

By way of summary, the editor would observe that both the individual articles and the collection as a whole have been instructive and provocative for him, and hopes that other readers will be affected similarly. To the extent that the book stimulates further research and fresh thought about the reciprocal influences between the corporation and other sectors of society, it will have, as the economists say, a multiplier effect, thereby greatly increasing its own contribution.

A NEW FRAMEWORK FOR GOVERNMENT-BUSINESS RELATIONS: HOW DO WE RESPOND BEST TO THE CHALLENGE OF A WORLD ECONOMY?

by John B. Anderson

As 1987 began, that national barometer of American public opinion, the Gallup Poll, showed that 49 percent of those who were surveyed cited economic problems as the nation's most important issue. International tensions, the spread of terrorism, drug abuse, and a host of other problems relating to both foreign and domestic affairs were far down the scale. This reading occurred as we began the fifth year of recovery from the great recession of 1981-82. That unhappy event was the worst such development since the economic collapse of the early 1930s. One would have expected the recovery from that recession, among the most robust and longest of the postwar period, to have generated widespread optimism. It did not.

This contrast between present prosperity and public fears about the economy may be easy to explain. The public may be expecting a "correction," and it may be right.[1] As the year 1987 proceeded, mounting evidence that stagflation was replacing prosperity was seen in the statistics on producer and consumer prices, on industrial production, and on interest rates. Moreover, per capita growth in real income entered a period of actual decline. The historic growth rate in productivity halted, and might even have declined.

The budget deficit persists--and we rely on foreign investors to fund a major part of it. The trade gap seems unconquerable, despite the fall of the dollar. The financial markets fluctuate with increasing instability.

In 1986, Americans consumed about 4 percent more than they produced, and financed this deficit through borrowing. That policy was possible only because the U.S. government was able to rely on foreign capital to finance the more than one trillion dollars of additional public debt that we as a nation have accumulated since 1981.

The day may soon approach when we will be unable to rely on such capital. In the spring of 1987, a three-day refunding operation of the U.S. Treasury attracted inordinate and unusual attention. The most important single question was the ability of the U.S. government to market its securities at prevailing rates of interest. This, in turn, depended on whether or not Japanese investors, concerned about the falling U.S. dollar, would be willing to participate in the offerings. On that occasion they made the investment, but they may not continue to do so in the future.

Moreover, it is increasingly clear that if our current economic performance continues at its present level, we will no longer be the world's preeminent economic power. Indeed, we will be the world's preeminent economic headache. In fact, a good case can be made that we have already lost our dominance. By some measures, for example the application of technology to manufacturing, we appear to be in second place.[2] Also, in 1986 we became the world's number two financial power, measured by the quantity of capital effectively available to influence global financial markets and investment patterns. And by some standards, our securities markets are also now number two.

We no longer dictate macroeconomic policy or economic performance to the rest of the world. To the contrary, for well over a year, we have been imploring both the West Germans and the Japanese to pursue economic policies designed to boost demand in those countries. Needless to say, we are not doing this out of some altruistic sentiment that is prompted by a desire to see the West Germans and the Japanese live better. Our advice is based on the hope that if people in those countries consume more, it will be in the form of imported American goods.

To be sure, we remain the world's largest economy, but size is not always the equivalent of power. Other countries have become proficient in exercising economic power beyond their size. We, on the other hand, exercise less economic power today than the size of our economy normally would seem to dictate.

Although we still have more real wealth than any other nation, this condition is the product of our past successes. A strong argument can be made that in recent years we have become net consumers of our accumulated wealth, not net contributors to its growth. Economic worries, therefore, may center as much on long-term decline as on the expectation of short-term recession.

I

Given these new realities, we face several important challenges. One is to meet the overseas competition to our economic position in the world. A second is to maintain and increase our standard of living and the quality of life for our citizens at home. A third is to help others in poorer regions of the globe to do the same.

Government must play a major role in achieving all these objectives, and to be successful it must creatively redefine its relationship to the business community. Let us examine first the challenges, and then some possible solutions.

The nation that bids to replace us as number one, is, of course, Japan. The success of its economy has been based on a number of well known factors: manufacturing and marketing competence in a highly competitive and capitalistic domestic economy; a market penetration strategy internationally designed to take full advantage of the product cycle phenomenon; governmental policies designed to encourage the substitution of knowledge for resources; a moral drive to win by excelling, and therefore to compensate for the humiliation of defeat in war; a long-term perspective which has encouraged both a public and a private preference for investment over consumption; and, perhaps most important for our discussion, a strategy of conducting a perpetual "upscale" restructuring of the Japanese economy and its role in the international economy. It is the success of this last strategy (which builds on the others) that Americans find so challenging today.

Japan has become a successful upscale economy for two reasons. First, it has adopted a strategy of shifting its manufacturing base away from low-value-added products to high-value-added products, so that as a nation it can produce (and therefore either consume or invest) more wealth. It began with textiles, moved to cheap electronics and motorcycles, then up to expensive electronics and autos, while gradually liquidating low-value-added industries. Consistent with this strategy, Japan now threatens to become a major producer of aircraft and large computers.

Second, as Japan nears the top of the value-added product line, it is shifting its emphasis to continue the upscale strategy. The new emphasis seems to be not on the production of goods, but on the development and production of the systems necessary to produce goods. Japan today is putting an enormous emphasis on the technology of industrial production: robotics, materials, control systems, new generation computers, and automated production systems generally. We must assume that the strategy behind this emphasis is not only continually to upgrade the productivity and competitiveness of Japanese factories at home, but also to export this technology overseas in the form of capital equipment, capital systems, or entire factories. Exports of autos will level off or decline; exports of auto factories, and auto-making equipment, and parts-making equipment will accelerate.

This shift, which is currently underway, has several advantages for Japan. First, factories--more accurately industrial systems--easily leap over protectionist barriers. If a country limits the importation of the world's most advanced production processes, it destroys the competitiveness of its own industries. Most governments, if not their citizens, realize this. Second, industrial systems can be exported to Third World countries as well as to industrialized countries. Third, although direct sales of such industrial systems seem not especially profitable because their selling price is low compared to the value of the products they produce, Japan nevertheless can share extensively in the wealth they generate. This is true regardless of where the systems are located, because Japanese companies can finance, lease or directly own them. Fourth, if Japan is successful in achieving global domination of industrial technology, it will be in a position to decide, in effect, which countries and which companies will produce which products. The economic power created by such a monopoly position, given national incentives to produce manufactured products, can easily be translated into enormous political power. Finally, the export of real capital systems, through financing and leasing arrangements, can contribute mightily to the building of Japan's global banking position, and thereby underwrite the third stage of Japan's upscale strategy.

We are all familiar with Tokyo's recent leap into the position of major world financial player. Japan now has at least seven of the world's ten largest banks; we have two. It has the world's largest securities market, one of the largest insurance industries, and its role in financing the American debt is giving it enormous leverage over our economic policies.

Thus far, the speed with which Japan has achieved financial prominence has been primarily the result of our own economic folly-- the domestic budget deficit, which accelerated the trade deficit; the falling dollar; and related matters. But this folly has only served to hasten a previously existing growth in Japan's financial power.

Japan's underlying economic position has been improving for years. It may be that its banking system is potentially more sound and powerful than our own. The Japanese system is evidently built upon the financing of an expanding industrial network composed of the world's most efficient producers of manufactured products and upon the well-supervised export of real capital equipment and capital systems. The U.S. banking system is increasingly based upon uncollectible, but in many cases still growing, foreign loans to commodity producing countries; on loans to domestic commodity producers, ranging from oil to wheat; and on consumer credit, which is expanding faster than the economy itself.

In short, Japan seems to be rapidly turning its industrial position into a very powerful financial position, and such a strategy seems to be the culmination of Japan's immediate economic objectives. Global financial dominance is the key goal in a strategy of upscaling the nation's economy.

Moreover, if American industrial competitiveness continues to deteriorate, and is not compensated for in other areas, the value of our currency with respect to the yen will continue to decline. This will occur either through market forces or through conscious policies of devaluation designed to "protect" American jobs, and allegedly, American competitiveness.

Although many factors determine which nation's currency serves as the world's major reserve currency, economic ones play a significant role in this regard. Therefore, it is not unreasonable to expect, if current economic trends continue, that the yen will perform this function by the end of the century or before. In such a circumstance, the dollar's role will decline--just as the pound's role did with respect to the dollar in the 1920s. People and countries simply have an enormous incentive to hold currencies which do not steadily decline in value. Such a downgrading of the dollar's role will severely limit our ability to maintain any form of freewheeling economy, and we might well find ourselves in the kind of "stop and go" cycles that the British found so frustrating before the North Sea oil came on line.

We face one of the largest challenges in our history. Unless we meet it, our own standard of living will deteriorate, our ability to aid others will lessen, and our global potential will change from that of generous benefactor to miserable supplicant.

The foregoing is not a polemic against the Japanese. This caveat is necessary because "Japan-bashing" has become a popular sport among many groups, from solons on Capitol Hill to those on assembly lines. The accomplishments of the Japanese, however, should not be denounced. They should be recognized for what they are: extraordinary applications of strategic analysis, exemplary cooperative efforts, and enormous amounts of old-fashioned hard work--the virtues we used to think so highly of here in America. Japan has moved into the number one position in so many areas, not because of some demoniac conspiracy against us, but because we ourselves have pursued foolish policies which have enabled Japan to beat us at what hitherto had been our own game.

II

If we believe that the threats to our global economic position, our domestic standard of living, and our ability to assist others are real, then we cannot deny that a democratic government, which should be responsive to the chief concerns of its citizens, has a major role to play in the economy. Nor can we deny the necessity for closer cooperation between government and business to meet challenges at home and from overseas.

What keeps these convictions from becoming mere tautological propositions is that the official policy of our national executive for more than six years has been decidedly to the contrary. We have eschewed anything with even a vague resemblance to industrial policy. Our trade policy has oscillated wildly between 1) simply reciting the words "free trade," as if they were a mantra to inspire correct economic decisions; and 2) brass-knuckled protectionism. If we have any real investment strategy, it is not discernible. If the administration has any serious commitment to ending the deficit, it has neither revealed it, nor convincingly practiced it.

But do others have a realistic and viable approach? There has been a profusion of literature on this general subject of our economic weakness, as well as on the relationship between business and government. Much of it is helpful; some is very helpful. Perhaps there is a direct connection between this profusion and the fact that serious cracks have appeared in the economy.

Yet the economics profession has suffered increasing doubts about its ability to offer with any degree of unanimity the necessary prescriptions for this age of cascading change. We are no longer in a period of economic certitude, as we were in the 1950s, or even the 1960s. When Juanita Krebs, Secretary of Commerce in the Carter Administration, left office at the end of the 1970s, she did not return to her former position as a professor of economics. At the time, she said she was no longer sure that the answers to our problems were to be found in that discipline. However, people continue searching for answers to these imponderables, notwithstanding the loss of confidence by at least some economists in their ability to find the correct answers.

What has been the response of the political system? This article is being written about a year and a half before the 1988 American presidential election. As the electoral pace quickens in the months prior to the first primaries, the role of government in economic policy and the relationship between government and business will be in the vortex of the debate. It is doubtful that the high level of concern about the economy, as measured by the Gallup Poll, will decrease appreciably between January 1987 and November of 1988. Indeed, the chances are better than even that concern with the economy will heighten, despite Irangate, Contragate, or any other issues that may emerge. The percentage of those who view economic problems as foremost will still be the leading political indicator. But will the politicians respond?

The New Right, supply-side Republicans, once vocal, have become very quiet of late. Their policies of limiting the growth of government have not brought forth "The American Renaissance," to use the descriptive phrase of Jack Kemp, a supply-sider and current Republican presidential candidate. Such familiar rubrics as deregulation and tax reform, and a policy of allegedly "getting government off people's backs and out of their pockets," has failed to produce desirable economic results.

Attempts at budget cutting by the government were really only successful in the first full-budget year of the Reagan administration. Thereafter, despite tax cuts, revenue "enhancement" measures, and tax reform, we have seen an exponential growth in both public and private debt. Most, if not all, economists perceive a linkage between the dreary succession of budget deficits and a deficit in our international balance of payments that has more than quintupled since 1980. Supply-side economics, put quite simply, has failed to do what it promised to do. Nor has the conviction that government is synonymous with disincentives, while only the private sector is equated with incentives, been a helpful basis for successful policy.

It is therefore not surprising that among the more old-line Republicans, the brightly focused beam once cast by supply-side economics has given way to a more penumbral appearance, judging from the efforts of numerous Republican candidates to differentiate their position from that of the supply-siders. Nonetheless, government remains the archenemy for all of them. Or, if one de-escalates the rhetoric, government is at best a bumbler when it intervenes in a market economy.

Within the Republican Party, there is no "left left." That is, there is no Republican Jesse Jackson, or even a Nelson Rockefeller, to explore strong action by government to solve economic problems and define a cooperative, not conflictual, relationship between government and business.

In fairness, some Republicans like Kevin Phillips, whose credentials as conservative have been many years in the making, saw the trap into which we had fallen. In 1984, Phillips took issue with the false notion that in all instances affecting economic policy government simply should be dismissed as an incompetent, meddlesome bungler intent only on regulation to achieve its goals of social engineering.[3]   He has recommended a fifteen-point program, which included a Department of International Trade and Industry, which looked suspiciously like Japan's Ministry of International Trade and Industry (MITI); expansion of the Export-Import Bank; sweeping revisions of federal antitrust laws, so that government could encourage consortiums of American business to undertake research and development on advanced technology; vastly increased direct government support for this new technological research, with even a government-sponsored trust fund for neglected basic research; and an exponential increase in federal funding across-the-board for education in scientific and technical subjects.

Unfortunately, when Phillips parted company with his fellow conservatives by proposing these broad prescriptions for federal aid and activity, he brought few conservatives with him. The basic outlines of "Reaganomics," especially the role of government vis-a-vis business in the formulation of policy, has changed very little.

What contribution has the Republic President made recently? On January 27, 1987, the White House released a program which was called "The President's Competitiveness Initiative." Although we heard continuously that global competition is the new reality, the forty-three separate recommendations which made up his Special Message to Congress were almost immediately analyzed as a "patchwork of mostly old proposals."[4] One Democrat who has taken a particular interest in the subject, Senator Max Baucus of Montana, complained that it was put together with bailing wire, paste, and glue.

The report, of course, may not have been intended as a series of serious proposals. Rather, its purpose may have been merely to reflect basic attitudes. Indeed, Richard Darman, formerly Deputy Treasury Secretary, indicated that the President's chief contribution regarding the competitiveness issue would be simply to launch a grand dialogue on a national scale. It seems to be the Administration's view that the real movers and shakers should be members of the private sector. Moreover, although many of the President's proposals were concerned with the improvement of educational standards, Mr. Reagan has always regarded education as the province of state and local school, not federal administrators.

A close examination of the one-thousand page report reveals that it has both positive and negative aspects. On the one hand, there is a proposal to establish new, university-based, interdisciplinary "Science and Technology Centers," which would focus on fundamental science that directly enhances our ability to compete. This idea is parallel to a proposal I made several years ago for the establishment of Regional Technology Centers. Similarly, there are proposals to expand the functions of the National Science Foundation and to accelerate intersectoral technology transfers. A particular emphasis in this regard is placed on technologies that could be spun off from defense research and development.

However, the voluminous document is not a call for a carefully coordinated program of government policies and programs to address our key international economic problems. Nor does it deal in any seriously creative way with the relationship between business and government.

The Democratic candidates offer little more. To be sure, Gary Hart, prior to his political demise, advanced a series of "New Ideas," but, taken together, they constituted more of an ad hoc collection of suggestions than a comprehensive framework within which to rebuild our economy and creatively redefine the relationship between business and government. Perhaps later in the campaign Hart would have undertaken to synthesize his views to accomplish this latter goal. Alas, we may never know.

The most liberal candidate in the Democratic Party, Jesse Jackson, has already proposed a federal budget based on "quality of life," which would significantly increase both federal spending and governmental intervention in the economy in order to halt everything from farm foreclosures to plant closings. Although many of his objectives are valid, his approach contributes little to the debate on increasing American competitiveness and maintaining the American standard of living across-the-board.

More centrist Democrats speak in nebulous terms of a government that has a "significant" or "important," but "limited," role. Presumably this reflects a less redistributionist stance than that of prior years, but where are the recommendations for stimulating competitiveness, productivity, and sustained healthy economic growth?

The neoliberals, with their concepts of "sunrise" and "sunset" industries have offered extensive plans for industrial targeting, but in an age of rapid technological change, targeting industries may be a very bad plan indeed. A few years back they spoke of targeting the high-technology industry, but today the manufacture of computer chips, for example, has seemingly joined the ranks of sunset industries in America, such as steel and autos, which demand protection against foreign competition.

As an opponent, over a decade ago, of the Chrysler bailout, I have been skeptical about government designating winners or losers. A good argument can be made that it should not concern itself with whether we have a "Big Two" or "Big Three" in the automobile industry. Rather, it should go beyond the preservation of a particular corporate entity to the larger issue of preserving our industrial capacity to produce the goods that will not only help to satisfy our own essential needs, but maintain our role as a great trading nation.

Protectionism, of course, has become the overriding cause of many other Democrats. It does seem inevitable that the 100th Congress will produce a trade bill. The Democratic House passed one last year, but the Republican Senate refused to go along, objecting particularly to provisions crafted by Representative Gephart, the Democrat from Missouri. Those provisions would have mandated retaliatory action if surpluses of our trading partners, in their trade with us, were not reduced. But this year, so far, Gephart is winning, and with an election in the air, some trade restrictions may be enacted. The fact that tariffs and quotas will make stagnation permanent and reduce our standard of living is often ignored in the interest of short-term political advantage.

III

What must we do? We face a set of economic challenges at home and overseas, which will require for their solution the kind of national effort that in the past we have expended only on major war. To succeed, the government must take a dynamic and active role, not just in mobilizing the opinions and efforts of others, but also in acting directly itself.

However, the government must have a comprehensive plan to guide its actions in the economic sphere, and it must enlist the full-fledged support of all major sectors of the American public. Important among them is the business community.

I believe that business is willing to respond to creative initiatives of government, as long as it is convinced that governmental objectives are valid and governmental instruments are effective. The United States Council of International Business, in a position paper released last February, sensibly set forth a series of policy objectives that are both a good starting point for thinking comprehensively about economic policy and good evidence of business support for effective government action. The paper argues that:

> the highest economic policy priority for the Administration and the 100th Congress in 1987 should be to implement policies and legislative programs aimed at enhancing the competitiveness of the U.S. economy as a whole, in an open global economic system. Domestically these include fiscal and monetary policies and actions, such as those affecting education, labor mobility, and R & D. Internationally, greater economic policy coordination and exchange rate cooperation, a forceful and concerted policy to deal with indebtedness, and an enhanced and more open trading system will add to the greater competitiveness of the United States.

In both the domestic and international spheres, dynamic and progressive political leadership should enlist the support of the business community in formulating policies, enacting legislation, and implementing those policies, even in the areas of regulation. The business community has an interest in responsible government regulation. That community needs a sound financial system, a reputation for honesty, and an image of producing safe products of high quality.

But we need more than objectives. We need, also, a coherent philosophy, which defines the extent to which government can and should play a strong role in the economy. Notwithstanding my many reservations about supply-side economics, it did demonstrate one important proposition. A joinder of economic philosophy with specific objectives is needed to achieve any real gains of even a semipermanent nature. This much President Reagan clearly understood. His general approach of cutting taxes, while doubling defense outlays, was consistent with a conservative philosophy that required the building of a firebreak against what he viewed as the consuming flames of ever-expanding government in domestic economic policy. That philosophy was more than the nostrum that supply creates its own demand. It was deliberately designed to curb the notions that big-government objectives are valid and that governmental instruments are effective.

President Reagan, however, had the wrong philosophy. Government should play a creative role in the rebuilding of the American economy. It is necessary to dispel the myth that government is never creative. This myth comes in part from a confusion of government action in the social realm with government action in the economic sphere.

This co-mingling of views is unfortunate. It is incorrect to look at some of the failures of the Great Society legislation which was designed to deal with poverty and the social problems of America's underclass, and draw conclusions about what government can accomplish in areas quite unrelated. The views on political economy that shaped the debate on the Great Society are tangential, at best to the current, unprecedented challenge resulting from our lack of competitiveness. For example, George Gilder's thesis in Wealth and Poverty was that government intervention in the economy was totally ineffective in solving the problems of the poor. He believed that the most effective and powerful incentive which would bootstrap the poor out of their impoverishment was the very fact of their poverty itself. A little later Charles Murray argued in Losing Ground that government intervention in the decades of the 1960s and 1970s had stymied efforts to aid the nation's poor whose plight was so ably described in Michael Harrington's The Other America. Murray said that government actions caused the poor to slide backward and deeper into the mire of failure and despair.

These arguments, however they may be judged, are simply irrelevant to the argument over government's ability to act effectively in the economic sphere. They are not helpful in defining what should be the relationship between government and business in our battle to be, once again, on the cutting edge as a world economic power.

In saying that the lessons of one area will be misleading in another, let me add that I do not personally believe that our concentration on one should be at the expense of the other. As a nation we do not need to become absorbed in the problem of competitiveness to the exclusion of our concerns about poverty and economic inequality. Greater economic equity should continue to be a primary concern.

In arguing that the government must have a coherent plan of action in order to exercise a creative role in rebuilding the American economy, I use the word "plan" advisedly. I am well aware that it raises the hackles of those who regard any form of governmental economic intervention as insidious. And yet, we have a five-year defense plan which sets forth what our defense needs and priorities should be. The Joint Chiefs of Staff certainly rely on a Single Integrated Operations Plan to maintain an adequate future-oriented defense. In the private sector large companies, unless they want to end up in Chapter Eleven proceedings, engage in detailed long-range planning. That process may not invariably demonstrate foresight and vision--as the auto makers of Detroit so egregiously illustrated in the 1960s and 1970s. However, there are innumerable other examples of success, rather than failure, in the implementation of the planning principle.

Now, let me be very clear: by planning, I mean something very different from what is usually meant by the word. To tell companies what to make or how much to make is a recipe for disaster. The decentralized decision-making process of the marketplace has time and again proven its superiority over centralized planning.

In fact, I am even hesitant about industrial targeting on the Japanese model. We are, quite simply, a very different country from Japan, and much can be said for an economically innovative society being permitted to grow without central direction.

But there are two fundamental levels on which we can use well-constructed plans. Both are based on redefinitions of the role of government and business. The first is to increase the government's role in providing the infrastructural base of the American economy. The second is to open an era of genuine cooperation between government and business.

A national infrastructure, broadly defined, must be a very high priority in America. In traditional societies, infrastructure has included such basic items as roads and electric generating plants. But in modern society, it should refer to the whole support system upon which our capitalist economy rests.

What is this support system, and what is government's legitimate role in making it work? As I recall my introductory course in economics, we were taught that any production system needs six things to make it work well: capital, resources, knowledge, labor, entrepreneurship, and management. We were even required to memorize that interest was the return to capital, rents to resources, royalties to knowledge, wages to labor, profits to entrepreneurship, and salaries to management.

These concepts from microeconomics may well be useful in a macroeconomic context. Not only individual companies need capital, resources, knowledge labor, entrepreneurship and management. The economy as a whole needs them as well. And government can plan to ensure that companies operating in a free market can have access to those infrastructural necessities, which are as important to our modern economy as roads and canals were to the economies of old. We must also recognize that the government can play an important role in ensuring that all of these elements of a support system are adequate.

It is at this level that I favor serious and sustained economic planning. Such planning implies research, which can give us a better understanding of how these factors are important to the overall economy, how they relate to each other, and what we can do to ensure that the marketplace is adequately supported in a larger infrastructural way. In this view, the fundamental role of government in the business-government relationship is to provide a rationally planned support base upon which a free market can thrive.

Let me illustrate with a few examples. Capital: How can we restructure our private banking system so that it will make the maximum contribution to our economic growth and development? Resources: Can we have an intelligent and coordinated resource policy which will fight cartels and ensure access by American firms to overseas resources? Knowledge: How do we best encourage the development of science and technology; do we need additional institutions to do so? Today, as the result of deliberate government policy, our research and development facilities are being directed more to defense research than to research which has commercial possibilities. Is this wise? Can we develop the means of encouraging direct transfers of independently developed technology to commercial enterprises? Most agree that our scientific plant needs rebuilding. Perhaps we need a plan for such rebuilding which encourages a much less defense-oriented approach than we have today. Labor: Do we need a plan to overhaul our current educational system, so that the worker of the future is much better trained (or retrained) for the jobs of the future than that worker is today? Entrepreneurship: Has government employed effective policies to encourage entrepreneurship in America? What new ones must be adopted? Do we need an informal "entrepreneurship impact statement" when we enact economic legislation? Management: Are our managers of the future being adequately trained to meet the demands of the future? Does our industrial structure today give managers the right incentives to manage their firms properly?

In each of these six areas, government in cooperation with the private sector, can play a significant role. But this role should be exercised in conformity with an intelligent plan for support-system development aimed at encouraging an upscale restructuring of the American economy. Such a restructuring would embrace in a coordinated way all the elements that I have mentioned, and would represent a really genuine "supply-side" economics.

Will such infrastructural development be adequate? I do not know. But I do know that it is necessary.

Moreover, infrastructural planning has many advantages over industrial targeting. The sunrise/sunset industry approach will face enormous difficulties in our political process. Attempts to select what industries to target and what industries not to target will quickly degenerate into a policy of protecting or subsidizing every industry of any size and any industry that can remotely make a "national security" argument. The history of tariff legislation before the existence of the General Agreement on Tariffs and Trade is instructive in this respect. Also, industrial targeting assumes that one can predict the nature of technological change over the next decade, industry-by-industry. I'm not persuaded that this can be done effectively.

With an infrastructural approach, we can initially support research and technology transfer capabilities between a wide range of industries. We can then let the marketplace ultimately dictate which industries will prove commercially successful, and at much less cost than industrial targeting.

Let me offer some examples of the kind of proposals that the government might offer in the areas of capital, labor, and knowledge.[5]

Capital:

A major restructuring of the American banking system is needed. One part of that restructuring might involve the creation of innovative and nontraditional sources of capital to be made available through a network of "venture capital banks." Such banks could own equity in companies, as is the case in Japan, so that managers could raise large amounts of equity capital without having perpetually to look over their shoulders at quarterly reports. We may need to charter other kinds of banks to perform other specific objectives. Otherwise, entrepreneurship could be neglected and even ignored as we gradually witness first the evolution of regional networks and ultimately a relatively few national networks of large banks. As these "super banks" become wholesalers, rather than retailers of finance capital, many small entrepreneurs could be ignored in the process, despite the rise of independent venture capitalists.

The use of government-chartered and supported venture capital banks would be a far more flexible and decentralized approach to financing than we would have if we created a Japanese-style national development bank. Venture capital banks would be consistent with our principle of diversity, and be a modest step towards meeting our challenges. They would preserve market discipline. They could encourage, through a plan for mixed public and private capital contributions, broad-based local support and participation, which would be important in sustaining such efforts. Business would be expected to be intimately involved with these banks, both as an investor and as a borrower.

Also, it recently has been observed that the present commercial banking system, with few exceptions even among the large money center banks, has lost interest in export financing. Senator Heinz, among others in Congress, has complained bitterly about the inadequacy of the Export-Import Bank financing of American exports. Another governmental institution, the Overseas Private Investment Corporation, has been criticized for its timidity in promoting the effort to manufacture and sell to overseas markets. In too many cases government agencies have exercised a distinct preference for dealing with well-established, so-called-old-line companies, rather than late arrivals or new entrants.

Yet if capital requirements of new ventures are not met, a good many ideas will be stillborn: ideas which could result in new designs, new products, and new competitiveness. Moreover, it is demonstrable that the behemoths of American industry do not have the job-creating capacity of newer and much smaller counterparts. So both from the standpoint of improving market share in the world economy to aid our balance of payments, and improving the health of the U.S. economy by increasing employment, we need to promote new capital flow to emerging enterprises capable of innovation and flexibility in the manufacturing process. These suggestions, of course, would take their place in a larger restructuring of the banking system.

Labor:

An upscale economy will increasingly be a knowledge-based economy. And those who work in it will have to have skills far superior to those of the average worker of today if we are to produce those high-value-added products we need to sustain a high standard of living. Hence "labor" in the future means "education" today.

Since the enactment of the Ordinance of 1787, we have accepted education as a proper function of government, and the federal government has always played a major role in supporting education. From setting aside sections of land to be devoted to that purpose, to the broader aims of the Morrill Act establishing land grant universities, our young country came to the realization that our democracy and our economy would always depend on an educated citizenry.

Later, a Vocational Training and Education Act, and even later, in the 1980s, the Joint Partnership Training Act, recognized the importance of job training. The post-Sputnik National Defense Education Act recognized the relationship between improved instruction in science and mathematics and our desire to play a catch-up game in the exploration of space. However, despite these salutary developments in the past and advances at the state and local level as well, we have recently let our support for education decline. Today we lag behind other countries we once led. There is virtually no analysis of Japanese economic strength which does not refer to an educational system where students work longer and harder and are generally more skilled in both mathematics and the physical sciences than in the great majority of American schools.

It has been pointed out that only a few years after Admiral Perry sailed into Tokyo Bay, a Rutgers professor, David Murray, submitted a remarkably prophetic memorandum to the Japanese government.[6] Writing 115 years ago, he predicted that Japan could become the great commercial nation of the East by developing an effectual meritocratic educational system capable of producing the best-trained labor force in the world. As the result of their adoption of Murray's advice, and particularly their emphasis on equality of opportunity arising out of the U.S. occupation after World War II, the Japanese have been able to excel in electronics and many other fields of high technology. Their young people are better trained in science and mathematics than young people in any other country in the world. In a mathematics achievement test conducted among 13-year olds in the ten most industrially and economically advanced countries, Japanese students received the highest mean scores. U.S. students ranked ninth. Among the reasons commonly cited for their superior test results is the fact that Japanese schools offer a demanding curriculum and operate at least 240 days a year, compared with 180 days in the United States.

It is true that in recent years, particularly at the state level, commendable efforts have been made to improve teacher proficiency and to emphasize the need for a vastly improved curriculum in both science and mathematics. However, it is still far from being the overriding national priority, either regarding funding or standards, that it must become. Here business, which has an enormous stake in a more educated work force, can interact with government in a much more positive way to spur such a maximum national effort. Business should be in the forefront of the lobbying efforts against such proposals as the one in the FY 1988 budget for an overall cut of around $5 billion in the federal government's expenditures for education.

I agree with Seymour Papert of the Massachusetts Institute of Technology, who has said that just as it would be unthinkable to have a classroom without a pencil for every student, so also it would be unthinkable in the electronic classroom of the future not to have an individual computer for every student. This would be a truly revolutionary development. Considerable government support and incentives might be required and cooperation with business would be helpful. It already has been in many localities.

In a world changing as rapidly as ours, we do not show sufficient concern about the role of government in promoting and conducting the retraining and continual postgraduate upgrading of skills which will be needed to meet the intensely competitive environment of a world where one of the most obvious megatrends is an accelerating rate of change. Shortages of skilled labor can clearly develop in a country like the United States where the demographics indicate that the fastest growing groups in the labor force tend to be the least well educated. Mario Cuomo, the Governor of New York, in an address last spring to the Association for a Better New York, said to a thousand business leaders:

> The majority of the work force in this country in the twenty-first century is going to be minority. Currently, one out of two of them is being raised in poverty. What kind of work force are you going to have? Who are going to be your sophisticated people who will outthink the Japanese and the West Germans? How are you going to make it without them?[7]

Included, no doubt, in what the governor had in mind was the Immigration and Naturalization Reform Act which becomes effective this year. Many workers will emerge from the twilight zone of all-too-often underpaid and menial jobs where their illegal entry into the country is easily concealed. They constitute a valuable potential source of labor to meet what might otherwise be a much tighter labor marketplace in the 1990s. However, to be truly available, to be brought up to standard in the skills where future shortages might otherwise exist, and to be the valuable resource to the economy which they potentially are, truly massive educational and training efforts must be made. We should be developing right now, not five or ten years hence, a cooperative plan, which would engage commerce, industry, and labor together with government in this mammoth undertaking.

The governor quite properly coupled his plea for better awareness of this developing problem with a call for business and industry initiatives to develop training programs. I would reassert the need for government encouragement through both positive incentives and coordination. With enactments like the previously mentioned Job Partnership Training Act we have barely scratched the surface of government initiatives that need to be taken.

We have often heard the challenge that although we must work harder to achieve an increase in productivity, we must also work smarter. That will not happen magically. It will require government action, and it will require a plan.

Knowledge:

We have already made the point about the centrality of technology to our economic future. Despite abundant warnings that our once unchallenged and presumed impregnable lead is eroding, we are not devoting the resources that we should to research and development. Despite some recent increases in the grant-awarding authority of the National Science Foundation, it is important, as I have recommended for several years, that this expansion continue during the foreseeable future at a rate of at least 15 percent annually in real terms.

Under the aegis of the National Science Foundation, we should endow programs for colleges and universities as the backbone of an effort to have a permanent support system for scientific research, training, and instruction. Such an endowment to colleges should be supplemented by federally supported endowments for graduate and postdoctoral fellowships. Also, on a matching basis in which states would be encouraged to participate, there should be special endowment funds established to conduct specific research. The most important point about these various proposals for endowed research and training in science and technology is that they represent the long-term commitment and investment that is essential.

We need to do even more to improve the opportunities for basic research in America. True, the announced intention of the federal government to proceed with the funding of the super collider is welcome news.   But I do not believe we should rely on the vagaries of chance that a particular and glamorous project in basic research will attract presidential support and congressional funding.   Again, we need a comprehensive plan.

Business can play a major role even in the case of basic research. To make such a role profitable in the long run, we need an institution capable of helping to spread the risks and benefits of basic research over a wide number of companies.   Basic research cannot be geared to a quarterly balance sheet or even an annual profit-and-loss statement.

To meet this problem, we might create an Industrial Science Foundation (ISF).   Briefly stated, it would have the authority to accept funds contributed by industry on a nonrestricted basis.   Government would match these funds and the ISF would award grants to scholars doing basic research, and also supervise the equitable distribution of the economic benefits that could be expected to flow ultimately from this endeavor.

Perhaps, even at the risk of complicating the new tax code in small measure, an arrangement could be worked out where contributions from private industry would not only be tax deductible, but a portion would be eligible for status as a tax credit.   (Because of the long-term nature of the program, these incentives might be required to elicit private sector support.)

The ISF would make its own independent judgment on the funding of specific projects and the recruitment of scientific personnel.   Peer review of projects supported for funding would be important.   Our national laboratories, such as Los Alamos, Livermore, Argonne, and Oak Ridge should not suffer a diminished role in basic research because of an ISF. Indeed, in the present climate favoring arms control and a possible reduction in strategic nuclear weapons, the national laboratories should be a much more important component of the government's contribution to this new public-private partnership in basic research.

We also need to expand the effectiveness of applied research.   We hear repeatedly that other countries, notably Japan, have compressed the time frame for research and development followed by product marketing to a point where U.S. firms are left at the starting gate.   American companies may need additional help to meet this new threat.

One way of providing such help would be to create a large system of Regional Technology Institutes (RTIs). They could play a significant role in inaugurating a new era of government-business cooperation in applied research.   Modeled after the land grant college, they could be an autonomous institution, or, in some cases, an organic and integral part of an existing institution of higher learning.   Their primary role would be to overcome the time gap between research and development, and thereby to enhance our ability to have new products ready for market in time to beat the competition.   In other words, I believe the new era of government-business cooperation, at a time when overcoming the trade gap is clearly a national goal, must bring vastly improved new methods of production.   The RTIs could be active in developing and transferring new technology in such areas as microelectronics, robotics, flexible manufacturing systems, computer-aided design and manufacturing systems, telecommunications environmental protection systems, automated warehousing and inventory systems.   In this way we can begin to act to meet the Japanese threat to dominate the production of capital goods and capital systems, and hence world manufacturing.   The RTIs therefore should give great attention to production systems and the software required to program the newly emerging automated systems and processes involved in manufacturing.

Not only is technology per se important, but also the dissemination or transfer of new technology.   Individuals trained at RTIs could help to accomplish that objective as they take their place in industry or rotate in and out of industry.   The institutes could also play a powerful and important role in the retraining of engineers and technologists.

None of the suggestions just offered will solve our problems overnight.   They require that longer time so frequently lacking in American politics.   But major initiatives on the scale of these suggestions are needed to rejuvenate our industry.

IV

Government must not only forge a new relationship with business in infrastructural support systems.   It must also help create a new climate of direct cooperation between itself and business.

That is not the truism that it may sound like to some.   After seven years of unabashed laissez faire attitudes about the roles of business and government, more cooperation requires a sea change in currently popular attitudes.   In the campaign of 1984, it was often noted that politicians of both parties avoided the phrase "industrial policy."   Even among Democrats there was fear that it could be regarded as simply a code word for "planned economy."   The sea change, therefore, must come not only in public attitudes generally, but more specifically in the attitudes of our policymakers and office seekers in both the executive and legislative branches of government.

Again, we might look to Japan for examples that we can modify to meet our own requirements.   The Japanese penetration of markets in the People's Republic of China and the enormous potential this market offers in future trade has already so far outdistanced that of the United States that many fear the battle may already be lost.   In 1986, 29 percent of the goods imported by China came from Japan, against only 11 percent from the United States.

Why? Among the reasons commonly assigned are that the Japanese have a long-term perspective. The Mitsubishi representative who finances much of the China trade was quoted as saying, "For now Japanese banks commit hara-kiri. Later we will recover a profit."[8] Another reason is that under the Japanese tax code the Japanese firms can offer lower interest rates. However, there is something more important then the specifics of the Japanese tax code itself. That is the fact that decisions are formulated within a framework where, along with other steps encouraged by the Japanese government, there is a cooperative and planned effort by Japanese business and financial interests to win market share. Perhaps we, too, can find the means by which government encourages companies to look as much at market share as at short-term profits.

Another excellent example of cooperation with a view to the long term is provided by the race to develop superconductors. These are the materials which are capable of revolutionizing the use of electricity. Press reports indicate that the Japanese have been quick to form so-called "Special Committees" which have brought together top minds from both the public and private sectors--from government ministries, universities, and Japanese companies--to see how government aid can mesh with plans for commercialization.[9] In other words, the Japanese government has already begun to act as a facilitator and coordinator of a truly national effort. Where is the United States in all of this? Our scientists were the pioneers in superconductivity research. However, the White House and Congress seem to be at loggerheads on the important question of where do we go from here.

The White House Office of Science and Technology Policy insists that government efforts cannot go beyond the area of basic research, and that industry alone can make decisions relating to commercialization. It is this rigid separation, apparently deemed necessary to maintain the purity of free market doctrine, that alarms Congress. There is a bipartisan coalition in both the House and the Senate which has introduced legislation to create a Japanese-style commission to monitor the U.S. effort in superconductors and also to provide direct oversight. It would have the authority to study and recommend changes in the antitrust laws. Government would play a role as a facilitator to encourage joint efforts by industry in the race for commercialization. What the executive branch still does not seem to understand is that in recent years we have been the tortoise in this race to proceed from research and development to the actual marketing of a design, process, or product. Unfortunately, unlike that of Aesop's fable, we have not been the tortoise who ends up winning the race. John H. Gibbons, Director of the Congressional Office of Technology Assessment, summed it up succinctly: "There's a twilight zone between basic research and its application to the marketplace, and it is in that zone that we need to learn to operate."

Yet another and even more familiar example of public and private-sector cooperation in Japan involves the computer industry. We have recently engaged in a "chip war" because of pervasive evidence of cooperation between the Japanese government and chip manufacturers which permitted alleged dumping at subsidized prices.

To go back one step in the process and examine the ability of chip manufacturers to sell at subsidized prices is to discover the handiwork of such industrial structures as the Japanese Development Bank and MITI. The linkage between these structures involving government and private manufacturers is clear. Although I agree that the mere replication of these organizations in the United States would perhaps be unavailing, that is not the point. The real lesson is the imperative need for the United States to develop a measure of cooperation between business and government which will enhance our ability to be on the leading edge of new technologies which hold the key to our economic future.

In my campaign for the presidency in 1980, I advanced some very specific suggestions as to how we might move in this direction. One idea which I believe has become even more meritorious in the intervening years is to pass enabling legislation to create an Industrial Development Council. The staff, headed by a Presidential Advisor for Industrial Development, would operate at the very highest level of government. Indeed, the Council itself would be chaired by the President, and its membership would be composed of cabinet secretaries and representatives from business and labor, who would serve on the Council by presidential appointment. Its mandate, very broadly stated, would be to coordinate and review those government policies touching on industrial policy, with the object of fostering cooperation between leaders of both business and labor. It would also be charged with making specific recommendations to American industry about the ways in which the latter could adapt to the rapidly changing developments in international economics, terms of trade, emerging technology and consumer preferences.

These examples are by way of suggestion, but they do shed light on one basic weakness in our economic system. For all too long, both government and American industry have suffered from what some have called "cultural inhibitions" against the kind of business-government cooperation that is essential in a globally interdependent economy. Our traditional two-ocean insularity may be part of the problem. However, just as global political concepts have changed to enhance our national security, our economic vision must be focused on the need for a new level of thinking about the mutuality of the government-business relationship.

The Great Seal of the United States, adopted early in the history of our republic, carries beneath it the legend: "Novus Ordo Seclorum." Literally translated, it stands for the proposition that there must be a new order of the ages.   That phrase was not intended to carry any chilling overtones of a regimented concept of government and society.   To the contrary, it was an affirmation of the belief that the American experiment was unique: that a new birth of freedom was compatible with both a willingness to cast off the dead hand of a past where men and women had been bound in economic and political servitude, and also a willingness to innovate, plan, and create something for the future.   We must commit ourselves once again to a vision for the future where we usher in a new age of mutual cooperation, mutual respect, and mutual dedication to rebuild our economy along new and creative lines.

NOTES

1. After this article was written, that "correction" took place with a vengeance when the stock market plunged in October 1987. [Editor]

2. For a contrary view see Robert Z. Lawrence, Can America Compete (Washington, D.C.: The Brookings Institution, 1984).

3. Kevin Phillips, Staying on Top: The Case for a National Industrial Strategy (New York: Random House, 1984).

4. The Wall Street Journal, February 12, 1987, p. 58.

5. Many of these suggestions appeared in the August 29, 1980 platform released by the independent ticket on which I ran for the Presidency. The official title was "Rebuilding a Society that Works: An Agenda for America." The entire 80,000 word text, together with commentary, has been published as A Campaign of Ideas: The 1980 Anderson/Lucey Platform, compiled by Clifford W. Brown and Robert J. Walker. In light of the recently discovered issue of competitiveness, it is interesting to note that the introduction to the section of the platform entitled "The Economy" appears the following statement: "Something has gone wrong. A nation whose productive capacity made it the arsenal of Democracy and the envy of the world today finds itself plagued by shrinking capacity to produce and a growing inability to compete in the world marketplace" (pp. 28-29).

6. Sam I. Nakagama, Economic Perspectives, vol. 12, no. 26, September 7, 1982.

7. The New York Times, April 29, 1987, p. B1.

8. The New York Times, April 29, 1987, p. D8.

9. See, for example, The Washington Post, May 20, 1987, p. 1, 16.

CONVENTIONAL DETERRENCE AND THE AMERICAN INDUSTRIAL BASE: SECURITY CHALLENGE FOR THE NINETEEN-NINETIES

by Robert S. Wood

The United States is dependent upon foreign sources, especially Asian ones, for many components of military items produced by American corporations for U.S. conventional forces. This essay discusses the magnitude of that dependence, some of its causes, and its implications for national security and America's relations with its allies, both European and Asian. Potential solutions and their ramifications are also explored.

Negotiations between the United States and the Soviet Union on an agreement to remove and dismantle intermediate range nuclear forces from NATO and Warsaw Pact Europe, if followed by the removal of short-range and battlefield nuclear forces, as some suggest, would signal a substantial denuclearization in practice, if not yet in principle, of NATO strategy. Such a development would suggest the need either to negotiate a similar agreement on conventional forces or to bolster conventional deterrence by increasing NATO non-nuclear forces--or both. In any event, many commentators have argued for some time that the nuclear balance between the Soviet Union and the West and our total inexperience with nuclear war make the early, or indeed late, use of nuclear weapons in a Eurasian conflict unpromising as a rational strategy and potentially catastrophic in its global implications.

This is not to imply that nuclear weapons no longer serve a role in deterring attack, say, in Central Europe. Would any statesman readily launch a war on the premise that there is, for instance, only a 10 percent likelihood that nuclear retaliation would ensue? At the same time, if Western conventional forces are seen as inadequate, it is possible to conceive of difficulties in Eastern Europe or other motivations arising from fear or ambition that may well impel the Soviet Union, however improbable currently, to attempt a territorially limited but rapid, massive strike on its periphery on the calculation that war could be successfully terminated before reaching the nuclear threshold.

This consideration has led a number of analysts to support not only an improvement in Western conventional forces but the development of a strategy aimed at conducting a protracted, conventional conflict with the Soviets, most likely on a global basis.[1] Those who advocate this approach argue that, from the Soviet political-military perspective, if the Soviet leadership believed that circumstances warrant war, the battle should be geostrategically limited and conducted in such a way as to minimize damage to the Soviet Union while rapidly overwhelming its adversaries. Such a campaign, in the Soviet view, should be characterized by the highest degree of clear control and exact timing.

Many Western analysts thus argue that it must be precisely the West's aim to persuade the Soviets that they cannot with any degree of certainty look forward to the happy outcome outlined above. Instead, they must face a possibly global, protracted conflict in which crucial elements of their military capabilities and political control are put in jeopardy. In other terms, the West must have the ability to reconfigure the terms of the conflict.

Conceptually, it should be emphasized that this philosophy is not entirely new and is at the heart of current NATO strategy--with a nuclear difference.   Those who choose to deter by early reliance on an intercontinental nuclear strike are also, in effect, threatening global war as the price for a successful Soviet thrust into the central front of Europe.   And, as has been noted, this capability, and hence threat, remains.

The difference from those who advocate greater reliance on conventional deterrence is not on the global character of war, but on the sequence, duration, and probably negotiated outcome of the conflict. Advocates of this conventional school contend that Western credibility is strongly reinforced if the Soviets understand that they cannot confine the battle to the central front, even at the conventional level.   A genuine threat in the North and the South of Europe and as far away as the Northwest Pacific, with the prospect of an adversary mobilized for pro-longed conflict, should strengthen the Western position simply by making it difficult for the Soviets to discern clearly an acceptable war termination position.

Not all advocates of conventional deterrence support the global dimensions of this approach but believe that the limited availability of forces and the intensity of the battle will most likely confine the conflict to the central front, with perhaps minor operations on the northern and southern flanks.[2]   Yet, even this approach assumes a rather protracted engagement, one not calculated in days but perhaps many months, if not years.

Nuclear force might well preserve the relative immunity of the Soviet heartland and the continental United States but the clash of arms and the expenditure of resources would be the most intense in history.   In effect, however one views a conventional conflict, it has the flavor of a World War II under nuclear conditions.   And herein lies the rub--and the most troublesome difficulty in these strategies: the ability to sustain conflict and to prevail during World War II was undergirded by the enormous American industrial base.   The extent and character of this base have dramatically changed in recent years.

An analysis of recent trade deficits indicates the dimensions of the problem.   In September 1987 the gap by which imports exceed exports was the lowest since May and led to some cautious hope that the decline in the value of the dollar, by lowering the cost of U.S. goods on the world market and raising the cost of foreign goods in the American market, was finally improving the trade balance.   And although the October trade deficit hit a monthly record of $17.6 billion, the November deficit was significantly lower than expected--$13.2 billion, a decline of 25 percent from the October figure. Whether the September and November figures pointed to a trend or were a mere blip, however, the nature of contemporary U.S. manufacturing complicated the picture. Jerry J. Jasinowski of the National Association of Manufacturers, as reported in the press, noted that American manufactured goods "have an increasingly high content of imported parts, a factor that helps keep imports at stubbornly high levels. One-third of imports . . . now become industrial parts and thus a given increase in exports represents a smaller contribution than formerly to the trade balance."[3] Moreover, a survey conducted by the National Association of Purchasing Management found that 88 percent of American manufacturers use foreign components. At the same time, American multinational corporations fill a large bulk of their foreign orders from their overseas factories rather than from their domestic plants.

In addition to the fact that many U.S. products include components not directly part of our industrial base, U.S. imports of industrial products have grown in recent years for a number of other reasons, including increased income, which expanded demand for foreign goods generally, and changes in the comparative cost of production between the United States and other industrial countries, which shifted demand from domestically produced products to imports.

Changes in comparative costs have not been even among different sectors of industry. Generally speaking, the United States has retained its cost advantages in the capital-intensive and high-technology lines of production, but has been less successful in the labor-intensive and low-technology areas. The high ratio of labor costs to capital costs in the United States, relative to other countries, explains this phenomenon. U.S. advantages in the costs of capital have been eroded in recent years, however, as labor/capital cost ratios have declined in many foreign countries because of rising wages and capital subsidies.

The recent high exchange value of the dollar has, of course, further increased the price-competitiveness of manufactured imports. And it is this one element of the equation which may improve with the decline in the dollar value. Some economists argue, however, that the dollar will not only have to decline to levels well below 120 yen but will have to stay there for some considerable time before there is likely to be a shift back to domestic production and purchases. Indeed, many businessmen believe that a persistently weak dollar is not in the cards and have actually increased their imports of offshore industrial components. Even if one assumes a persistently weak dollar, manufacturers may continue both to base their plants and to purchase abroad because of higher quality and lower transportation costs. The New York Times recently cited the decision of the pharmaceutical company, Pfizer Inc. to continue to buy European molasses, a key component of the citric acid manufactured in its North Carolina plant. The company found that European molasses is superior to the Middle West variety and that bulk ocean shipping rates paid in dollars are considerably cheaper than American railroad rates.[4] This homely example apparently is reproduced across a wide spectrum of products. At the same time, the fact that a substantial portion of our domestic manufacturing capability has already been lost means that it may take as long as 10 years to recover--assuming there were concerted efforts in that direction. And, of course, to the degree that U.S. multinational firms are selling abroad, many of them believe that marketing is easier if the plant is located near the customer--a calculation, it should be noted, that is leading Japanese and other firms to locate in the United States, interdependence being a many edged sword.

The trends in U.S. imports, in terms of volume, composition and country of origin, are of importance for defense planning. This has long been recognized with respect to a variety of raw materials. More recently, it has become evident that the United States depends on foreign suppliers to support production of many military end items. Denied access to those foreign suppliers in time of emergency, U.S. mobilization efforts would be severely restricted.

A number of studies have identified aspects of this problem. The Defense Science Board 1980 Summer Study Panel on Industrial Preparedness, for example, estimated that up to 90 percent of the semiconductors used in military applications in the United States were assembled and tested abroad, primarily in the Far East. Japan was identified in that study as the source of a large percentage of the ceramic packages, lead frames and high-technology electronic components. Indeed, on 7 April 1987 then Secretary of Defense Casper W. Weinberger declared that "in one form of semiconductor chips (dynamic random access memory), the U.S. market share has dropped from almost 100 percent to only about 3 percent in only 10 years."[5] And he placed this within the broader context of the rate of productivity growth in which between 1975 and 1984 Korea outdistanced us by 15 times and Japan by 10 times. The 1980 report of the Defense Industrial Base Panel of the House Armed Services Committee drew attention to the negative implications for U.S. ability to sustain military conflict arising from the growing dependency on foreign sources for parts and components of U.S. built weapons systems.

In January 1985 the President's Commission on Industrial Competitiveness reported to President Reagan that by 1984 the U.S. had lost world market shares in 7 of 10 advanced technologies categories, i.e., microelectronics.

In a 1986 study sponsored by the Air Force Logistics Command, the Applied Concepts Corporation and the Analytic Sciences Corporation undertook the most comprehensive and detailed analysis of this problem that had been attempted up to that time. That study examined 13 weapons systems to identify dependencies on foreign suppliers. It employed a vertical-tier methodology to determine sources of supply not only for prime contractors, but for subcontractors and vendors further down in the supply network as well.

The study concluded that foreign dependencies were pervasive in U.S. defense industries. It found significant foreign inputs in 8 of the 13 weapons systems examined, including the Sparrow missile, M-1 tank, CH-58D helicopter, F-16, F-18, and AV-8B aircraft, sonobuoys and the

AR-5 chemical protective suit.   The authors expressed the view that their methodology probably had failed to detect other existing dependencies.

In addition to lower costs enjoyed by foreign suppliers, the study cited superior foreign technology, U.S. environmental restrictions, geographic distributions of raw materials, NATO standardization and corporate strategy decisions as the primary reasons U.S. producers of weapons systems imported so many parts and components.

If foreign supply sources were disrupted during an emergency, the principal result would be to halt U.S. production of affected weapons systems and spare parts.   Domestically produced substitutes for most of the items purchased abroad could be developed in time.   The study estimated, however, that production typically would be disrupted for 6 to 14 months.

At the same time, the committee figures, however gloomy on the time necessary to gear up the productive base, may still be optimistic because of an inadequate level of effort now to improve the base.   On 9 March 1987 Senator Jeff Bingaman (D-NM), Chairman of the Senate Arms Services Committee's subcommittee on Defense Industry and Technology, argued that the U.S. technology base is being consumed faster than it is growing. Indeed, he noted that spending on the technology base as a percent of Pentagon research and development had moved from 15 to 9 percent since 1985 and the FY 88-89 budget request pegs it at 8 percent.

Broadly speaking, two policy responses to the foreign dependency problem suggest themselves, both of which entail certain risks.   The first is to do nothing.   This approach recognizes international economic and industrial interdependencies as facts of life arising from the interplay of market forces.   It would promote the efficiency and vitality of the U.S. economy and those of Japan and our NATO allies, who have been identified as the major sources of our dependencies.   This alternative views economic and industrial cooperation in a major war as a natural extension of the military alliances we view as necessary to conduct such a war.   The risks inherent in such an approach are obvious, however, as mentioned earlier in this discussion.

The second alternative involves the United States instituting programs to reduce reliance on foreign suppliers of items essential for the production of military hardware.   Complete self-sufficiency could not, of course, be obtained, but by systematically identifying foreign dependencies and adopting a combination of measures to eliminate or reduce them, their effects could be significantly mitigated.   That approach would be costly both in terms of budgetary considerations and economic efficiency.   It further risks negative political consequences as a result of deliberately restricting trade with our allies.

The first alternative--that is, essentially to let global market forces work unimpededly while trying to improve U.S. efficiency in the market-- implies a continuing high level of external dependency, including in the military weapons sector, however improved our economic performance. The strategic implications of this situation should be clear.

In a real sense, Japan and a number of other Asian producers will increasingly become the "arsenals of democracy." Thus, any conventional war scenario for Europe will depend on access to these producers with continuing availability of key military components. A conventional deterrent posture for Europe and, a fortiori, a wartime posture are crucially linked to the cooperation of a number of Asian powers. This in turn implies the protection of those areas and the maintenance of the lines of communication between them, on the one hand, and the U.S. and Western Europe, on the other.

If we consider the growing defense industrial support capacity in Japan and the Pacific rim countries, an interesting strategic map emerges--one with the United States in the middle instead of "at the left edge" of the chart. Instead of envisioning the lines of communication running solely from the U.S. East Coast to NATO Europe, for some key war materials these supply lines could now stretch across the Atlantic, across the U.S., and across the vast Pacific to countries such as Japan, which could augment NATO's defense industrial capacity in the event of a major NATO-Warsaw Pact war.

Should we begin to conceptualize the problem in this way and develop the necessary links through political understandings and military exercises, the deterrent impact on Soviet calculations should be patent. This presents a far more complicated military problem than Soviet planners are likely to welcome. At the same time, such a perspective should shape the thinking of those Western theorists who believe that our strategic concentration can be almost exclusively on the central front and the Atlantic lines of communication.

The second alternative policy--intervening in market forces in order to reduce external dependency on items needed in the production of military hardware--is unlikely to exclude a rather high-level dependence on global market forces because of important political and economic reasons. Nonetheless, there is widespread sentiment for some market intervention to decrease dependence. However, the decreased dependence will be a matter of degree--hence continuing the imperative for a global strategy.

U.S. dependency on the world market, not only in the sense of global trade but of the internationalization and establishment offshore of much of the U.S. industrial base, arose not simply from a generalized policy on free trade but also from specific governmental decisions and socioeconomic changes in the American polity. U.S. policy since World War II has aimed at encouraging an industrial "two-way street" with our NATO allies and Asian associates and in recent years at providing preferential access to our market, generally within quota limits, to developing countries. The primary instruments of trade liberalization with our key economic partners have been the reduction of tariff and quantitative barriers and the removal of the more obvious, non-tariff barriers that directly and intentionally limit access to each other's markets. Many tax and investment policies, laws on trusts and monopolies, governmental-industrial-academic networks, cultural mores--all of these factors have guaranteed that the competition was not on an "even playing field." Moreover, not only have U.S. governmental business policies affected the competitive position of the American firm but so too have American educational policies, the nature of the U.S. work force, and the cultural propensity of a citizenry that favors credit and spending over savings.

Moreover, defense acquisition policies have been to a substantial degree based on economic criteria--that is, the purchase of the best military weapons components at the cheapest price. At the same time, U.S. national security policy aimed at the maintenance of friendly and independent regimes and of coalitions robust enough to contain Soviet opportunism and regional threats, constrains tendencies toward purely economic calculations on our part in dealing with those same states.

The result of all of these forces has been a level of dependency and perhaps of vulnerability that is not easy to overcome completely without doing grave damage to our security, economic well-being, and social stability. Nonetheless, the dimensions of that dependence should be appreciated if some remedial action is to take place. For example, the rising dominance in the 1980s of Japanese manufacture in ceramics, electronic components and parts, machine tools and parts, and telecommunications equipment and parts has been impressive by any standard and, most significant, this manufacture constitutes a substantial portion of the U.S. market (see Table 1).

An examination of the critically important semiconductor industry shows how in an area where U.S. science and technology, have indeed been path-breaking, the American market has nonetheless been increasingly penetrated by foreign, especially Japanese, manufacture (see Figure 1). In February 1987, a number of key scientific breakthroughs in semiconductors were announced by U.S. concerns only to be followed within days by the organization of a Japanese consortium of experts to develop and commercialize the new materials. This led U.S. Senator David Durenberger to complain that "we go on inventing and the Japanese go on producing. . . . The stakes are just too high to let superconductivity go the way of the VCR industry." Some have noted that the time between invention to commercialization is simply too long in the United States compared with Japan--ranging from 3 to 5 years in the first case to 1 to 2 years in the second. It is this environment that has led to demands for a joint government-industry approach, not to throttle the free market but to improve the U.S. manufacturers' position in it.

Some steps, however inadequate, have already been taken. Under the Reagan Administration, an Industrial Modernization Incentives Program (IMIP) and a Manufacturing Technology Program (MANTECH) have been undertaken, although the level of effort is considered far too low. The IMIP is aimed at providing government funds for research and development investment as a stimulus to private sector capital investment and MANTECH is basically an effort to discover new defense-relevant manufacturing technologies.   Both programs suffer from the lack of a consistent, comprehensive industrial policy and from limited funding.

Technology experts and public policy analysts have advanced a number of suggestions to strengthen the "bite" of the government's program.   First, and expectedly, there is call for a substantial increase in federal funding of research and development, as high as an immediate influx of $100 million in the semiconductor industry alone.   An argument against such a level of support is the chronic federal budget deficit.   On the other hand, this is precisely where policy is required--i.e., a curb on current consumption via public funding and individual discretionary spending in the interest of increased production.   Budget cuts and tax increases should be evaluated in terms of industrial policy as well as other criteria.

Second, the time may have come to evaluate our federal antitrust laws by reference to a global rather than a purely national market.   Some relaxation of these laws to allow researchers in large firms to pool their research efforts seems desirable, at a minimum.

Third, in some cases a single U.S. laboratory might be designated as coordinator of research and development in critical high-technology areas not only in order to avoid duplication of effort but to insure important areas are not neglected.   Again, the superconductor field may be a logical candidate for such an enterprise.

Fourth, if the country needs to accept a level of government-industry-academic cooperation often resisted in theory if not (fortunately) always in practice, a similar effort may be required among the industrial countries.   For instance, some have argued that Japan and the United States should agree on cooperative efforts in basic research, engineering, and commercialization.   Such an approach appears to counter the drive to moderate U.S. dependency.   But U.S. security ties and the depth of interdependency dictate intergovernmental as well as national policies.

Some analysts have argued that, as stockpiles of vital strategic raw materials have been established, so the country should build a national critical items list along the lines of the military critical items developed by the Joint Chiefs of Staff and to include the manpower skills, natural resources, production capabilities, and finished goods essential to military and civilian needs in time of war and incapable of being generated in a matter of weeks.[7]   Guaranteed government purchases and tax and investment incentives, as well as cooperative efforts by industrial associations, private and public laboratories, and the government would undergird efforts to establish criticality and substitutability of items and the necessary steps in the industrial process.   Such a process could be folded into the Joint Industrial Mobilization Planning Process (JIMPP) initiative of the Office of the Secretary of Defense in concert with the Joint Chiefs of Staff.

To state this vision, at its logical extreme, is, of course, to raise the prospect of America, Inc., with all the implications of a general industrial policy and the attendant impacts on a free market. Should it be thought desirable to develop along these lines, however, a major issue will be how to limit such impacts and the accompanying costs, either to the taxpayer or to the consumer or to both.

One thing is certain: the demands of a conventional deterrent are far more strenuous than many of its proponents suspect. It requires an external policy aimed at linking a number of industrial producers and resource states not party to the North Atlantic Treaty and an internal policy that would at the same time in some form recapture U.S. technical and industrial leadership. Such a conventional deterrent posture also implies a strategy that would maintain the integrity of those same states and the lines of communication among them in wartime.

Many Western statesmen have long understood that a nuclear-reliant strategy exacted less economic and direct military costs. That calculation is still largely true. Ironically, however, reliance on a conventional strategy could potentially undergird the "reindustrialization" of America and a more orderly linkage among the Western economies.

NOTES

1. See for instance, Admiral James D. Watkins, USN; General P.X. Kelley, USMC, and Major Hugh K. O'Donnell, Jr., USMC; John F. Lehman, Jr.; and Captain Peter M. Swartz, USN, The Maritime Strategy, U.S. Naval Institute (January 1986). Also Colin S. Gray, Maritime Strategy, Geopolitics, and the Defense of the West (New York: National Strategy Information Center, 1986). Also Captain Linton Brooks, "Naval Power and National Security: The Case for the Maritime Strategy," International Security, Fall 1986, pp. 58-87.

2. See John J. Mearsheimer, Conventional Deterrence (Ithaca and London: Cornell University Press, 1983). Also, Mearsheimer, "A Strategic Misstep: The Maritime Strategy and Deterrence in Europe," International Security, Fall 1986, pp. 3-57.

3. The Providence Journal, 13 November 1987, p. A2.

4. The New York Times, 14 January 1988, p. D6.

5. "Technological Leadership, The Industrial Base and National Security," remarks delivered by Secretary of Defense Casper W. Weinberger to the Electronics Industries Association Annual Government and Industry Dinner, Washington, D.C., 7 April 1987.

6. The Providence Journal, 7 June 1987, p. B3.

7.   For one important example of this approach, see Albert M. Bottoms, Defense Systems Management College, Ft. Belvoir, VA, "Toward National Security Resource Preparedness: The Resource Citadel." 3 February 1987.

TABLE 1

KEY INDUSTRIAL IMPORTS TO U.S.
(IN MILLIONS OF DOLLARS)

	1980	1981	1982	1983	1984
CERAMICS (LAB & INDUSTRIAL)					
WORLD	8.6	12.3	16.6	17.0	25.1
JAPAN	2.6	6.2	10.5	6.4	8.3
% OF JAPANESE IMPORTS TO TOTAL	30%	50%	63%	37%	33%
ELECTRONIC COMPONENTS & PARTS					
WORLD	3,592	3,959	4,524	5,388	8,228
JAPAN	522	553	732	1,095	2,229
% OF JAPANESE IMPORTS TO TOTAL	15%	14%	16%	20%	27%
IRON & STEEL					
WORLD	7,364	11,211	9,613	6,791	10,871
JAPAN	2,864	3,829	3,605	1,940	3,161
% OF JAPANESE IMPORTS TO TOTAL	39%	34%	38%	29%	30%
MACHINE TOOLS, PARTS & ACCESSORIES					
WORLD	1,575	1,794	1,638	1,136	1,725
JAPAN	547	760	649	459	787
% OF JAPANESE IMPORTS TO TOTAL	35%	42%	40%	40%	46%
TELECOMMUNICATIONS EQUIPMENT & PARTS					
WORLD	2,562	3,247	1,899	2,534	6,583
JAPAN	1,067	1,525	1,623	1,985	3,202
% OF JAPANESE IMPORTS TO TOTAL	42%	47%	85%	78%	49%

SOURCE: BUREAU OF THE CENSUS: U.S. IMPORTS (FT 150 & 155)
BASED ON CUSTOMS VALUES FOR IMPORTS

Origins of U.S. Semiconductor Imports - 1972, 1978, and 1984***

FIGURE 1

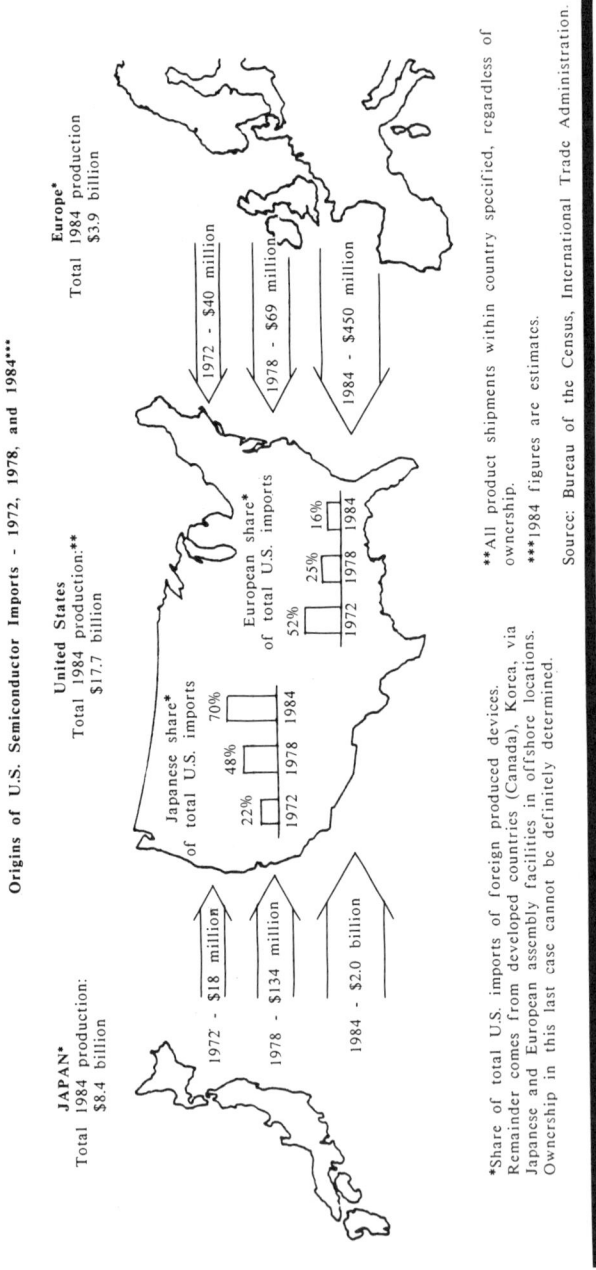

Origins of U.S. Semiconductor Imports - 1972, 1978, and 1984***

JAPAN*
Total 1984 production:
$8.4 billion

1972 - $18 million

1978 - $134 million

1984 - $2.0 billion

United States
Total 1984 production:**
$17.7 billion

Japanese share*
of total U.S. imports

22%   48%   70%

1972   1978   1984

European share*
of total U.S. imports

52%   25%   16%

1972   1978   1984

Europe*
Total 1984 production
$3.9 billion

1972 - $40 million

1978 - $69 million

1984 - $450 million

*Share of total U.S. imports of foreign produced devices.
Remainder comes from developed countries (Canada), Korea, via
Japanese and European assembly facilities in offshore locations.
Ownership in this last case cannot be definitely determined.

**All product shipments within country specified, regardless of
ownership.

***1984 figures are estimates.

Source: Bureau of the Census, International Trade Administration.

THE DEPARTMENT OF DEFENSE, DEFENSE INDUSTRY AND PROCUREMENT: FATAL MISCONCEPTIONS

by Lawrence J. Korb

Problems between government and defense industry over procurement are not new. However, during the Reagan Administration relations between industry and the Pentagon hit an all-time low. Each side blamed the other for the difficulties. Reforms recommended in 1986 by the Packard Commission will help, but unless certain underlying biases or misconceptions are understood there is the potential for another outbreak of hostility between the government and industry.

The problems fit into four categories: inaccurate perceptions of how industry and the Pentagon view each other and how they are both viewed by the American people; desire of both government and industry to have things both ways; lack of appreciation for the American political system; and rigidity in corporations.

I

INTRODUCTION

During my career, I have served at high-level positions in both government and defense industry. From 1981 to 1985, I served as Assistant Secretary of Defense, Manpower, Installations and Logistics [ASD (MI&L)]. In this position, I administered about 70 percent of the entire defense budget and was responsible for ensuring the readiness of our armed forces. From 1985-86, I served as Vice President Corporate Operations of Raytheon, a $7-billion-a-year Fortune (100) corporation that consistently ranks among the top ten defense contractors. I was responsible for running the Corporation's Washington office, that is, directing the marketing, congressional relations and planning functions that were conducted in the Washington area.

As ASD (MI&L) and as a company Vice President, I was in effect a "corporate officer" of both the Department of Defense (DOD) and Raytheon. Hence I was involved in all the major policymaking meetings of both organizations and had frequent interactions with the heads of both groups. The major policymaking body in DOD was the Defense Resource Board (DRB), composed of the Under and Assistant Secretaries of Defense, the uniformed and civilian heads of the armed services, and the Chairman of the Joint Chiefs of Staff (JS). Raytheon's equivalent to the DRB was the annual corporate strategy meeting composed of the corporate officers and general managers of its 10 divisions and 12 major operating subsidiaries. The DRB's job was to review the five-year programs of DOD's components (the armed services and defense agencies) for consistency, fiscal soundness, and adherence to the policy guidance of the

Secretary of Defense and the National Security Council. At Raytheon's annual corporate strategy meeting, each of its 22 components presented its five-year programs to the corporate officers.

The heads of DOD were the Secretary of Defense, Caspar Weinberger, and the Deputy Secretary of Defense who handled the day to day management of the Pentagon. In my time in the Pentagon, three men occupied this post: Frank Carlucci, Paul Thayer, and William Taft IV. In the case of Raytheon the leaders were the Chairman of the Board and Chief Executive Officer, Thomas Phillips and the President, D. Brainard Holmes.

Essentially I was on the corporate staff of both bodies. In DOD, the line organizations were the three military departments, Army, Navy, and Air Force, plus a host of defense agencies ranging from the mammoth Defense Logistics Agency (50,000 people), to the tiny Defense Advance Research Projects Agency with about one hundred people. In Raytheon, the line groups ranged from the large Missile Systems Division to the tiny Raytheon Marine Company and D.C. Heath Publishing Company.

II

THE PROCUREMENT PROBLEM

During my tenure at DOD and Raytheon, relations between government and the defense industry were at an all-time low. In the mid-1980s, there seemed to be a procurement scandal a day. It was as though a plague was infesting the acquisition system. DOD was charged, or payed, outrageous prices for such mundane items as a hammer ($435), diode ($110), wrench ($9,600), plastic cap ($917), toilet seat ($640), pliers ($748) and coffee pot ($7,000). Major companies were found to be billing the government for such administrative costs as kennel fees for the chief executive officer's dog. Companies were apparently making up for losses in their commercial lines by transferring overhead expenses to defense contracts. Expensive weapon systems like the Division Air Defense Gun (DIVAD) and the B-1 bomber simply did not perform as advertised. Rather than shooting down enemy helicopters, the DIVAD homed in on an outhouse fan! Despite an expenditure of some $28 billion, the B-1, a penetrating bomber, was found to have neither the defense avionics or the aerodynamic capacity to get through Soviet air defenses properly. It was no wonder that President Reagan's Blue Ribbon Commission on Defense Management, the Packard Commission, reported to the President in 1986 that the acquisition system was "fundamentally ill."

For its part, defense industry claimed that DOD was a terrible customer. It seemed to change its mind from year to year on the types and quantity of weapon systems it wanted. The laws and regulations governing acquisition were extremely cumbersome. For example, there are some 400 different regulatory requirements that are pegged to some 60 different dollar thresholds. DOD seemed to be interested in competition for competition's sake and prosecution of companies for publicity purposes. Moreover, government seemed to have no understanding of or respect for the proprietary rights of companies or the need for industry to make a profit. Finally, defense contractors were forced to spend more time dealing with inspectors and auditors than working on the product. DOD proudly proclaimed that it performed in excess of 10,000 audits of defense contractors per year.

Defense industry argued that its record was pretty good, although there were some problems. It noted that DOD executed about 15 million contracts per year and that on a percentage basis the number of mistakes was less than 1 percent of 150,000 per year. Moreover, compared to other public sector projects or large private sector projects, defense industry's record was excellent. Major weapon systems cost growth was smaller than public sector water projects and public buildings, and such large private sector projects as the New Orleans Superdome, the Concorde, and the Trans-Alaska Pipeline.

Problems between the defense establishment and defense industry date at least from the Civil War. During that conflict, Congress enacted the so-called Abraham Lincoln Law, the False Claims Act of 1863, because of stories that contractors were overcharging the Union Army; engaging in such practices as selling the Union Army dead mules; or selling the War Department live horses, stealing them back, and then reselling them.

There will always be some conflict between DOD and defense industry. Indeed some conflict or tension is healthy because the aims of the two sides are fundamentally different; DOD wants to minimize cost while industry wants to maximize profit. However, the level of tension and conflict need not be as high as it was during the Reagan Administration. Neither DOD nor industry wins when they declare war on each other. The hostility which came into the open during this decade had as much to do with undermining the defense consensus as did the massive federal deficit. In the first Reagan Administration defense spending grew by over 50 percent in real terms and spending on weapon systems purchases more than doubled in real terms. However, following the publicity surrounding the procurement scandals, the five-year plan of the second Reagan Administration was slashed by $600 billion (30 percent) and the defense budget has now dropped for three consecutive years.

III

PERCEPTUAL PROBLEMS

The Packard Commission has laid down a sensible formula for improving the procurement system. Its recommendations for streamlining the system, stabilizing programs, balancing cost and performance, using technology to reduce cost and expanding the use of competition and commercial products will help cure some of the most egregious problems. However, the Commission could not alter the biases or misconceptions on which both DOD and industry operate. In my view, until these are understood and ameliorated there will be more conflict in the process than necessary and everyone, DOD, industry and the nation, will lose.

These biases or misconceptions can be broken down into four categories: First, neither group has a very accurate perception of how it is viewed by the American people. Nor do DOD or industry officials realize how they are viewed by each other. Top defense industry officials see themselves as patriots providing America with the arsenal of democracy at less profit than they could make doing commercial work. The American people view them more as merchants of death or the insidious part of the military-industrial-complex. For example, according to a Harris poll conducted in 1985, 85 percent of the American people view defense contractors as dishonest.[1] Moreover, their counterparts in government perceive them as overpaid and avaricious individuals who would cheat the government if given half a chance. Terms like Beltway Bandits, Crystal City Crooks and Roslyn Robbers are commonly applied by government workers to their counterparts in industry. Thus, government workers feel little compunction in unleashing hordes of auditors on defense contractors.

Defense officials also view themselves as selfless patriots, working long hours for low pay with no other motive than serving the public good. They are unaware that the public sees them more as lazy bureaucrats without much common sense who invent rules and regulations to protect themselves and their cushy jobs, rather than as persons committed to serving the public. This helps to explain why the spare parts horror stories struck such a responsive cord with the public. They confirmed what the public already believed: that is, government officials, even in DOD, are just like the bureaucrats they encounter at the post office or the motor vehicle bureau.

The view of corporate officials of their counterparts in DOD is no more flattering. They see the career people as bureaucrats protected by civil service tenure who are incapable of making a decision or assuming responsibility and who are closet specialists, deeply suspicious of the glories of capitalism and the rewards of free enterprise. Business leaders perceive political appointees as hacks, more concerned with pleasing political interests than in producing good weapons.

These misperceptions explain how both government and industry responded to the crisis brought about by the spare parts horror stories and why their responses were inappropriate. DOD launched a blitzkrieg of studies and reorganizations which resulted in some 600 initiatives with fancy sounding acronyms like BOSS (Buy Our Spares Smart), all the while denying that any problems existed. This only reinforced the perceptions of the public and defense industry.

Industry responded by claiming that it was within its rights to maximize profits wherever it could. I can remember dealing with officials of the Lockheed Corporation on the price of the toilet seat (it was actually a lavatory cover). Their initial offer was to take $100 off the price, as if they would appear less ridiculous with a $540 instead of a $640 toilet seat.

Second, both groups want to have it both ways. Defense industry wants all the benefits of free enterprise but none of the risks. If all goes well during the research, development and production phases of the weapon systems acquisition process, defense industry wants to keep the difference between their costs and the amount of the government contract. If, however, problems arise in the execution of the contract, industry wants DOD to pay for these difficulties, even if they result from industry's own bad management. In 1983, General Dynamics actually had the gall to sue the Navy for mistakes made by its own management at Electric Boat in carrying out a submarine construction.

Similarly, when calculating profits on defense business, contractors usually present them in terms of a return on sales rather than as a return on investment or assets. Since in many cases DOD actually owns the plant in which the system is produced (for example, the General Dynamics plant in Fort Worth which makes F-16's), or pays the initial costs of research and developing or tooling, return on investment or assets is a much better indicator of the profitability of defense work. Moreover, when return on sales in defense work becomes high, industry tries to mask the full extent of profitability by lumping defense in with commercial work in its public reports. About half of Raytheon's business was with government, but the vast majority of its profit came from defense work.

DOD officials exhibit the same tendencies. They want to take credit when the weapon's acquisition process goes well and blame industry when things go wrong, even when the fault lies with the government. For example, in the 1970s Lockheed almost went bankrupt as a result of a fixed price contract for the C-5A which DOD "forced" upon it, even though both sides knew that such a contract was inappropriate.[2] Recently DOD blamed industry for the problems of the B-1, even though the Air Force itself served as the system integrator and the Secretary of Defense himself reviewed the program every two weeks.

Third, for the most part, neither group understands or appreciates the American political system. Both DOD and industry view Congress and the press as nuisances, rather than the fundamental underpinnings of our way of life. Government officials are constantly complaining about the inordinate amount of time they have to spend testifying before Congress, rather than looking at that time as an integral and necessary part of their job. What could have higher priority than explaining to the people's representatives why we need to spend a full 6 percent of our GNP on part of our budget? Similarly, government officials constantly complain about Congress destabilizing their programs. It is as if the legislature were not a coequal branch of government, with the constitutional power to raise an Army and a Navy, and with the constitutional obligation to oversee expenditure of the funds it appropriates. Accountability, both financial and political, is a bulwark of our system, however burdensome to implementors of policy.[3]

Many defense officials treat the media like a cross between the Soviet Union's Committee for State Security and Pravda: that is, one organization from which all important information must be kept and another one that should echo the party line. On more than one occasion, I heard the Secretary of Defense say that he wanted to start his own newspaper to get the "truth" out. Very few people in DOD recognize or accept the constitutional role of the press to act as a check on the power of government by informing people of the facts and presenting options other than those espoused by DOD.

Defense industry officials have an even more pernicious view of Congress and the media than do their government counterparts. They perceive the members of Congress as motivated primarily by parochial considerations and greed. This view stems from, among other things, industry's expectations about congressional behavior. Defense contractors expect members who represent districts in which they have plants to support their programs blindly. Many officials of Raytheon, which is the largest employer in Massachusetts, just assume that the Massachusetts delegation will go along with even the most dubious Raytheon defense program because, "What is good for Raytheon is good for Massachusetts."

Similarly, defense industry expects money to talk. Corporations assume that those members whom they help will do their bidding. Moreover, when the contributions do not achieve that objective, they soon dry up. In my discussions with some Raytheon executives, they found the idea of a member of Congress voting his conscience or looking out for the national interest incomprehensible, and if such a person existed, they often argued that he or she was not worthy of "our" support.

Defense industry perceives the media as illegitimate, with no right to discuss anything about the corporation, even if the latter is publicly owned. When Business Week reported (correctly) how poorly Raytheon's top management handled the retirement of the company's president, the company cancelled its advertising in that magazine. Similarly, when asked by the media to comment on a story, the standard response is, "No comment," or some pious platitude.

These attitudes toward Congress and the media also explain the way in which industry and government dealt with the procurement scandals. Rather than recognizing that the acquisition system was fundamentally ill; they blamed the messengers, who, in their view, had no right to be involved in "their" business. Both DOD and industry blamed the Congress and the media for hyping the scandals merely to get publicity or to sell newspapers.

Fourth, contrary to the standard wisdom, there is actually much more diversity, openness, and tolerance for dissent, and thus less rigidity, in DOD than in industry. Based upon my experience at Raytheon, I believe defense industry needs a Packard Commission much more than DOD. At

DRB meetings or in the Secretary of Defense's morning staff meetings, I never felt intimidated about speaking up. In fact some DRB meetings or morning staff meetings became pretty raucous. At Raytheon's monthly staff meetings or the annual corporate strategy meetings no one, except the CEO or the president, said a word. About 50 people sat there once a month for one hour and once a year for 16 hours listening to the "party line" with nary a murmur. DOD's leaders may make some mistakes, but it will not be because they did not have opposing points of view to consider. Raytheon's leaders may make correct decisions, but it will be in spite of the fact that they do not have all the views of their immediate subordinates.

I can remember sitting in Lexington, Massachusetts in the fall of 1985 listening incredulously to glowing reports about how Raytheon's defense business would continue to increase rapidly because of the "growing defense budget." I naively asked another corporate officer when I could correct the assumption, but he merely laughed and said that that was not done. Subsequently, I made my controversial, but accurate, statement about the defense budget in a public forum (it had declined in real terms for three consecutive years), and was summarily fired after some government officials complained to the company. The efficiency of American industry suffers substantially from such rigidities, and therefore the national interest, which is dependent on a productive economy, is ill served. The problem, a serious one under any circumstances, is a deepening one, given the increasingly competitive international environment within which American industry operates. In contrast to the Raytheon incident, when someone in DOD occasionally allowed his disagreements with official policy to become public, that individual might be reprimanded, but never fired, especially if he or she apologized.[4]

Another sign of stagnation in our industrial sector concerns women and minorities. At no Raytheon corporate meeting did I ever see a black or a woman. Those meetings were more like sessions of some Ivy League fraternity circa 1920 than a modern progressive corporation in the last decade of the twentieth century. By contrast, women and minorities have been represented at the higher echelons of DOD (although not in sufficient numbers).

While DOD had many problems, they will be easier to fix because of its comparative openness and tolerance of dissent. The rigidity I found at Raytheon makes me sympathetic to those who claim that the lack of competitiveness in American industry is self-inflicted. If that rigidity is characteristic of the industry as a whole, I do not have much hope that the abuses in defense procurement which have come to light in this decade will be eliminated, or even substantially reduced.

IV

CONCLUSION

The solution to these biases and misconceptions is easier to sketch out in general terms than it is to achieve, but the articulation of some basic propositions represents at least a beginning. The solution will have to involve: ensuring that people who rise to positions of importance in government and industry be aware of these mistaken frames of reference; encouraging people to go back and forth between government and industry;[5] and making sure that people in these organizations receive a good liberal arts education that helps them develop an appreciation for our system. Without broad acceptance of these three basic principles, no viable solution is possible. However, since very few people in either industry or government even recognize the essential elements of the problem, I am not optimistic that anything will be done. Thus, warfare is liable to break out again between the Pentagon and defense industry.

NOTES

1.   Joseph Kruzel, American Defense Annual, 1986-87 (Lexington, MA: D.C. Heath, 1986), p. 57.

2.   Since DOD is the only customer, industry either accepts its terms or does without the business. These unrealistic contracts are often drawn up for political purposes with the expectation that terms will be adjusted when the political heat is off.

3.   Manifestations of this attitude were graphically demonstrated by the testimony of executive branch officials to the secret committee investigating the Iran-Contra situation.

4.   Ironically, after DOD's inspector general found that some defense officials had acted improperly by complaining to Raytheon about my remarks, they were not fired or even publicly reprimanded.

5.   Obviously, one has to ensure that appropriate safeguards exist so that the integrity of the procurement process is maintained. I have in mind people like Norman Augustine and Frank Shrontz, who served in high-level positions in DOD in the 1970s, and who now head Martin-Marietta and Boeing, respectively.

LIBERAL ARTS COLLEGES AND CORPORATE CREATIVITY: SOME PRELIMINARY REFLECTIONS[1]

by David Riesman

The principal concern of this essay is with the private liberal arts college (church-related or secular), which is small (1,000 to 3,000 students at maximum), demanding and correspondingly selective, residential and hence capable of producing an esprit de corps, attracting students and sending them forth again beyond their narrow geographical catch basins. I have in mind something on the order of 100 colleges, primarily in the East, Southeast, Middle West, and Far West, with two exemplars in the Mountain States (Colorado College and St. John's College in Santa Fe). In the various college guides, these are the colleges which are reputed to have produced an astonishing number of corporate leaders, many of them directly after the baccalaureate. Others, often aiming toward corporate work, have gotten there via a law degree or an MBA or, infrequently, through graduate work in arts and sciences. I do not believe, and I shall say more about this anon, that there is any inevitable connection between becoming liberally educated and attending any particular version of liberal arts college, or indeed any kind of college. Nevertheless, there is evidence, though I can touch on only a fragment thereof, that half a hundred liberal arts colleges play a very large role in furnishing future academic leadership to the major research universities, public and private. Thus, the liberal arts colleges contribute indirectly, as well as through their graduates, to the personnel and to the scientific infrastructure which support corporations that aim to be competitive. At the same time, the private liberal arts colleges are facing increased competition with public colleges and universities.

I

There is no single type of successful corporate leader. In the American context, many people in and out of corporate life are rediscovering that the most effective leaders are capable of building a team, while maintaining independence of judgment and willingness always to listen to, but occasionally to differ from, the collaborative group they have developed.

In contrast, America presents today in toxic abundance the hyper-individualism in which every lone ranger has her or his lawyer-gun for hire, suing at the drop of an expected raise or promotion or allegedly unfair pension plan. Also in superabundant supply, coming out of law school in some cases, business school in others, are consultants for hire who have never since childhood, and perhaps not then, experienced any institutional loyalty, including loyalty to the firm for which they are currently working. Business executives of this orientation are prompted by their inner drives, and by the market forces both they and the corporation face, toward under-maintenance of people and plants and under-funding of research and development. The goal is to have themselves and their company's stock look good on Wall Street in the current quarter, but not so positioned as to tempt a raider.[2]   What is also present, although perhaps not superabundant, is the willingness to work hard, or at least long hours--a willingness supplemented by the fierce ambitions of the new generations of career women determined to outplay the men at the men's own games. Indeed, some of these women, taking competitive men as their models, but only beginning to be aware that the road to the boardroom leads through the locker room, find it even more difficult than many men to adapt to the teamwork requisite in today's corporate leadership.[3]

What are the qualities in short supply among corporate leaders? In short supply are curiosity; empathy, though not necessarily sympathy; knowledge of another quite different culture; and a capacity for judgment which is independent yet cooperative, nonanarchic, and nonrapacious. Leaders must be prepared to defend institutional interests, which means that they must become facilitators of a going concern. This may require tough judgments vis-a-vis particular individuals, and a capacity for self-criticism and self-development in contrast to solipsistic defensiveness. It helps if in college or in later life they have learned what it takes to become an expert in a specialized arena (whether directly germane to business tactics or not). Going through that process one begins to learn how to judge the expertise of others, while being neither awed by it nor, in the American populist grain, hostile to the expert and the bureaucrat.[4]

Some of what I have just said is perhaps captured by a statement that may seem paradoxical, namely, that unconventional ambition is also in short supply. Such ambition involves an eagerness to accomplish something that is not necessarily "making it," in terms of money or status on a quick career ladder, but rather a longer-run, more inventive ambition, based on one's unfolding powers, one's ability to develop oneself, and one's hope to leave an institutional as well as a personal legacy.

II

The ability for cooperation is unevenly distributed. Therefore, there is a common and understandable complaint about today's students at the major research universities, such as my own. These renowned institutions recruit and prepare often exceedingly intelligent individuals who jostle one another as they seek to get on the "fast track" for positions that may be highly remunerative, but who still do not betoken unconventional ambition. If these comments are not too wide of the mark, where then might corporations look when they seek individuals who are cooperative, not in some sentimental sense, but with a combination of independent thinking and the ability to work in a team and to build a team?

In the big research universities, primarily cosmopolitan and secular in outlook, there is sufficient diversity to produce enclaves which are out of sympathy with the typical ethos (on the faculty and in the student body) of competitive yet also cautious individualism. However, it is in the church-related institutions, often in isolated settings, that one finds illustrations of the ability of Americans to combine individualism and team spirit. The largest academic institution I have visited where personal rivalry is muted by fraternal spirit is Brigham Young University in Provo, Utah, with nearly 25,000 undergraduates, virtually all of whom are Latter Day Saints, that is, Mormons. Most students have had field missions abroad before entering the University. Many of them, however, have agreed with my observation that they went abroad too young to take full advantage of their cross-cultural exposure. It is strong family ties and the organization of the church into stakes and wards that maintain a sense of collegiality for Mormons.[5] Brigham Young University does excellent work in some of the sciences, engineering, and the study of law, business, and education--the notation, "God is Intelligence," is a Mormon staple. What is less common is imagination, an ability--rare, as I have indicated at the outset--to transcend time and place. Curiosity, too, seems to be channeled, rather than at large.

Other church-related colleges and universities nurture the combination of collegiality and individuality found at BYU. Hope College in Holland, Michigan, linked to the Reformed Church in America, the former Dutch Calvinist Church, is not perhaps as well-known as Calvin College, which is more strictly evangelical. Wheaton College in Wheaton, Illinois, and Gordon College in Wenham, Massachusetts, are nondenominational evangelical colleges. Talladega in Mississippi (United Church of Christ); St. Paul's College in Lawrenceville, Virginia (Episcopal); and others are examples among the traditionally black colleges. None of these institutions, nor, for example, Furman University (Baptist) in Greenville, South Carolina, with 2,300 undergraduates, have the religious near-homogeneity of Brigham Young. But on a small scale they often turn out to be locales where individualism, religious ties to some traditional values, and a cooperative, friendly spirit go hand-in-hand. Some notable inventive industrialists have come out of Hope College, with 2,500 students; Gordon College sends people into high-tech industry in this state from a student body of 1,200.[6]

In general, for reasons I shall come to in a moment, it is in the private liberal arts colleges, those with and those without a religious orientation, that I find inculcated some of the qualities, in fact the missing ingredients, needed for corporations to prosper when they combine stability with flexibility and innovation. Throughout, I am talking only about residential students and about traditional college-age student bodies, for my focus is on the capacities cultivated in a cohort that studies together and lives together during an important stage on life's way.

III

With its size, its wealth, its strong alumni support, Brigham Young University is not at risk in the foreseeable future, nor is the Ivy League, nor Stanford, Notre Dame, Emory, or Duke. The most eminent liberal arts colleges in the Northeast, including Bowdoin, Amherst, Williams, Trinity,

Wesleyan, Haverford, Swarthmore, and, I would hope also, Wellesley and Bryn Mawr, have the endowment and eminence to continue to prosper. However, one can make no similar guarantee concerning the future of the less fortunate, smaller, private, liberal arts colleges. If I am right that it is these colleges which in small but crucial numbers prepare potential corporate leaders, then I would suggest that corporate leadership today needs to continue its concern in philanthropy as in recruiting for this particular genre of institutions.

I say this fully recognizing that corporations provide an increasing amount of higher education through their own in-house programs. Not only in teaching skills but also in broader aspects of intellectual development, corporation in-house educational enterprises have the advantage of working with motivated adults who are not worrying about paying back loans or about whether or not they will get a job on graduation. Corporations can provide state-of-the-art equipment. They can pay market rates for faculty without subjecting themselves to what I sometimes call the campus socialism of trying to pay the same amount of money to a tenured professor of philosophy or fine arts as they have to pay to an assistant professor of computer science, or decision theory, or perhaps microbiology. However, neither IBM nor AT&T is able to sustain programs such as AT&T's program for Humanistic Education of Executives that was developed in 1953 at the University of Pennsylvania--the most intense educational program I have ever had a hand in. AT&T had to give up that program, not because it failed, but because other companies would not join in. Thus, AT&T felt exposed to stockholder objection to the development of what Thorstein Veblen called idle curiosity, not geared to specific corporate tasks. The closest analogues to that AT&T program are found in the private liberal arts colleges, although there are arenas in the research universities, public as well as private, where of course liberal education of all sorts flourishes.

Diversity among institutions (in contrast to diversity within them) which allows for the play of the market, religion, state and regional pride, and non-centralized control, has been, in the view of foreign as well as American observers, the principal reason why American higher education has achieved its present international eminence, despite the lackluster quality of much precollegiate education. However, private higher education is steadily losing ground to publicly subsidized state colleges and universities; each had half of the student population in 1950, whereas today the private institutions have only 20 percent, and that share continues to decline.

It is widely recognized that higher education is capital-intensive. There is also, unevenly in different regions of the country, sharp demographic decline in cohorts of high school graduates. Despite low tuition, some state colleges have shrunk, but these are harder to eliminate even than an Army base. In private colleges, tuitions have gone up in an attempt to meet rising costs, even while federal loan and grant support for the middle-income students attracted by these colleges has been curtailed. In this situation, many small liberal arts colleges, already precarious, can lose any sense of mission and elan and then fold. Conversely, the major private research universities in the Ivy League, along with Stanford, Rice, Hopkins, Emory, Northwestern, Duke, and others, which are well-endowed and in many cases metropolitan, will actually gain recruits, since they can afford to subsidize students, and since attitudes of students and their parents make them the "best buys" in parental and student assessment alike. Williams, Amherst, Wesleyan, Trinity University in San Antonio, Haverford and Swarthmore, by reason of combinations of endowment, eminent alumni, locale, and of course eminence, are likely also to remain "best buys."

Nevertheless, even the topflight, private, liberal arts colleges face hazards which corporate leadership can help minimize. In the past, the competitive relations between public and private higher education reflected a sort of tacit treaty, albeit one often broken and seldom fully adhered to. The treaty is refracted in the Pell grants and state and federal programs such as Bundy Aid in New York and federal low-interest loans which help middle-income as well as low-income students to have a real choice between attending private and public institutions. Currently, the Reagan Administration refuses to raise taxes. This is one, but not the only, reason why the President and William Bennett, the Secretary of Education, want to cut Pell grants to students from middle-income backgrounds, and also to raise interest rates and make loans more difficult to obtain. That would further unbalance the private-public competition, which already gives competitive advantages to what have been called the Public Ivies, for example Ann Arbor, Berkeley, Chapel Hill, Urbana, Madison, Charlottesville, and Austin--all of which offer middle-income and even upper-income residential students what is often commodious state-subsidized education.

The squeeze on the private colleges and the private sector generally is tightened by the greatly enhanced ability of the "Public Ivies" and other less eminent public universities to establish foundations with large development staffs and then to pursue corporate philanthropy, often through the attractive device of matching grants. The University of Minnesota has announced a huge capital campaign. The corporations of the Twin Cities are notable for their philanthropy for education and cultural institutions in the area and beyond, which includes such fine liberal arts colleges as nonsectarian Carleton, residually Presbyterian Macalester, Lutheran St. Olaf, Methodist Hamline, and Catholic St. Catherine's, St. Thomas, and St. John's University and many others. The corporations will be expected to make substantial gifts to the University's drive and will want to do so because of many reciprocal ties, including, of course, many alumni and alumnae among their employees, as well as the fear of being deemed elitist and "unpatriotic" to the state if they favored only the private sector. At the University of Connecticut the genial, energetic John DiBiaggio, president since 1985, watched capable students who chose not to seek loans available to them to attend private colleges or whose parents were unwilling to make the sacrifices private-college attendance would entail enrol at his institution, not yet a Public Ivy. Beyond that, he was able to garner large sums from Hartford, Bridgeport, and Stanford corporations for the University's Foundation, in competition with the elite and non-elite private universities in the state and nation.

Almost every state college and university now has its foundation, and this is one of the growing elements of generally unobserved risk to private higher education outside the charmed circle of the heavily endowed.[7]

I recognize how important private philanthropy has been in improving the quality of education in some of the public colleges and universities. The accoutrements of the stunning residential Colleges at Santa Cruz; the special programs for honors students at Charlottesville and Chapel Hill; the seed money for pedagogic experiments in ever so many public institutions-- all these come from what in our complex mix of what is public and what is private we term the private sector. There are also colleges in the public sector that have a "private" quality, notably the College of William and Mary and, far less well-known, St. Mary's College of Maryland. The question is one of proper balancing between private contribution and public fiscal policy.[8]

IV

I want to state a proposition that I cannot prove: namely, that students in the smaller liberal arts college settings are more willing to take intellectual chances in an independent, rather than a showy, way than their counterparts of comparable academic caliber in the leading research universities. I am discussing differences of degree: there are students at Stanford or Harvard, Yale or Pennsylvania, at least as inventive and intellectually venturesome as the students to be found anywhere in the country. However, as I have already suggested, the ethos is different in the two settings, even within the private sector. Some quantitative sense of the difference was presented in a report released at Oberlin College in June 1985.[9] The report was commissioned and the conference convened by the presidents of Carleton, Franklin & Marshall, Mount Holyoke, Oberlin, Reed, Swarthmore, and Williams, and brought together the presidents of 48 colleges, including a number of less well-known institutions, among them Hope and Albion in Michigan, Wabash and the College of Wooster in Ohio, and of course such eminent and well-endowed colleges as Bryn Mawr, Haverford, Davidson, Wesleyan, and the College of the Holy Cross. The report focused entirely on the natural sciences, with a side glance at mathematics. It called attention to the dramatic decline in students intending to major in the natural sciences in the private research universities, where the percentage has fallen from 26 percent to 15 percent. The decline means that students are headed toward law, business, and what I believe to be, on the whole, marginally less-demanding subjects as undergraduate majors. In the 48 "research colleges," as they called themselves, the decline has been much smaller: from 32 percent to 27 percent in the past ten years.[10]

This finding about one segment of the curriculum is, in my judgment, illustrative of a much broader phenomenon which distinguishes the scholarly liberal arts colleges from the undergraduate colleges or my own and other research universities. The pressure to excel, in order to enter the Ivy League and Ivy-type, private research universities, does not abate when students have been admitted. In prestigious Japanese universities, say Tokyo or Kyoto, students, once admitted, relax and cultivate their senses and, now and then their souls; our students do not stop competing. The graduate of a major Japanese university has gotten into that setting by extraordinarily demanding pre-collegiate exertion, and the label of Tokyo, Kyoto, Waseda, assures a position in a government ministry or an appropriate company.

Our less well-educated college entrants cannot well afford a Japanese-style university moratorium. The question arises, therefore, as to the degrees of anxiety and constraint students in our selective institutions feel. These students are under parental pressure to enter a profession in which one can make a living sufficient to avoid downward economic mobility--a living which enables one to buy a home and send one's children to an expensive residential college.

I do not believe faculty should see themselves as tempters to engage students in their own fields at the risk of the students' own future. But in today's climate in the research universities especially, and even at some of the research colleges of the Wesleyan level of quality, students feel themselves under pressure to regard college as a way station on the road to somewhere else--medical school is only a more extreme case. Such students cannot afford to get too deeply engrossed in a subject's fascination, or a professor's interest in encouraging further work beyond the syllabus. They must spread their energies over their courses, much as a careful investor cannot get too interested in a particular security for fear of overcommitment and under attention to the rest of the portfolio.

While this mode of education does not invite, and even appears to penalize, curiosity and imagination, it is not without virtue. Schooling today in the more progressive environments may have moved too far away from anything involving memorization, whether of poetry or the periodic table. One is unlikely to be well-educated if one is unable to do for a bit without sleep, and if one is not prepared for spells of slogging, uninspiring work. The terms in use at MIT and elsewhere of "science jock" or "computer jock" have the interesting connotation that these individuals bring the same qualities of endurance and sometimes indeed of enthusiasm to their studies that the best athletes bring to sports.

There is, however, one enormous difference between studies and sports in a scholarly setting. In sports one is often part of a team, and one's activities benefit the team and the institution, whereas in studies it is more of a zero-sum game, in which one person's A may indirectly lead to another person's B+. The sense of camaraderie and teamwork important in the corporate context is often defeated in the academic context.

It is not irrational for students to be frightened when they face the occupational and global uncertainties of the future, as well as for many the repayment of the loans they may be carrying, which often severely limit choice or, indeed, rationalize a short-run career choice.[11] But what is dismaying is their herd-like behavior. Although economics is seen as a practical major and as a road to law or business school, students seem not to have learned anything about business cycles, and possess little knowledge of demography or the ways in which the composition of the labor force will change. Hardly any students I see at Harvard College appreciate that by the time many of them have finished doctoral training there will be job shortages in the fields they have not entered. And, in fact, in many academic fields there are job shortages of able candidates currently. Conversely, there are already looming surpluses in many medical specialties as well as in the law, and small changes in governmental policy or in the economy could minimize opportunities to work in the now-booming investment banking areas.

What is equally dismaying, and indeed puzzling, is that students from highly privileged backgrounds who have already established their academic capabilities appear to act with no less fearfulness, sometimes even more fearfulness, than students from less affluent backgrounds with less proven mastery of their studies. It is as if the privileged ones feared even to think of themselves, let alone appear, as an elite; they must persuade themselves that they are not special, and behave with almost the same degree of competitive preoccupation as their peers. The latter, looking at the well-situated students who are running scared, then have to redouble their own anxieties, for if the most privileged are frightened, then they too a fortiori must be facing a precarious future.

When I occasionally suggest to somewhat uncertain seniors, who have never been outside of New England except to Florida and Washington, that they might consider two years in the Peace Corps, not at all as a down payment on anticipatory guilt for making money later on, but as an opportunity for de-provincialization and something that might contribute to self-development and a later career, some of them are interested. They hesitate, however, fearing to have something that might look dubious on their resumes.

V

Herd-like behavior in the pursuit of individualistic yet unoriginal short-run ambitions may be somewhat less rampant in the liberal arts colleges than elsewhere. Student test scores at Swarthmore, Carleton, and Williams are at the level of some of the Ivy League institutions. However, self-selection brings to the liberal arts colleges, especially those in nonmetropolitan settings, young people who are seeking a good education which is not necessarily defined as "the best" in the national ratings, but that is, nevertheless, in their view, optimal for their own development. Although small classes are not necessarily superior classes,[12] in such classes a student is not likely to be what at Harvard is sometimes referred to as a "phantom." "Phantoms" congregate in large courses where they will not be called on, and in ones where no faculty member is likely to read one of their essays and then make higher demands or even supportively encourage the students to exert themselves.

The engagement of the students with their material is facilitated in the liberal arts colleges of high quality where, as already suggested, undergraduate majors are often the de facto research assistants, as well as the refectory companions of those among their faculty who remain oriented to scholarship and to the discipline. Correspondingly, the tie to the field as a way of life, as well as a conceivable livelihood, may come across more vividly in the liberal arts colleges, as demonstrated in earlier studies of the high "productivity" of certain liberal arts colleges.[13] In contrast, of course, the converse can occur. As applications fall off and admissions become less selective, faculty accustomed to superior students can become demoralized.[14] Even the best liberal arts colleges struggle to maintain libraries and laboratories, to find support for faculty self-renewal, and to bring in new faculty as current faculty members age without retiring. In an anemic setting, there will still be close contact between students and faculty members, but the lives of the latter may appear dreary intellectually, as well as depressed economically, rather than invitational. This is particularly likely where most full-time faculty will be tenured and feel themselves stuck, with the college resorting for financial reasons to an increasingly numerous part-time or "gypsy" faculty.

To be sure, a truly curious person can learn in almost any setting. As a student, such a person does not require a professor who competes with television as an entertainer, nor do the tasks have to be continuously enjoyable. The curious student may still have to cope with dull and redundant moments in the process of learning, but does not permit these episodes to rationalize uninvolvement in learning. There are always some students who go beyond what is required to get a good grade, and care for more than making the grade. But also at any level of the educational enterprise, one can find tacit treaties of mutual noninvolvement between students and teachers, each cohort not disturbing the alternative preoccupations of one another.

VI

It perhaps goes too far to say that virtually any subject can be taught in a way that invites at once craftsmanship and curiosity, or can be taught in a way that deadens curiosity and encourages slovenliness. It is a self-serving mistake for professors, for example in the humanities, to see themselves as disesteemed vocationalists. A musicologist or a philosopher who is seeking to recreate in his or her students a specialized professional scholar of his or her own "school" and subspecialty is in fact providing vocational training. While the readings may be in principle emancipating, they may be read in a dehydrated way, with all the reductionist capabilities of scholarship which may be brilliant yet sterilizing for the student.

In contrast, the diversity of the American academic landscape provides examples of engineering schools which have made serious efforts to engage their students with the humanities and the social sciences. Some years ago, I served on an advisory panel consisting mostly of deans of engineering schools to help Worcester Polytechnic Institute develop a program in which engineers would have intellectual commerce with social policy and social science. Students and faculty were to work together to develop integrative projects. But where faculty members could not themselves continue learning, the projects sometimes ended up linking an engineering skill to what was thought to be a humane purpose, rather than something as difficult as seeking to reinterpret the work of engineers through understanding work place processes as affected by different sorts of automation, or analyzing complex tradeoffs between production costs and such externalities as acid rain.

In my judgment, Carnegie-Mellon University has been, over a period of years, particularly inventive in managing the curricular breadth required of students in its undergraduate preprofessional programs. It is significant that English and history are at the doctoral level taught partly as applied subjects, and not solely to advance the disciplines in the latter's own terms. At the undergraduate level, however, students in engineering or in management bring to their courses in literature, history, or sociology--all of which they are required to take--a level of motivation and interest that is rare in a commandeered curriculum where such courses are often dismissed as cultural bull, at best entertaining and at worst distracting. While the student subcultures at Carnegie-Mellon are not notably intellectual, the spirit of professionalism seems to be carried over to the required courses in the liberal arts.[15]

Carnegie-Mellon University seems to have developed a climate, under the leadership of President Richard Cyert, discouraging faculty members in engineering or management from making invidious comments to undergraduates concerning supposedly less rigorous fields they must study in the College of Humanities and Social Sciences under the provisions of the Core Curriculum. An unusual faculty monthly, Focus, serves for exchange of views among administrators and faculty members in all the schools; there is ample debate about CMU itself and concerning larger political issues. Focus is consonant with Herbert Simon's comment on the Core Curriculum: "We want to provide some common topics of conversation between sports, the weather, and sex." Simon has also observed that there are many "sociables" among the students, fraternity members who study hard and party hard. The undergraduate student body of 4,000 (students in the demanding College of Fine Arts hold themselves, and are held, somewhat separate from the rest) exhibits a somewhat different atmosphere from that of the prevailing student cultures in the Ivy League, reflecting the fact that three-fifths of the graduates go to work immediately after the baccalaureate. Correspondingly, the student culture at CMU overall is less sophisticated and rivalrous, but also, I would surmise, less likely than students in a comparably selective liberal arts college to envisage themselves as pursuing a special destiny all their own.

Thus, my impression may be too generous that undergraduates at Carnegie-Mellon University, spread among its different undergraduate colleges, mobilize what I have termed a professional intensity toward subjects in the liberal arts and sciences. At CMU as elsewhere, faculty complain that few students share faculty members' own professional--that is, academic--preoccupations, and few also share their wider intellectual ones.

One difficulty I find in writing about higher education is my awareness of the hazards of overgeneralization. For example, I have made reference to the "Ivy League" as if these were monolithic institutions within and vis-a-vis one another. In some respects, Princeton with its 4,500 undergraduates and a distinguished faculty's major preoccupation with them, and with its requirement that every senior have a thesis or comparable independent study project, is more like a liberal arts college (with a sizable engineering component) than it is like Harvard or Columbia. However, in general, as I have already indicated, mutuality of attention among faculty and students is most common at the private liberal arts colleges, where the student bodies more typically number 2,500 (as at Wesleyan or Smith) or 2,000 or less. Some of the institutions where students and faculty are evocative for one another are smaller still (around 1,000 students): Haverford, Bryn Mawr, and New Hampshire, for example. Hampshire College remains experimental but is not unstructured. In individuated but monitored programs, students progress through three phases: (1) a sequence involving Basic Courses, including hands-on work in the natural sciences; (2) a concentration which is frequently interdisciplinary, not only within Hampshire's Schools of Humanities and Arts, Communications and Cognitive Science, Social Science, and Natural Science, but among them; and (3) Advanced Studies, whose main requirement is a senior thesis or other comparable project, along with an Integrative Seminar in some related field, and in some cases opportunity to join a faculty member in teaching less advanced students. In the absence of grades, Hampshire College employs continuous faculty evaluations of student work and student responses to these to create what, at its best can be an intense effort by the students to extend themselves to meet their own increasingly high expectations for what they can accomplish.[16]

VII

What I am suggesting is that students in liberal arts colleges, as compared with students in other institutions, are apt to become self-starters in their academic areas. Of course, there are enormous differences among liberal arts colleges themselves: for example, coeducational versus single-sex institutions. This difference among liberal arts colleges appears to have an impact on the academic performance of women. Admittedly, there are many women who flourish in coeducational settings, including in the most selective colleges such as Wesleyan, Bowdoin, Williams, Amherst and Haverford, which only recently became coeducational. However, there is some research which indicates that many women, when they are in the presence of men, hesitate to perform outstandingly well in such traditionally male fields as the natural sciences, mathematics and engineering. In contrast, in the top-flight girls' schools and women's colleges such as Mount Holyoke, Bryn Mawr, Wellesley and Smith, girls and women feel freer to take an independent course without anxieties concerning a male audience. After graduating from a women's college, they feel sufficiently confident to pursue careers in what previously have been men's domains.[17]

The superiority that I believe the liberal arts college in general has in preparing students to be inventive and to become independent-minded later on does not come about because they have studied any particular subject matter in traditional areas of learning or even, as in the College of the University of Chicago (2,950 students), because they have experienced an unusually integrated program. But rather the issue is one that goes beyond particular courses and even particular departments to the general spirit of the place--remember that I am talking only about residential colleges, and only about those which still attract a selective student body. The relatively small numbers of students in the shrinking private sector of higher education and in the liberal arts colleges of that sector are important corporate and indeed national resources--resources for corporate life, for the faculties of research universities and their professional schools, and for the intellectual life which helps us discover and believe in our own curiosities.

NOTES

1. An earlier version of this essay was prepared for a symposium of the Corporate Council on the Liberal Arts, held at the American Academy of Arts and Sciences on September 3, 1987. I am indebted for helpful comments on an earlier draft of this essay to David Fowler, Paul E. Bragdon, Michael Maccoby, Chase N. Peterson, Richard F. Gross, Richard M. Cyert, Adele Simmons, Gerald Grant, Stephen J. Trachtenberg, Gordon J. Van Wylen, and Judith Block McLaughlin. For support for the work reflected in the article, I am indebted to the AT&T Foundation, the Ford Foundation, the Exxon Education Foundation, the Mellon Foundation, and the Lilly Endowment.

2. There is of course nothing wrong with consulting, which plays a significant role in academic as in corporate life. The problem exists in the rarity of well-educated individuals who are prepared to become attached to the day-to-day work and life of a corporation in all its ethnographic detail. My colleague, Winthrop Knowlton, of the Business and Government Center at the John F. Kennedy School of Government, distinguishes between those men and women of the corporation who leave an endowment of human and physical resources after their departure and those now so very common whose interest is only in short-term transactions, that is, those without institutional loyalty who are essentially traders.

3. Commenting on the foregoing passage, Gerald Grant has reminded me of the effectiveness of women's mutual support groups; skill in personal relationships has been a greater resource for women than for men, although at the same time concern for maintenance of such

relationships is now seen by some feminists as a handicap society places on women's ambitions.

4. Useful ruminations concerning the value of politicians and bureaucrats, so commonly defamed in America, are to be found in Stimson Bullitt, To Be a Politician (New Haven: Yale University Press, paperback, 1977).

5. Mormon collegiality has known schisms in the past, as well as more recently.   Currently it is under considerable strain with the succession of Ezra Taft Benson as President.   Culturally and politically liberal Mormons warily observe the tempering of Benson's Radical Right Wing ideology as the result of his age, his accession to the Presidency, and the influence of moderate colleagues. For an observant account of the Mormons' combination of individuality and cooperation, see Elizabeth Calkins, "The Sense of Optimism in the Mormon Church," honors thesis in the Program in Social Studies, Harvard College, March 1984.

6. Berea College in Berea, Kentucky, with 1,500 students, dedicates itself to serving low-income students from the Appalachian region; it has a work program and an extraordinary esprit de corps. It is not tied to a particular denomination, but seeks nevertheless to maintain a religious ethos of Protestant flavor. The story of the Catholic and once-Catholic colleges is too diverse and complex even to begin to explore here. Laicization of faculties, ethnic and credal differences among administrators and faculty members, as well as student bodies, have left extant a few Catholic colleges and universities with a combination of individualism and cooperation that is now generally more marked among the evangelical or sectarian divisions of Protestantism.   For fuller discussion see Riesman, On Higher Education: The Academic Enterprise in an Era of Rising Student Consumerism (San Francisco: Jossey-Bass, 1980), pp. 162-178.

7. For discussion of the tuition gap between the private and public institutions in Connecticut, see observations of University of Hartford President Stephen J. Trachtenberg, University of Hartford Observer, vol. 12, no. 7, March 26, 1986, pp. 1, 8.

8. For a variety of perspectives on the mix of public and private, see Richard Zeckhauser and Winthrop Knowlton, eds., American Society, Public and Private Responsibilities (Cambridge, Mass.: Balinger, 1986).

9. See David Davis-Van Atta, Sam S. Carrier, and Frank Frankfort, "Educating America's Scientists: The Role of the Research Colleges," Oberlin College, 1985. For an earlier study with similar findings, see R. H. Knapp and R. B. Goodrich, Origins of American Scientists (Chicago: University of Chicago Press, 1952).

10. With present levels of funding, the "research colleges" can continue to attract capable faculty to teach geology, which does not require laboratory equipment, but can make use of the field, and astronomy,

where everyone must take their turns at the great national observatories; there are subfields in physics and biology and possibly in chemistry which can be cultivated as things now stand in the "research colleges." Still, if these colleges are to maintain their outstanding record of producing natural scientists, they will need massive infusions of public and private support for equipment to assist faculty-student collaboration and attendance at professional meetings and released time for faculty.

11. The loans many students have taken out often shadow their choices of major in college and of post-baccalaureate career plans. Sometimes the loans loom larger than life because students rarely discount them for inflation or for their financial prospects, even in careers such as teaching which are not lucrative. I am one of those observers who believes that the country and, along with it, all of higher education would be better served by a national loan plan with income-contingent repayment collected by the IRS. Such a plan would eventually become self-financing (I cannot here go into the many actuarial complexities). It would help to counter the state "tariffs" which often charge out-of-state students extremely high tuition for the state's public colleges and universities, and would make it easier for students to leave home and nearby commuter institutions for places that could serve them better. Such a plan would make no assumption that it is attending college that makes one rich or leaves one relatively poor, but the "tax" and schedule for repayment (and provision for buying out of one's obligation) would bear somewhat more heavily on those who struck it rich than on those who became social workers or parochial school teachers.

12. It would be a mistake to conclude that teaching assistants are only a necessary evil and have no advantages in work with undergraduates. Since it is the department which carries the ethos of a discipline and conveys it to its initiates, the teaching assistants, especially in particular fast-moving fields, may be closer to the state of the art than senior faculty members at their own institutions or the majority of faculty members in the liberal arts colleges. Reed College, with 1,100 students, has a six-person department of physics; Bryn Mawr, somewhat smaller, five persons, plus a laboratory coordinator and-- since it is unusual in having a small graduate school--three baccalaureate assistants. Carleton, with 1,750 students, has an eight-person physics and astronomy department. Someone continuing from an undergraduate university college to a research university's graduate department, either in the same or a different place, is likely already to have had a postgraduate experience, and has commonly been in classes taught by graduate students and in classes shared with graduate students. Such a Ph.D. candidate may have picked up the gossip of which laboratories are the "hotter" ones, with the more responsive faculty, and will know the lingo, the jargon, of various small fields. With differences among particular undergraduate colleges of research universities, the undergraduate major will have been alerted to subspecialties of which only a few exist in liberal arts colleges. Those that do exist in such colleges do not require

enormously expensive equipment and teams of assistants. I have heard it said that the Reed College graduate in physics (at Reed more likely to be male than female) will find himself, at the outset, at a disadvantage whether at Berkeley or Cornell, seeing himself less competent than those who have come as majors from a research university background. But if such a person can manage through the first year of graduate study, the handicaps of acculturation attenuate, vanish altogether, and in some cases turn around completely. However, in other fields graduates of Reed and a few other colleges of like intensity can find the first year or so of post-baccalaureate study a letdown because, working closely in projects with their college teachers, they had anticipated some of the initial themes of graduate school training, as well as gaining confidence in their ability to learn.

13.   For earlier studies, see R. H. Knapp and H. B. Goodrich, Origins of American Scientists (Chicago: University of Chicago Press, 1952); and R. H. Knapp and J. J. Greenbaum, The Younger American Scholar: His Collegiate Origins (Chicago: University of Chicago Press, 1953); and discussion in Riesman, On Higher Education (San Francisco: Jossey-Bass, 1980), pp. 27-41. Several more recent unpublished studies are referred to in Gilbert T. Sewall, Small Independent Colleges in America (report to the U.S. Department of Education, March 1986), p. 47, footnote 3.

14.   Many colleges and universities, though few of the topflight ones, are now offering "merit" scholarships for able students who, in a sense, would pay their own way; in effect, bribes comparable to those paid to entice prospective athletes to enroll. As tuition and other costs are discounted, there is occurring a bidding war encouraging bargaining by students and their families for not the "best buy," but a good buy combined with a good offer--a process likely in the end to be self-defeating, as in other price wars.

15.   In addition to Worcester Polytechnic Institute, Clarkson University, Illinois Institute of Technology, and Rensselaer Polytechnic Institute, among others, have worked to develop connectedness between their undergraduate professional programs and the liberal arts.

16.   Although the general climate of Hampshire among the students and the faculty is liberal, even radical, a number of Hampshire College graduates have become self-starting entrepreneurs; having learned to navigate by themselves in the College's unstructured program, they have developed the confidence and often the technical virtuosity necessary for the small businesses they inaugurate.

17.   See, for example, the writings of M. Elizabeth Tidball, professor of physiology at George Washington University Medical Center: "Baccalaureate Origins of Entrants into American Medical Schools," Journal of Higher Education, 56: 385-402, 1985; and "Baccalaureate Origins of Recent Natural Science Doctorates," Journal of Higher Education, 57, no. 6 (November/December 1986).

This is not the occasion to explore all the hotly debated issues of gender. However, it should be noted that in the general decline of SAT scores that began in the middle 1960s, the sharpest fall has been in women's verbal scores, which overall are slightly lower than the men's verbal scores, while women's quantitative scores have remained as heretofore markedly lower than those of men.

THE NEW ALLIANCES: HOW STRATEGIC PARTNERSHIPS ARE RESHAPING AMERICAN BUSINESS

by Rosabeth Moss Kanter

The quest for competitiveness is leading some American business firms to seek partnership-like relationships with other organizations as a way to leverage their own resources, extend their reach into new territories, and gain an edge with respect to innovation. These new "partnerships" take three forms: multi-organizational service alliances, such as industrywide R & D consortia; opportunistic alliances, such as joint ventures; and complementary, or stakeholder alliances, which involve vendors, customers, and employees (via employee organizations such as labor unions). The complementary alliance is the main focus of this article, as it potentially could become the model for successful corporate activity, as well as bring about some basic changes in the nature of the organizations that constitute such alliances.

I

STRATEGIC PARTNERSHIPS: THEIR RATIONALE AND FORMS

In the face of heightened competitive pressures, many U.S. firms have established new cooperative agreements with other organizations that involve unprecedented (for them) levels of sharing and commitment. While American firms, particularly small ones, have always allied with other firms for specific purposes, the extent as well as the diversity of such activity has grown in recent years, moving from the periphery to take a central place in some companies' strategies.

In 1987, over 40 coalitions between Ford Motor Company and outside commercial entities were identified by Harvard professor Malcolm Salter. There were over 8,000 person-visits by U.S.-based Ford employees to Japan--and so much traffic between Detroit and Tokyo in general that U.S.-Tokyo flights now originate in Detroit rather than Chicago. Indeed, by 1986 General Electric had over 100 cooperative ventures with other firms, and even IBM, long known as one of the "great independents," had established formal partnerships with a number of other organizations, including Merrill Lynch and Aetna Life and Casualty. IBM was also trying to ally with potential competitors through agreements making them "value-added resellers"; McDonnell Douglas Automation, for example, would sell IBM products to their customers, adding their own to the package. In some sectors, there were more domestic joint ventures announced in a single year in the 1980s than in the previous 15-20 years combined.[1]

These relationships with "blurred boundaries," to use Joseph Badaracco's term, overlay or even replace market relationships with organizational ones, often creating close, even intimate connections between separate organizations. Firms do not lose their legal identity, they retain their own culture and management structure, and they can pursue their own strategies. But they reduce their autonomy by strengthening their ties with other organizations, thus sharing authority over certain decisions.[2]

Inter-organizational alliances are a fragile, intermediate form, often evolving in one of two directions. Some partnerships that begin as an alternative route to gaining a capacity or a resource may end with at least one organization better able to provide that resource for itself, so that it no longer requires the partner. Dependency is decreased over time. Other partnerships have the opposite dynamic. What begins as a limited alliance may move toward greater degrees of interdependence, and end with the organizations merging. Some analysts have compared "strategic alliances" to marriages, but they are really more similar to living together.

There is something entrepreneurially appealing about cooperative arrangements among firms. These relationships can help little firms compete with big firms. They offer flexibility and speed of access to new capacity. Getting the benefits of what another organization offers without the risks and responsibilities of "owning" it is the ultimate form of leverage.

Of course, the benefits and issues that partnerships create depend on the purpose of the alliance. I distinguish three kinds of partnerships: multi-organization service alliances, opportunistic alliances, and complementary (or stakeholder) alliances.

Multi-Organization Service Alliances

In service alliances, a group of organizations with a similar need, often in the same industry, band together to create a new entity to fill that need for all of them--an industry research consortium, for example. The service is one that is too expensive or difficult for an organization to provide for itself, and it cannot be purchased on the open market. So several organizations ally to establish a new organization, which they jointly control, to meet the need. The resulting consortium is one of the simplest examples of inter-organizational cooperation. The limited purpose of the consortium makes it possible for even nominal competitors to ally (both legally and strategically) in ensuring that a service is available across-the-board to all members. The effect is to lift the performance level of the whole group.

Consortia thus offer the benefits of larger scale through resource pooling. Each member gains some of the benefits of larger scale while still retaining its independence with respect to every other activity. For this reason, consortia are especially attractive in areas where the development of new technology is particularly important and particularly costly.

The National Cooperative Research Act of 1984 loosened antitrust restrictions to allow joint development through the prototype stage. By

1986, at least 40 R & D consortia were being organized nationwide, taking a number of forms. Pradco, organized by Borg-Warner, Dresser Industries, Ingersoll-Rand, and TransAmerica to design new boiler pumps for power plants, spreads research tasks among its own members. The 33 members of the Semiconductor Research Corporation, including AT&T, GM, IBM, and DuPont, sponsor research at a number of universities, as do the seven members of the International Partners in Glass Research. The Center for Advanced Television Studies--formed by ABC, CBS, NBC, PBS, RCA, and five other companies to improve the quality of television transmission-- spends its $1 million yearly research budget through M.I.T. And the Guided Wave Optoelectronics Manufacturing Technology Development Program, organized by six companies, conducts its research on fiber optics at the Batelle Memorial Institute in Columbus, Ohio.

Still other consortia create new, stand-alone organizations. Two of the better-publicized stand-alone consortia are Bellcore and the Microelectronics and Computer Center (MCC). In 1984, the regional telephone companies spinoff from AT&T formed Bellcore, a research center with a $900 million budget established to carry out research and development benefitting all seven companies. In 1983, 21 computer companies formed MCC in Texas, an industrywide research center with a budget of up to $700 million over ten years and a staff of 400 drawn in part from member companies.

Research consortia predate the current high-tech competitiveness frenzy, but the latter is now the driving force behind their emergence. The Electric Power Research Institute, a nonprofit, semipublic organization managing research and development for the entire industry, was established in 1973. Since its founding, its engineers have turned out over 430 products: hardware, software, manuals and guides, electrical devices, and entire electric-generation systems. About $4 in quantifiable benefits have been generated for each $1 invested.

While R & D consortia are by far the most identifiable, they are not the only examples of this form. In 1986, 34 companies, including IBM, General Electric, and Chase Manhattan, contributed $10 million each to form American Casualty Excess Insurance Company, a company that would provide them with insurance they could not otherwise obtain. Even more significant are consortia designed to allow smaller companies to gain joint purchasing or market power--such as the Independent Grocers of America.

Consortia are stronger versions of the weaker alliances that companies in the same industry form to conduct research or take action at the industry level. In consortia, as compared to the weaker alliances, membership is generally more restricted, membership costs are higher, and the consortium itself has more strategic significance. It is expected to produce specific benefits for specific companies, rather than generalized or abstract benefits. The stake in consortia is much higher than the stake in trade associations, and participation in governance is thus a more significant issue.

Opportunistic Alliances

A second cluster of partnerships is best labelled "opportunistic," with all the positive and negative connotations of that term. Organizations see an opportunity to gain an immediate, though perhaps temporary, competitive advantage through an alliance which gets them into a new business or extends an old business. The goal is venture development. The alliance opens up possibilities that would not have existed for either of the partners acting alone. Once that opportunity is exploited, there may not be a basis for the relationship to continue.

Joint business ventures are the generic example of this category. The partners get from the others a competence that will allow them to move more quickly toward their own business goals. For example, CBS formed a number of joint ventures in the 1980s--with IBM and Sears to develop and market videotex, an electronic information service; with Twentieth Century Fox to develop videotapes; and with Columbia Pictures (Coca-Cola) and Home Box Office (Time Inc.) to develop motion pictures.

The addition of the partner's competence explains why organizations would want to pursue a business opportunity with full-fledged, although possibly temporary, partners, instead of more passive lenders or investors. The ability to attain larger scale is also a motivating factor, though a weak one. The two principle driving forces behind these kinds of alliances both enhance competence: technology transfer and/or market access. And that is often the trade: one partner puts in the technology in return for the other partner's access to particular markets. But once one of the partners has gained experience with the competence or entered the market of the other, the alliance is vulnerable to dissolution--the opportunity can now be pursued without the partner.

Many joint ventures form because one partner is eager to learn something from the other--get a piece of technology, learn how to manage a process, gain technological expertise. Indeed, international joint ventures for R & D purposes were the fastest-growing subcategory of cooperative arrangements by U.S. firms in the 1980s, replacing wholly-owned subsidiaries.

How much "jointness" is entailed in many of these alliances is an open question, and one that makes direct comparison of costs and benefits difficult. My research on two advanced technology companies demonstrated that "doing a deal" with a newer, smaller company was a primary way that each got access to new technology. But the resulting 24 alliances all involved different degrees of investment and proportional ownership.[3]

A second opportunistic use of joint ventures is to gain fast access to new markets. Several studies have pinpointed the considerable odds against success, at least in the short term, when companies try to enter product-markets where they have not previously competed. Experience with similar products is not sufficient to compensate for lack of customer base or market experience.[4] Finding a local partner to provide access to a foreign market is particularly appealing to U.S. companies. After deregulation, for example, AT&T allied with the Dutch company Philips and the Italian company Olivetti to get access to the European market.

Complementary (Stakeholder) Alliances

Complementary alliances are defined by interdependence. They are partnerships between a set of stakeholders in a business process. Stakeholders are those groups on whom organizations depend--the people who can help them, or prevent them, from achieving their goals. They include vendors, customers, and employees.

The catalyst in the formation of complementary alliances is often the drive for innovation. Major innovations in technology or organizational systems require longer-term investments. When they also require similar investments from stakeholders, to ensure compatibility of systems, for example, then the basis for an alliance emerges. These complementary alliances resemble other forms of long-term relationships between companies with separate ownership--franchisor/franchisee relationships, for example, or the "quasi-firms" of building contractors and their subcontractors in the construction industry.[5]

Vendors. Facing imperatives to cut costs and improve quality, leading American companies are creating closer relationships with suppliers. Arms-length relationships do not produce the motivation for suppliers to invest in technology to improve quality or manage the complexities of just-in-time inventory systems. John Marshall, Vice President of TRW Safety Systems Division, described the change at TRW's automotive divisions to George Lodge:

> In the past we sought bids from a number of suppliers, and price was the principal issue. Now we want flexible relationships with a few suppliers, and we want our suppliers to help us in a variety of ways. We want better quality. We want them to help us reduce our inventories. We want their help and ideas about how we can improve the final product. It is not unusual these days for two or three engineers from our suppliers to be working in our plants for a while. We network through computers. I might call one of our suppliers and urge . . . [it]-- if not help . . . [it]--to locate a plant near us.[6]

In addition to making possible joint investments in technology and compatible systems that improve quality and reduce waste, supplier input into product design can improve innovation by taking advantage of suppliers' expertise regarding the potential of their technologies.

NCR has a particularly well-developed set of alliances with its key vendors, designed to ensure that the partnership works to the benefit of each member. To maintain its computer products based on the Intel 80000 family of integrated circuits and microprocessors, NCR established an internal role called the "Intel advocate." This has been so effective that

Intel has assigned its own in-house advocate to manage its relationship with NCR. The "supplier advocate" program involves the ten suppliers with the most important strategic implications for the company. NCR works closely with those organizations, making sure not only that the relationship is sustained, but that they each benefit from the other's particular strength and expertise. NCR also has a series of technological agreements with suppliers for developing and sharing knowledge on a worldwide basis. Executives say that they see such agreements as part of a broad commitment to supplier and customer education, which both improves the transaction of the moment as well as laying a foundation for enhanced relationships in the future.

Even "getting tough" with suppliers leads to closer alliances. Polaroid saved $27 million over two years by helping vendors to improve their cost structure. To do this required knowing the suppliers' businesses well and showing them ways to operate more efficiently.[7]

Customers. This is just the flip side of supplier partnerships, of course. There have always been strategic advantages to staying close to customers. Good customer relationships reverberate not only in current sales but in future effectiveness and growth. Satisfied customers are the single best source of new business. Timely knowledge of changing customer requirements makes it possible to guide production more efficiently, reducing waste, inventory costs, and returns. And experience shows that customers are also one of the major founts of ideas for innovation. Depending on the industry, up to 80 percent of all important industrial innovations have originated with users. These are among the reasons that innovation-conscious high-technology companies go beyond emphasizing service to create more formal ties: user councils, inviting customers to consult on R & D projects, joint promotions, and the ultimate partnership step, joint development projects.

Benson Shapiro has been following the evolution of the sales function in manufacturing companies from single transaction-oriented, to systems selling, to account management, to what he calls "strategic partnering"-- the "close encounter of a fourth kind." He comments:

> Even account management with all of its opportunities and rewards, as well as significant investments and costs, cannot satisfy the evolving need for closer, more permanent vendor/customer relationships. Joint products, service, and infrastructure development have led to an even more intimate buyer-seller relationship.[8]

One example he cites is the alliance between Electronic Data Systems (EDS), now owned by General Motors, and AT&T Information Systems (ATTIS). EDS has substantial skills in integrating computers, telecommunications gear and software into custom systems. ATTIS sells telecommunications equipment, computers, and related equipment. It does not have sufficient system integration skills to satisfy all of its customers. EDS and ATTIS therefore signed an agreement under which EDS will be considerably more than a routine supplier to AT&T; it will also play an important role as a systems integrator for AT&T customers.

At Ford's initiative, IBM has also departed from its past modus operandi with customers in winning a $200 million contract for office systems at Ford Motor Company. Ford had "asked to start with a blank piece of paper and redefine how the relationship between the two companies should work. So we did," reported an IBM executive. Under the new relationship, a team of 50 Ford and IBM executives is designing the system to fit Ford's needs and is jointly overseeing installation.[9]

Technology is not the only basis for customer alliances. A consumer products company is experimenting with another form of customer partnership with large retail chains. It is making part of its sales force available to store managers to provide a number of in-store shelving services.

Unions. A third form of complementary partnership involves labor organizations and management jointly setting policies or administering an area of company operations. The planning for General Motors' Saturn subsidiary, for example, has been conducted jointly with the United Auto Workers (UAW). The plans include a network of management-union committees running the plant; representatives of the UAW will sit on all planning and operating committees, including the strategic advisory committee formed by Saturn's president and staff.

In addition to those in the auto industry, several well-publicized but unstable labor-management alliances have occurred in air transportation. Eastern Air Lines made a deal with its unions in 1983 to exchange employee stock ownership, union seats on the Board of Directors, and a workplace participation program for wage concessions. (The alliance fell apart in bitterness when Eastern asked for further wage concessions and was ultimately taken over by Texas Air.) Western Air Lines developed a less-publicized but more successful partnership with its unions to cut costs; this returned the company to profitability before it was acquired by Delta in 1987.

Union-management alliances are occurring in industries undergoing rapid change, as a means to permit innovation. Thus, it is no surprise that telecommunications is joining autos, steel, and air transportation in seeking new relationships between labor and management organizations.

Many changes have occurred in telecommunications organizations since the breakup of AT&T on January 1, 1984, and the formation of seven new regional telephone operating companies. Perhaps the most remarkable one is the speed and effectiveness with which Pacific Bell, the largest part of the newly formed Pacific Telesis Group, and Nevada Bell, its tiny sister to the East, established a new "business partnership" with its major union, the Communications Workers of America (CWA).[10] This business partnership--Pacific's term--is considered vital to realizing its strategic goals of superior financial performance in a competitive environment.

While the idea of a dramatically different relationship with the union was seeded in the first year after divestiture, partnership activities got underway in the spring of 1985. Between May 1985 and September 1986, the following had been accomplished:

(1) A Memorandum on Employment Security was developed by Pacific Bell officers and CWA local presidents and ratified by the CWA membership in August 1985. The company agreed to undertake a variety of actions to save jobs and avert layoffs in exchange for greater flexibility in deploying people. A layoff of over 1,000 people was averted immediately.

(2) "Local common interest forums" (LCIF) were established to continue discussion of employment security issues--which were now broadened to include company discipline policies, introduction of technology, contract labor, and new venture development. These forums consisted of every company officer and the union local presidents representing the employees in his or her organization. Meeting monthly since the fall of 1985, they began gradually to include the next echelons in their activities, and by the fall of 1986 were beginning to act as policy boards or steering committees guiding a number of task forces working on specific organizational changes.

(3) Pacific Telesis conducted its first independent (post-divestiture) bargaining with its unions in the summer of 1986. Though AT&T and other regional telephone companies had strikes, Pacific and the CWA signed their contract a week before the contract deadline, and it was later ratified overwhelmingly by the CWA membership. The local common interest forums contributed heavily to the bargaining agenda--so that the contract negotiators were given a set of recommendations already developed jointly by the union and management. The contract itself set forth the principles for deepening the business partnership. The company gained several ways to cut costs through flexibility in labor deployment and the exchange of a portion of fixed compensation for pay and benefits that would partially float with company performance.

The Pacific Bell/Communications Workers of America (PB/CWA) partnership is an example of management-driven labor relations[11]--labor relations to realize management's strategic agenda, with union involvement as an aid to management's operational decisions at the worksite level. This does not mean that the union is getting hurt; indeed, the union may gain in power. But the origination of the PB/CWA partnership lay in business necessity, and the new role evolving for the CWA in California and Nevada is to serve its membership through helping management design programs and shape policies--and protect its members' interests in the process.

The decision to seek a new relationship with the CWA was a management-driven business decision. It was not done to "improve labor relations" in the narrower sense, and was not union-driven, and it was not even staff-driven by the labor relations and human resources function. It was not a matter of mounting an "employee involvement program," but rather creating a partnership with another organization--the union-- through its official leadership in order to ensue joint investments that would result in a flexible, appropriately-trained labor supply.

Thus, union-management partnerships such as the PB/CWA linkage are another form of strategic alliance across organizational lines.

II

HOW PARTNERSHIPS CHANGE THE ORGANIZATIONS FORMING THEM

The development of formal alliances with "external" parties changes internal roles, relationships, and power dynamics for the organizations entering into them.   Of course, the degree of change is likely to be minimal in cases where the alliance consists of a new stand-alone organization, but important and significant where the partnership's activities overlap with other organizational activities.   In general, service alliances such as research consortia would have the least impact, while complementary alliances would have the most.   Roy Shapiro's comments about supplier-customer partnerships could hold for other varieties as well:

> Consider a company that enters a long-term cooperative relationship with a supplier.   The company purchasing department no longer performs the essentially clerical task of renegotiating short-term price-based contracts based on precise specifications.   Instead, purchasing becomes a focal point for efforts to learn about the supplier's capabilities, aid in improving them, coordinate contacts between design personnel in the purchaser's firm and the counterparts at the supplier, and perhaps even finance equipment and inventory at the supplier. The purchasing department will grow in size and surely grow in expertise and responsibility, and important decisions may well be shared with the supplier.[12]

Managing alliances and partnerships creates several special organizational requirements.

1.   Partnerships require consultation as a matter of routine expectation.   The illusion of autonomy is lost.   Unilateral action decreases. The number of forums for cooperative decision-making increase.

2.   Simultaneously, partnerships make the activities involved in "external" relationships more important and reduce any one department's monopoly over them (e.g., labor relations to "handle" the union).   They can

increase the number of functions and the number of people involved with those "external" relationships. Where strong customer alliances prevail, both product designers and production workers get directly involved with customers.   In a union-management partnership, line managers relate directly to union officials, without any labor relations staff involvement. The former "boundary managers" can gain importance from the strategic significance given to their area, but they lose monopoly power and must change how they operate. If they do not, they risk being bypassed.

The task of such departments under a partnership is to integrate and coordinate rather than dominate. Indeed, partnerships in general tend to increase the requirements for intra-organizational integration.   With multiple contacts connecting partners, communication can be unmanageable or inefficient unless each partner is well-integrated itself.

Overall, the development of strategic alliances is one more force toward politicizing the role of managers, making it essential for them to be able to juggle a set of constituencies rather than control a set of subordinates.   Chester Barnard recognized long ago that the task of leaders was to develop a network of cooperative relationships among all those people, groups, and organizations with something to contribute to an economic activity.   Alliances and partnerships multiply the complexity of performing this task.   For example, Teknowledge Inc., producer of expert systems software, has development alliances with six major corporations, including GM, Proctor & Gamble, and FMC.   President Lee Hecht of Teknowledge told a Business Week reporter that he feels "like the mayor of a small city. I have a constituency that won't quit. It takes a hell of a lot of balancing."[13]

III

RESHAPING ROLES AND RELATIONSHIPS:
THE UNION-MANAGEMENT CASE

Nowhere were the impacts of a partnership on each of the partner's organizations clearer than in the case of Pacific Bell's formal alliance with the Communications Workers of America.

The establishment of the PB/CWA business partnership shifted the power dynamics and reshaped the roles and relationships within both the union and management hierarchies.   An extensive set of interviews and direct observation during the first two years of this alliance allows me to detail its implications in depth.[14]

It was important for participants to feel that each party had gained by working through difficult issues--an example of productive synergy, instead of the mere compromise (and sometimes stalemate) in their previous relationship.   In the first year, however, union local presidents gained the most.

Union Presidents: Role Changes

For the CWA local presidents, the empowerment was clear and direct, despite a few skeptical voices to the contrary. They had direct access to company officers, whereas previously they had dealt only with department heads. They were given information and data to better understand what drives business decisions, and they could get questions answered with a single phone call to a vice president. They were consulted on matters of business significance to the company before decisions were made. They were handed an opportunity to educate management about the pressures on union leadership. And they increasingly knew things before the rest of company management did, even becoming an information and influence source for middle management.

Pacific Bell executives readily admitted this. As one indicated: "I used to make decisions without taking their constituents' needs into consideration. Now I tell them first, lay out what I'm thinking of doing, ask for their input. Nine out of ten times their input alters what I would have done for the better." Agreeing, another officer reflected that "this has created a very different environment for our managers. Opening up decisions this way and listening to [labor's] input gives the union a chance to critique our actions."

For their part, the union local presidents contrasted this with how it used to be: "We've only gotten together for once-a-year meetings over the last 4-5 years, which was usually a report from the company. We were always met negatively, as potential grievances. We lacked the ability to present the union's concerns. We weren't as aware of business issues." Certainly, access other than the most strictly formal and official was missing. One CWA local president recalled: "I have never had access above the department head through the grievance procedure, and . . . [I had] never met a company vice president before. They were untouchable; they wouldn't know what's going on here with employees; they're driven by revenues . . . that's what we thought." Said another:

There are still some side deals, but now managers are coming to the union presidents to flex the contract. I have lots of phone calls coming in from third-level managers just before LCIF meetings, to get MY help to influence the management team on their behalf! . . . This is a return to the kind of subtle influence old unions had, prior to the advent of hard union lines. We are now back to the union presidents having some control.

Local union presidents were becoming much more important in the union hierarchy, too. They were more central in the communications flow because of their direct links to company officers, and they often had information earlier and more completely than district-level or national union officials. They were also more broadly connected with company management, because the structure of local common interest forums meant that local presidents sat on more than one company officer's forum.

In general, the labor-management partnership shifted the action away from events favoring professionals in the union and toward the events favoring local presidents; away from processes favoring the national union and toward processes favoring local decision-making; away from treatment of workers on a mass basis and toward differentiated treatment of individuals and local worksites. And the local common interest forums added new arenas for defining union strategy, arenas in which local presidents represented the union.

The increase in local presidents' power with respect to company matters was accompanied by a change in their roles within their own local organizations. At the simplest level, the considerable time commitment imposed by monthly meetings of at least 4 (and as many as 8) LCIFs meant that union presidents were outside their regular bailiwicks a significantly greater proportion of each month. Their regular attendance at these meetings can drastically reduce members' access to their presidents. This is particularly so in smaller locals, where presidents are part-time or have few staff to whom they can delegate official responsibilities (e.g., member communications, grievance follow-up and often bargaining preparation). To the extent that visibility in the field handling member problems was a major component of the local president's job, it was probably no coincidence that the most serious continuing member opposition to change was found in the smaller locals of northern California--those areas with the greatest expectation of direct personal service from union presidents.

While LCIF participation greatly changed the kind of representation local presidents provide their members, this change was considered positive--a significant move into the realm of proactive policy formulation. In the words of one president, "If union presidents don't support the LCIF process, they're not carrying out their elected responsibility to members. It is essential to complete representation to be there. . . . The difficulty is, we've always been in a position for reacting. It's very different to be part of the doers and to have to live with what we do." Another put it in stronger terms: "You can't play at being a union leader; you have to be one. You have to take responsibility and make decisions and explain your actions. This is always easier to do when you're passing blame onto someone else."

There were several components to this additional or heightened responsibility, among them the obligation not just to inform members of LCIF actions, but also to include and involve the union's secondary leadership. All presidents agreed, though, that they reported only outcomes of LCIF meetings. Too few among their members or local officers would understand the process component of the LCIFs--why so much time is involved and why consideration of various issues need take so long--that attempts to share this information could create more confusion or misunderstanding, something an elected official can ill afford.

Local presidents also felt an obligation to be careful about the information they exchanged within the LCIFs. Whereas they previously reacted to decisions made by company officials, with the advent of the

LCIFs such information provided the foundation upon which decisions were based. "You have to listen, check things out first, get facts and agreement" from both sides, one CWA president said. "The vice presidents say things they believe to be true, but that may not be true for all groups," or for all employees in all areas, another recognized. Moreover, instead of doing what he might have done in the past--accusing the company of deceit--the president noted that now "in cases of discrepancy I have checked back with the managing vice president, found out about why things might be different in different groups, rather than considering it another lie from the company." Instead of always complaining or filing grievances against management actions, then, local presidents were seeing it as within their role to investigate differences, and, if possible, resolve them short of the more traditional avenues.

Union presidents found themselves broadening their horizons. They were becoming more sensitive to relationships with their peers and to ramifications beyond their own area. Ironically, the local and decentralized nature of the LCIFs placed more responsibility on them to think broadly, not parochially. As one said, "It is more important for me to have good peer relationships. Before, the locals were autonomous, and now we must make decisions together. It forces you to be a clearer thinker. Before, we could handle issues individually without looking at their impact on other issues and decisions."

While LCIF participation brought local presidents greater influence with Pacific Bell, it also made presidents vulnerable to charges of neglect from the membership or to isolation resulting from disagreement with their peers. In response to the new challenges presented to union presidents by the LCIFs and to avoid attacks by their constituents, they developed new ways of selling the concept and new involvement techniques with their membership as they strived for rank-and-file acceptance of the process. The need for active selling was clear, given the shift in traditional roles that the LCIF represented--and the vulnerability of presidents who needed to be reelected. As one president put it, "Compared to the traditional [union] role, some members' secondary leadership may see the cooperative effort as selling out." So he redoubled his efforts to be sensitive to the dynamics within his local, and he has intensified internal communication efforts:

> There are feelings of powerlessness that influence the LCIF process, so I route the associated paperwork through the secondary leadership. However, our rules to limit the circulation of minutes until they were approved also caused problems. We are winning the battle in proving that we're not selling out or sleeping with the company. Through internal communication we are seeing results.

New methods of interacting with management, access to levels of management never before possible, and more time-consuming meeting requirements led several union presidents to develop new ways of involving and informing their membership of the output (and relevance) of the LCIFs. For the most part, presidents became more participative--in the way they carried out their duties, managed their staffs and addressed their issues. This approach produced new opportunities, but also caused a new set of problems: too many meetings and not enough time to touch all the bases in order to do all the necessary preliminary work. A number of presidents attempted to address these issues by further empowering those around them to carry out activities on their behalf. They delegated more tasks, had secondary leadership represent them on LCIFs, and held "shadow" LCIF meetings in the union. Still, pockets of more "traditional" thinking existed, and some presidents seemed to have adopted more of a wait-and-see attitude; they were not actively resisting, nor were they actively supporting further LCIF growth.

The new role for CWA local presidents was equivalent to learning an entirely new management style, one that was not "natural" to the traditional union dynamic. It required much greater sensitivity and political skill--not only with management, but also within the union. The "rules" no longer provided an objective, impersonal standard. Much more rested on the presidents' judgment and how they related to their constituents. One insightful union president framed the matter well:

> This is a much more difficult way to deal with each other. [Before] if we didn't like the decisions, we just complained. It was very easy, very comfortable, anyone could do this. Now, we must make advance decisions, exercise judgment and live with it, which is much harder and places much more responsibility on the unions. Laws regulate how unions are supposed to responsibly represent their members. [In the context of LCIFs], what constitutes fulfilling this responsibility? Under the old rules, we knew how to resolve objections. Now, if members dispute my judgment, what are their rights and my responsibilities? It's all new territory.

Organizational Role Redefinition

Surrounding individual role redefinition--how union presidents handled their new leadership challenges--was the question of organizational role redefinition within the union, a matter that only began to be addressed as the ramifications of the changes introduced by the LCIF process became clearer.

As the result of the presidents' LCIF participation, the CWA witnessed significant internal redefinition, not all of it smooth. Just as local presidents were becoming more participative with their members, so was the union structure above then beginning to involve them more and was beginning to allow and even encourage local autonomy--the union version of what Pacific Bell has called "self-management." One president reported, "The union is also changing its own operations, involving local presidents more, allowing more flexibility in the contract, encouraging new processes."

The commitment to change was further confirmed by CWA's hands-off attitude in letting the LCIFs be as autonomous as the participants wished.

A higher level union official made this clear. "It's not our intent to screen all the LCIF's actions," he said. "We may suggest an approach but most stuff they've worked out. Some things with legal ramifications they can recommend, then send to the bargaining level; e.g., contract jobs' wage and rate went to the bargaining level."

The role redefinition for union presidents also had ramifications for the union membership. The same union president that recognized the benefits of greater participation upward was also sensitive to the new strain it introduced downward. "This is creating internal problems within the union," he said, "specifically with executive boards, or chief or area stewards." In short, the traditional local union structure was also affected by the LCIF process and needed to manage change as well, like it or not. If the secondary leadership of union locals was not to become a "negative" force, as one president put it, then its role too had to change, and it had to be included rather than left behind.

Change sends out ripples that go well beyond the group initially affected by a new forum like the LCIFs.

Union Role Redefinition

Finally, at the broadest level, there was another important role redefinition occurring--what role the union in general would play under a "business/labor partnership" led by the LCIFs. The CWA as an entity was also in the process of inventing and learning a new role.

To the extent that any union is part of a checks and balances system originally organized to protect employees' economic livelihood, the opportunity to be proactive and constructive rather than reactive and confrontational looms as a major change in the way CWA leaders view the union's overall role. "The union is in business to put itself out of business" (eliminating grievances), said one local president. "I'm trying to get out of the grievance business and into the people business," said another.

At the core of this thinking was a challenge that has been present within the labor movement for some time, a challenge which one union president put in terms of industry change:

> How does one respond to the fact that our industry is changing [;that] technology is changing our business totally ...? Look at other industries and unions with large memberships who didn't deal with change--steel, railroads. If we don't recognize that transition now, we could wind up in the same situation. Instead, we are the right union in the right place at the right time with the right leaders. If we don't take this on now, we're not being effective, and we can't represent our people, or identify with the changes they're seeing. It's very easy to keep our old perspectives, and think that everything will stay the

same as it was for 30 years. But it is guaranteed that things will not stay the same for the next 30 years.

The local presidents saw these changes continuing. Said one, "It is a big role shift for the union, with 80 percent of its budget usually devoted to the grievance process. Now and in the future it'll be more like 20 percent, with the remainder to enhance lives, which is the goal of the process in the first place."

But the new role of the union in a longer-term business/labor partnership with PacBell was still being defined. And the union leaders are still learning new roles--from leadership styles to new ways of solving problems to what it means to be proactive business partners with management. They were well aware of the risks involved, as their jobs are political ones, dependent on the satisfaction of the electorate. But the accomplishments of the first year appeared worth the risk to the participants. As one said:

> There are big political risks. If the LCIFs fail, most presidents will probably lose next time around. But that's an acceptable risk, 50-50 probability, and the benefits of success are so high that it's worth it. There is a lot of activity in this local, any number of people who'd be after my job. I did have two elected VPs strongly opposed. Of four, one was pro-LCIF, one anti, two ambivalent. Now, all four agree, but one would say "I told you so. This was just another big brainwashing trick by the company."

The union presidents had a job security issue with CWA just as their members did with Pacific Bell: to manage their new roles so that they could keep their own jobs as elected officials. But ultimately the real, long-term issue of "keeping their jobs" was not just a matter of immediate, short-term constituent relations management. Instead, it would rest on the answer to the larger question of the union's role in Pacific Bell's business partnership.

One LCIF member phrased the challenge directly in terms of the need to invent a viable new role. "We may ultimately be facing an interesting paradox. The LCIF process is a clear demonstration of support for the valuable role unions play. However," he continued, "as this process further evolves, the need for unions, at least in their present form, may well be reduced. The question we will all have to wrestle with is: What will evolution do to the unions, their role and their future responsibilities?"

Company Officers: Skills and Behavior

There were many parallels between the new skills and attitudes that union leaders developed in order to be effective in the LCIF process and the new requirements for company management. With the advent of the LCIFs, company officers were also engaged in the creation of new roles, and such ongoing redefinition brought with it new learning needs.

For the officers, one of the first changes was a substantive one. The establishment of the LCIFs brought the most senior line managers into union territory--both literally, in terms of meetings at union halls, and figuratively, in terms of involvement with the labor relations process. The LCIFs made it important for them to be as conversant with the ins and outs of the CWA-PacBell contract as the local presidents. (For example, to the extent that items which are formally negotiated are "off limits," LCIF discussion must be restricted to specific instances requiring case-by-case resolution.) They had to get involved personally in labor relations, not through the discipline process, but as a matter of policy. They needed to become knowledgeable about career issues and work conditions for the unionized work force, and they were often learning about this directly from union presidents. This avenue represented both a new area of substantive knowledge for some company officers and a new educational source.

In addition to the formal learning, there was another kind of more subtle knowledge required--sensitivity to the nuances of union members' reactions to things company people either take for granted or regard as trivial. The managers had to be aware of a range of details that do not "normally" or "traditionally" concern an officer--from making sure to hold meetings in unionized hotels, to being aware of protocol in terms of who got meeting minutes first, to anticipating the reactions of union members when they saw photos of their leaders smiling alongside managers.

The union leaders were very adept at "reading" signals that indicate whether managers can be trusted or not. After all, they were "politicians" who rose to their positions through elections, and they had clearly learned to tune in to people. Thus, in the LCIFs they distinguished "vice presidents that are serious" from others "who were just reading the script." They looked not for rhetoric but for concrete gestures that show management's sincerity, such as one officer keeping people in their jobs despite negative financial implications which could lower his incentive pay. While commenting favorably on these gestures, they also pointed out contradictions and inconsistencies--for example, management asking them to help sell a new program whose credibility was undercut by another management action elsewhere. "I make a commitment to my members based on an agreement in the LCIF," one president said, "and then other managers turn around and do something else." Or, in another instance, union presidents questioned the officers' sincerity about "partnership" when the officers were sent minutes from a major joint meeting to review first, with the union getting the second, "revised" version.

Thus, nearly every managerial action carried the additional weight of being scanned for "messages" about "real" motives, attitudes toward the union, sincerity, and the meaning of partnership. Company officers needed to develop increasing attention to a new range of details, signals and danger zones, as well as a greater self-awareness about the impact of their behavior.

LCIF involvement required new skills for company officers, just as it did for union leaders. Managers who were accustomed to acting decisively and presenting full-blown plans (in part to look good to their underlings) needed to learn the patience that participative consensus building required, and they needed to learn to present half-formed ideas for discussion before making decisions. "Coming in with prepared documents" and "not fully consulting and collaborating" were two reasons for union presidents to resent and distrust a company officer. Because the process was far less amenable to packaging or control by any one player, managers accustomed to always having their homework done and their case flawlessly persuasive found that such behavior could be seen as manipulative, disingenuous, and counterproductive. Instead, the LCIF process rewarded managers who are prepared, yes,--but more important, flexible, informed, forthcoming, and candid.

This standard could easily make an executive who likes to look as though everything is fully under control feel vulnerable and exposed. And it created dilemmas even for those who handled it well, because sometimes union officials carried old expectations that company officers always knew what they wanted. For example, some union presidents attributed hidden agendas to a company officer who was genuinely opening up issues for discussion--in part out of disbelief that management would not have a preset agenda.

Because of the premium placed on group leadership skills, those managers who had more experience with participative leadership approaches, or had received formal training in it and who felt more secure about their position in the company, were better able to handle the LCIF role from the beginning. For such managers, the new roles came more naturally, and they were better able to share power in an everyday sense with the union presidents in their LCIF. Thus, in some LCIFs the company officer did not set the meeting agenda, as happened more typically in others. Instead it was jointly determined. Furthermore, in the "high participation" LCIFs, the chair rotated between the company officer and each of the union presidents. In addition to participative skills, of course, this process required more participative attitudes, a gut feeling of basic equality. As one of the high participation officers aid, "We're all just a bunch of people trying to do our best."

Organizational Role Redefinition: The Management Hierarchy

The second arena for new role creation and learning was organizational. Just as we saw with the CWA, redefinition of the roles of top Pacific Bell leaders sent ripples out to the rest of the organization, opening up the need to invent new organizational roles, particularly for middle management.

The opportunity for direct union presidents/VP contact that was provided by the LCIF effectively eliminated a whole slice of the middle management chain of communication. In certain respects, the LCIF became a vehicle to circumvent or end run the standard management chain of command. In some instances, vice presidents said that they were getting brought to them problems previously handled by middle managers. And at times, Pacific Bell middle managers found themselves in the position of learning more about emerging company issues from union representatives than from their own superiors.   One officer saw the LCIF process as producing a "squeeze" at the middle and, perhaps, bottom levels that required a redefinition of the appropriate first level management role.

"Middle managers see this as a joke," a union president asserted, claiming that communication with them was the key to success.   The presidents recognized the impact of the LCIF on the management hierarchy.   "Pre-LCIF, local presidents didn't meet with PacBell vice presidents, except very rarely," a union official reported.   "Now our meetings make the district managers nervous, but they are all very authority conscious, so they don't complain."   But one union president did not want middle managers included in the LCIFs.   In fact, in his view even consideration of their participation indicated that it was high time to redefine upper management roles away from details (the things in which middle managers had a stake and could easily feel disempowered if excluded) and toward broad strategic issues.   As he put it:

> I don't agree that having no middle management is a problem, anyone thinking in the Old Bell way would say that. We on the LCIF don't need middle management there all the time.   We would get bogged down in day-to-day details.   This way concepts are developed and we let implementation happen according to districts' specific needs.   That's the role of the LCIF and the local presidents.   The main job of a leader is to teach.

However, company officers were aware of the need to be sensitive to middle managers' needs and feelings, and to not undercut them, but they were not sure how to go about this.   Newer roles did not so much have to be learned as to be defined in the first place.   This created a dilemma. To accomplish this also required opening up the LCIF process to wider involvement, something that itself had to be approached cautiously given the initial agreement to keep LCIFs small and to retain information within the LCIFs in order to build a foundation of trust.   According to one officer, a LCIF set up a task force to look at how to communicate to those outside the LCIF, "in contrast to the previous sensitivity regarding circulation of LCIF minutes.   LCIF members didn't want them published to anyone but us.   [But] now we realize we [cannot remain] an island."

The importance of middle manager involvement stemmed not just from the potential for hurt feelings, but also from the material harm these managers could inflict on the process if new roles were not invented for them.   Said a union president, "The third level managers make it difficult if they're not on board.   A [company officer] and I wrote letters saying we had no surplus [employees], when in fact the division manager had eight undeclared surplus, making us look foolish.   Management thinks it can place those people.   But at that time, communication between [that officer] and his next level was not great."

Middle managers occasionally communicated dissatisfaction with their indirect representation through the VPs, leading to the earlier-quoted union leaders' description of support for the LCIFs below the VP level as "a joke." From the company officers' perspective, "The LCIF has the potential of being one of the greatest things that has happened, but it still needs buy-in from lower levels and all parts. They need to trust that their positions are being represented. We can't move the meetings down from the vice president level because the VPs have the middle levels, but we do need to better include their thoughts."

The Labor Relations Function: From Central Control to Decentralized Consultation

Middle managers were not the only company actors outside the LCIF group whose roles had to be redefined in order to make the process work. The role of the Labor Relations staff underwent two subtle shifts that cumulatively resulted in a significant role redefinition.

In the past, LR provided counsel and support to managers in contract interpretation, and, when grievances arose, stepped in at the latter stages of the grievance resolution and arbitration procedure. With the advent of "Business Partnership," however, two things changed. First, the LCIFs were given a role in addressing the conditions that might previously have led to grievances, and second, the LCIF participants, i.e., the company VPs and the CWA local presidents, were now vitally involved in the development of potential contract proposals and language. No longer were Labor Relations personnel the main company actors involved in the two primary processes of formal union interest.

Yet, rather than seeing a complementary decline in the volume of their work as the number of formal grievances declined, the Labor Relations department found itself increasingly called upon by managers for counseling, advice and support in the handling of interactions with the union and unionized personnel. In addition, as the role of Labor Relations is increasingly seen by CWA as more that of internal counsel than external advocate, there has been an equally subtle shift in the influence attributed to the staff by at least its outside observers. Many CWA interviewees said that Labor Relations had lost power in the redefined roles accompanying the LCIFs, by virtue of the fact that new players, both company and union, are now involved in both the dispute-cum-grievance and resolution and contract development processes.

Finally, to the extent that the old labor relations structure was dependent upon continuing adversarial relations between PB and CWA, and given that the new structure was showing some success in reducing the adversarial nature of company-union relations, several interviewees pointed out LR's stake in the continuation of adversarial relationships, and questioned its commitment to the new, less confrontational processes. Several interviewees pointed out that LR could be in danger of losing its function altogether. But the LR department itself disputes these views.

"We never saw ourselves as having power in the first place," a spokesman commented. CWA's questioning might reflect either a distrust lingering from the old relationship or a subtle acknowledgment of its own increasing empowerment in the realigned relationships under "Business Partnership." Whichever is the case, there is little doubt that Labor Relations will find itself playing a different role as PacBell's explicit strategic decisions pull the company increasingly away from confrontation (and from systems that work in that context), and move it more towards cooperation (and towards the internally supportive and coaching systems that enable the cooperative approach to succeed).

Management's View of the Union

Finally, the broadest redefinition was a rethinking of management's role vis-a-vis the union, a reexamination entailing the very notion of "business/labor partnership."   "Partners" are welcome allies, not manipulated adversaries. This was hard for some officers to see.

Experts on union-management cooperation make clear that any enhanced union role must be accomplished via a sincere company acknowledgement that such influence is a right of the union, given the latter's explicitly central role in today's common interests and tomorrow's common directions. This required a new attitude for some officers who might be prone to feel that the LCIF is a management "gift," not a partnership, in which management temporarily agrees to "give" the union some of the company's rightful power, to voluntarily bequeath something in order to win cooperation--something that can be withdrawn at will. Such a paternalistic attitude could undermine the essential core of the effort and its future potential.   And so the officers were under pressure to reexamine their assumptions and change their traditional ways of thinking.

IV

THE MANAGEMENT CHALLENGE: TAPPING THE "SIX I'S"
OF SUCCESSFUL PARTNERSHIPS

Strategic partnerships form because they bring value to the organizations entering into them.   But their existence also changes how the individual organizations operate and how their managers manage. Unless partnership activities can be segregated from other organizational activities (as in the formation of a stand-alone, arms-length unit that is only sphere of jointness), then the need to relate to partners in ways that reap the benefits of partnership inevitably changes how each partner operates as well.

Thus, in profound ways, the new alliances may change how American business operates. The PB/CWA case, though concerned with only one kind of alliance, provides evidence for a number of changes inside both parent organizations: in the roles of top management and the behavior required to succeed; in communication and decision-making channels; and in the influence and role of staff functions. Furthermore, the goals and strategies of each organization now embrace the goals and strategies of the partner. These findings from the PB/CWA case match what I am seeing in supplier-customer alliances, in investigations just underway. Alliances with high degrees of interpretation--in which each partner becomes involved in processes formerly "internal" to the other--change the nature of the management task.

Perhaps one of the major reasons that the number of inter-organizational partnerships is still relatively small is the management difficulties they entail. For each partnership, there are three areas of management challenge: managing the inherently fragile relationship between partners, and then managing the changes in each of the partner's own organizations. Until these new management challenges are mastered, corporations will not be able to take advantage of the benefits of strategic partnerships.

The kinds of partnerships I have outlined still represent, by any measure, only a small proportion of all American corporate activity. This is true across all three types. In 1985, cooperative research represented only $1.6 billion of the over $50 billion corporations spent on R & D, including the $1.4 billion spent by research organizations serving noncompeting electric, gas and telephone utility companies. Investment in joint ventures is still minuscule when compared to the multiple billions spent on mergers and acquisitions. Supplier-customer alliances are difficult to enumerate unless they take the form of an identifiable joint venture (since they represent a more cooperative or intimate extension of an existing relationship), but I propose that they are probably still more apparent in rhetoric than in practice. And although union-management partnerships are identifiable in a few large companies, they are still rare.

Those cases in which partnerships tend to have in place six factors--to make them memorable, let's call them the "six I's." The relationship is Important, and therefore it gets adequate resources, management attention, and sponsorship. There is an agreement for longer-term Investment, which tends to help equalize benefits over time. The partners are Interdependent, which helps keep power balanced. The organizations are Integrated, so that the appropriate points of contact and communication are managed. They are each Informed about the plans and directions of the other. Finally, the partnership is Institutionalized--bolstered by a framework of supporting mechanisms, from legal requirements to social ties to shared values, all of which make trust possible.

These I-factors reflect a different way of thinking about the management and organizational tasks of a modern corporation. Yet, for companies to gain the benefits of allying with other organizations--from the power of combination to flexibility and innovation--these must serve as the basis for a new philosophy for American enterprise.

Much important strategic improvement in economic competitiveness may be occurring in partner-like relationships--rather than "inside" the "boundaries" of one organization. This makes it especially important to understand what it takes to manage the new alliances and how they reshape the ways America does business.

NOTES

1. Kathyrn Rudie Harrigan, Strategies for Joint Ventures (Lexington, MA: Lexington Books, 1985).

2. Joseph Badaracco, The United States Business Corporation: An Institution in Transition (tentative title) (Cambridge, MA: Ballinger Publishing Co., 1988).

3. Study in progress on entrepreneurial vehicles in established organizations, supported by Harvard Business School Division of Research.

4. Ralph Biggadike, Corporate Diversification: Entry, Strategy, and Performance (Boston: Harvard Business School Division of Research, 1976).

5. Robert J. Eccles, "The Quasi-Firm in the Construction Industry," Journal of Economic Behavior and Organization, 2 (December 1981): 335-57.

6. George Lodge and Richard Walton, "The American Corporation and Its New Relationships," Harvard Business School Working Paper, June 1987.

7. Dan Baum, "Polaroid Corporation Is Selling Its Technique For Limiting Supplier Price Increases," Wall Street Journal, February 13, 1985, p. 36.

8. Benson Shapiro, "Close Encounters of the Fourth Kind," unpublished paper, Harvard Business School, 1985.

9. William J. Hampton, "How IBM Wooed Ford into a More Meaningful Relationship," Business Week, March 30, 1987, p. 87.

10. Rosabeth Moss Kanter and Erika Morgan, "The New Alliances: First Report on the Pacific Bell/Communications Workers of America Business Partnership," Harvard Business School Working Paper, March 1987.

11. Thomas A. Kochan, Harry C. Katz, and Robert B. McKersie, The Transformation of American Industrial Relations (New York: Basic Books, 1986).

12. Roy D. Shapiro, "Toward Effective Supplier Management: international Comparisons," Harvard Business School Working Paper, 1985.

13. "Corporate Odd Couples," Business Week, July 21, 1986, pp. 100-105.

14. The discussion of this case is based on direct observation and over 50 personal interviews conducted between January and September 1986. All quotes are from interviews.

SOURCES AND IMPLICATIONS OF STRATEGIC DECLINE: THE CASE
OF JAPANESE-AMERICAN COMPETITION IN MICROELECTRONICS

by Charles H. Ferguson

The crisis of the American semiconductor industry represents the
first public appearance of an issue likely to assume great prominence in
the years ahead. The past decade has seen severe erosion of America's
technological and competitive position in a number of areas critical to
future economic growth and military power--robotics, microelectronics, and
advanced materials, among others.[1] The ultimate effects of continued
decline, though impossible to predict in detail, could be quite large. They
may include lower living standards for the American people; a major
increase in Japan's leverage in American, and indeed global, affairs; and
rising tension over relationships between government policies and national
economic performance.

One symptom of, and contributor to, the erosion of U.S. economic
and technological hegemony has been the decline of the U.S. semiconductor
industry in the face of Japanese competition. Between 1978 and the
present, Japan's share of the world semiconductor market (now about $30
billion) rose from 28 to 50 percent, the American industry's world market
share declined rapidly, and the United States became a large net importer
of advanced semiconductors.[2] Japan now leads in several technologies and
continues to progress more rapidly than the United States.[3]

Microelectronics is a rapidly growing sector increasingly critical to
the computer, telecommunications, aerospace, robotics, automobile, and
defense industries.[4] Hence--and as recent political events demonstrate--it
is not an arena in which U.S. failure, and/or Japanese hegemony, will be
taken lightly. But the significance of U.S. decline, and the optimal policy
for reversing it, depend upon the forces which underlie the industry's
competitive dynamics. And here, the semiconductor industry offers some
interesting cautionary lessons. Many analyses of U.S. industrial difficulties
have focused upon mature, concentrated, and unionized sectors, citing
attendant rigidities and/or macroeconomic forces as the causes of U.S.
decline. Yet the semiconductor case shows that American troubles extend
to an entrepreneurial, fragmented, nonunionized high-technology industry.
Furthermore, close analysis of this industry calls into question the
adequacy of several frequently advocated policies, as well the economic
models of markets, firm-level behavior, and international trade upon which
some recommendations are based.

In particular, Japanese-American semiconductor competition has
fundamentally been driven by strategic and institutional forces, and
accordingly must be understood as a contest between two sectoral systems
(including relevant governmental components) more than as market
competition of the sort typically described by economic theory. Although
traditional economic variables (such as national market access or closure,
exchange rates, industry structure, and the costs of capital and labor)
certainly played a role, they were often the consequence of strategic
processes and institutional performance as much as their cause. Hence, in

order to understand U.S. decline, we will need to consider the institutional system which shaped the decisions and performance of the U.S. industry. Both in the U.S. and Japan, successive actions by employees, firms, and government policymakers reflected and continuously reinforced systemic incentives.   Their result is the international contrast in industrial structure, conduct, and competitive success which confronts us today.

The Japanese industry succeeded because its strategic regime encouraged external predation, rewarded investments in future productivity, and provided rigorous competitive discipline, while simultaneously restraining consumption and unproductive distributional conflict. Conversely the American regime encouraged short-term calculations, distributional conflict, and consumption relative to investment, so that in the long run Americans were collectively inefficient relative to Japanese producers.   Moreover, the American regime was not only chronically inefficient, it was also inflexible and self-destructive when placed under stress.   In the presence of external challenges, U.S. firms faced incentives to practice lifeboat diplomacy--to betray each other, their customers, and their suppliers rather than to improve the sector's collective, long-run productivity.

Hence when Japan entered global competition, the resulting American decline was largely predetermined. Whether the American regime can now be changed enough to preserve a competitive industry remains unclear. However, policy measures which do not recognize the strategic deadlocks facing the industry will be ineffective or even detrimental.   Successful policy interventions must lengthen the time horizons of industrial actors and ensure that assistance yields enduring productivity gains, rather than short-term profits, inflationary wage spirals, or zero-sum distributional competitions.   Otherwise the industry will waste or consume government support just as it wasted the technological superiority it once enjoyed.

I

THE DEVELOPMENT AND COMPARATIVE STRUCTURE OF THE
U.S. AND JAPANESE INDUSTRIES

Until the late 1970s, the U.S. and Japanese semiconductor industries evolved quasi-independently.   Japan imported U.S. technology and capital equipment,[5] restricted both import penetration and direct foreign investment by U.S. semiconductor firms,[6] produced for its domestic market (particularly the consumer electronics industry), but largely refrained from export drives directed at the United States.[7]   The U.S. industry sold technology to Japan, generally acquiesced to closure of the Japanese market, but also controlled the rest of the world market.   At the height of its success in the mid-1970s, the U.S. industry held 95 percent of its domestic market, half of Europe's, and 60 percent of the world market-- though less than a third of Japan's.[8]

The Japanese and U.S. national industries also diverged structurally. The Japanese industry became a relatively stable oligopoly[9] protected by the national government from foreign competition. Imports were controlled, and direct foreign investment was effectively prohibited. Semiconductor production was dominated by diversified, vertically integrated firms such as Nippon Electric Corp. (NEC) and Hitachi, for whom semiconductors accounted for 10 to 25 percent of total revenues.[10] These firms used roughly a quarter of their semiconductor production internally in the electronics products which constituted their principal businesses. They also maintained close, enduring relationships to their suppliers, the Tokyo city banks, the national government, and sometimes each other.[11] Entry into the Japanese industry came only through the diversification efforts of other large industrial complexes (Kawasaki, Sanyo, Sharp, Sony), rather than through the creation of new firms confined to semiconductor production. The industry's major firms also followed typical Japanese personnel practices such as lifetime employment, so employee turnover was consequently low.

In the United States, by contrast, there evolved a two part industry, divided into "captives" and "merchants." The few major and relatively stable "captives," such as IBM and AT&T, produced for their internal use but refrained from market competition. Conversely the open-market "merchant" industry, which at its peak accounted for 70 percent of U.S. production and dominated the world market,[12] evolved into a structurally unstable, fragmented, highly entrepreneurial arena.[13] Most U.S. merchant producers were young, relatively small firms whose semiconductor sales represented at least 40 percent, and often the entirety, of their total revenue.[14] Market leadership, employee loyalties, and supplier relationships were transitory; many semiconductor and capital equipment producers rose and fell rapidly, and employee turnover averaged 20 percent across the industry.[15] For twenty years this pattern of instability, frequent mobility, and new venture formation was considered a critical factor in the industry's success,[16] though by the mid-1970s the performance of IBM, AT&T, and the Japanese industry should have suggested otherwise.[17]

Equally striking, and analogous, is the contrast between the two nations' semiconductor capital equipment, materials, and services sectors. Once again, the Japanese industry is dominated by relatively large diversified firms, either semiconductor producers themselves or major firms with experience in relevant optical, chemical, mechanical, or construction technologies. And where the equipment producers themselves are small, they are linked to larger firms which consume much of their output.[18] For example, Fujitsu owns 22 percent of Advantest (test equipment), NEC owns 50 percent of Ando (testers), Hitachi owns Hitachi Electronic Engineering (various products); Hitachi and Matsushita manufacture their own automated assembly equipment; Toshiba and Hitachi produce electron beam machines used to make masks, the blueprints for integrated circuits; Nikon and Canon produce advanced lithography equipment; and Shimizu, a large construction firm, builds clean room facilities.[19]

The American capital equipment and services industry, in contrast, resembles its semiconductor producing counterpart in its extreme fragmentation and entrepreneurialism.[20]   A few stable, relatively large, established equipment firms (e.g., Teradyne and Perkin-Elmer) coexist and compete with innumerable "startups"-- newly founded ventures such as Trillium, Master Images, Zycad, and hundreds of others.   As of 1986, 55 percent of U.S. equipment and services vendors had annual sales of less than $5 million.[21]   Nearly half are less than ten years old;[22] many are already failing.   And even the established firms are having difficulties; for like its domestic clientele, the U.S. semiconductor equipment and services sector is decaying rapidly.

II

THE ONSET AND EXTENT OF AMERICAN DECLINE

American decline began roughly a decade ago, and coincided with the transformation of semiconductor production from an artisanal endeavor to a complex, large scale, capital intensive activity.   With the advent of Very Large Scale Integration (VLSI) in the late 1970s, microelectronics came of age.   Capital intensive, automated production became essential, as did large initial investments in product design, a wide technology base, large R & D efforts, and close relationships to equipment suppliers and final systems producers.   As integrated circuits became in effect complete systems, they became strategically critical to a wide range of major industries including consumer electronics, computers, and weapons systems.[23]

These developments offered a potentially large advantage to Japanese semiconductor producers as a consequence of their technical diversification, large resources, and vertically integrated structure.   This structural advantage, together with the rising strategic value of semiconductors, also offered the possibility of large future rewards in downstream industries based upon leadership in microelectronics. Beginning in the mid-1970s the Japanese industry, in part assisted by its national government through such means as the VLSI Project sponsored by the Ministry of International Trade and Industry (MITI), acted accordingly.

The ensuing decline of the American industry, which had previously dominated all advanced semiconductor markets, was noteworthy for its rapidity.   Japanese firms now hold 75 percent of world markets for Dynamic Random Access Memories (DRAMs), 50 percent of world microprocessor markets, 70 percent of world microcontroller markets, and 40 percent of the world market for Application Specific Integrated Circuits (ASICs).[24]   Japan's share of the total world market nearly doubled to 50 percent in less than a decade, while the U.S. industry's world market share shrank by 20 percent.   Six of the world's ten largest open-market semiconductor producers are now Japanese.   The U.S. is a major net importer of semiconductors.   Japanese capital spending has surpassed that of the U.S. merchant industry and the Japanese domestic semiconductor market is now larger than that of the United States.[25]

Less widely appreciated, but probably equally important, is the concomitant and similar decline of U.S. capital equipment, materials, and services technology. Over the past decade, the Japanese equipment industry's world market share has more than doubled to over 30 percent, primarily at the expense of U.S. firms.[26] Moreover, Japanese suppliers have reached parity or even superiority in major technologies including packaging, automated assembly equipment, various ultrapure materials, some categories of fabrication equipment, and specialized procedures such as maskmaking.[27] For example, Hoya and Shin-Etsu now hold 90 percent of the world market for mask quality glass and quartz; IBM's new East Fishkill facility is being built by Shimizu; and Japanese firms supply nearly half of Intel's masks.[28]

Relative R & D performance has changed as dramatically. While the U.S. still leads in many areas of theoretical research, it now trails in applied R & D. Between 1975 and 1982 the United States' share of world integrated circuit patent activity declined from 43 percent to 27 percent, while Japan's share rose from 18 percent to 48 percent.[29] By the mid-1980s, over 40 percent of papers presented at the IEEE Solid State Circuits Conference came from Japan, as did over 20 percent of all semiconductor technical publications worldwide.[30] Japanese efforts in X-ray lithography, which will probably dominate semiconductor production by the mid-1990s, appear to be far larger than those of the United States. NTT and its largest suppliers have embarked upon major programs for cooperative R & D, while among U.S. firms only IBM has a comparable effort.[31] Japan leads the United States in gallium arsenide research, and appears to have reached at least parity in laser systems, optoelectronics, and several other major technologies.[32]

Absent major structural, behavioral, and policy changes, then, the prospect is for continued decline within the relevant American industries, and for Japanese dominance of most semiconductor technologies and markets by the mid-1990s. This prognosis is strongly reinforced by consideration of the structural sources of U.S. decline.

III

THE SOURCES OF THE U.S. INSTITUTIONAL REGIME

The American industry's decay was the result of a systemic pattern involving a number of interrelated forces, of which three are particularly salient. They are (a) chronic failures of government policy; (b) persistent disadvantages in the costs of capital and skilled labor; and (c) an entrenched sectoral regime whose member firms were unstable, immature, and shortsighted. The result was an industry incapable of developing the technologies, institutions, and skills required in global markets, and the

CHARLES H. FERGUSON

creation of strong incentives to maximize immediate cash flow rather than
long run productivity. Moreover, each failure reinforced the others. The
resulting institutional regime reduced the American industry's efficiency,
perpetuated the perverse incentives shaping corporate strategy, and
blocked productive responses to macroeconomic, political, and competitive
problems. Let us therefore consider this regime's principal ingredients,
and then how they combined to form a strategically inferior sectoral
regime.

Government Policy Decisions

Government actions affecting the semiconductor industry, to the
extent they exhibit any systematic pattern, have tended to fragment the
industry and to shorten its time horizons, while failing to supply adequate
levels of the resources, such as engineering education, required for long-
run growth.

Although many early semiconductor innovations came from AT&T and
General Electric,[33] by the 1970s the industry was dominated by smaller,
entrepreneurial firms. In retrospect, this change appears partly to have
been a byproduct of government actions focused on other issues--albeit
one permitted by the initially small scale of early production and markets.
In 1956 AT&T, then the dominant presence in semiconductor technology,
agreed as part of an antitrust settlement to license upon demand its
patents and to refrain from open market competition.[34] In effect, the
history of the industry started over. There followed a rising flow of
defectors from established, large firms such as AT&T and GE, into dozens
of small, relatively new firms which sought to fill the vacuum left by
AT&T's departure.[35] Hence, antitrust policy favored fragmentation over
either concentration or industrywide cooperation. Until the early 1980s,
when the 1969 IBM case and the 1976 AT&T case were both resolved and
new legislation exempted cooperative research from antitrust constraints,
antitrust policy was clearly antagonistic to the industry's concentration
and/or rationalization.

In the 1960s this trend was furthered by Defense Department
procurement policies at a time when the military dominated U.S.
semiconductor markets. Throughout the 1960s, defense procurement
demanded technology more advanced than commercial uses, was cost-
insensitive, often paid for R & D and early production experience, but also
often required firms to license second sources.[36] These policies, too,
favored new firms over large established ones, and tended to fragment the
industry. They may also have contributed to the industry's emphasis upon
product R & D to the neglect of manufacturing efficiency. Thus early
military procurement policy probably contributed to the industry's later
structural problems. But it also performed valuable functions by reducing
firm-level risk and funding generic R & D.

Unfortunately, these positive contributions largely ended in the 1970s,
while new negative effects appeared. By the mid-1970s, the military
ceased to provide substantial, commercially useful industrial support via its

R & D and procurement spending. The military's share of total demand declined from 50 percent of U.S. consumption in 1965 to about 15 percent a decade later, and for several reasons military demand came to lag severely, rather than lead, commercial technology.[37] Concomitantly, in the 1970s defense procurement policies shifted away from support of generic R & D and towards specifically military technology, reducing commercial spinoff and drawing resources from commercial efforts, while remaining insensitive to manufacturing costs.[38] No commercial policy replaced the void left by the relative decline and changing nature of defense purchasing, so the industry's growing requirements for skilled labor, long-term capital investment, structural change, and Japanese market access remained unmet.

Other, nonmilitary, policies contributed seriously to the industry's fragmentation. The creation of new ventures through employee defections from established firms was subsidized by tax expenditures. Capital gains differentials, the tax treatment of losses, and the R & D tax credit favored new startups by making venture capital available on favorable terms and lowered the capital costs of startups relative to those of established firms.[39] Worse, tax and regulatory changes greatly increased venture capital flows in the early 1980s, just as the industry's rising strategic importance and scale requirements made stability more important. In addition, the taxation of individual income--particularly of capital gains and incentive stock options--permitted startups to offer higher effective compensation than more mature firms.[40]

Capital and Labor Market Effects

Macroeconomic forces and national differentials in factor costs (for both capital and professional labor) certainly seem to have played a significant role in the industry's competitiveness. For decades prior to the recent rise of the yen and of Japanese living standards, American salaries for professionals and managers were perhaps double those in Japan. Several studies have indicated that capital costs were substantially higher as well.[41] Altogether, these disadvantages probably constituted a significant drag on the U.S. industry's competitiveness.

But economywide factor costs are not, by themselves, the principal source of the industry's problems. Even where factor cost differences were important, their effect upon the semiconductor industry was substantially worsened by problems whose basic causes lay elsewhere. High U.S. professional labor costs, for example, were raised further by the need to use wage increases to reduce personnel turnover, and high turnover also discouraged training which would have alleviated skilled labor shortages. U.S. microelectronics firms also faced higher effective capital costs as a result of their instability, through their obligation to pay risk premiums for debt and to maintain greater relative liquidity to cushion against external shocks such as recessions or exchange rate changes.

Even including these effects, however, factor cost differences cannot fully explain the American problem. The U.S. industry already showed signs of decline at a time when its aggregate R & D, capital spending, and resources still dwarfed Japan's, and prior to the dollar's rise in the early 1980s. As early as 1978, Japanese producers captured 40 percent of the world market for 16K memories, and Japanese products were judged superior in quality to those of the U.S. merchant industry.[42]

Nor do factor costs explain why the U.S. industry maintained its fragmented structure and entrepreneurial behavior despite steep, technologically-driven increases in capital intensity, scale economies, and vertical integration requirements. By the early 1980s an efficient-scale semiconductor factory cost well over $100 million, and efficient production demanded both organizational sophistication and computer systems expertise.   Similar forces were transforming capital equipment and materials technologies. Yet U.S. startup creation actually accelerated in the early 1980s,[43] and sectoral rationalization is coming only through competitive decline, rather than through foresighted strategic decisions.

The Institutional Regime of the U.S. Industry

The forces acting upon the industry during its seminal period, then, included antitrust policies and decisions, the evolution of defense procurement, incentives for new ventures derived from tax effects, high capital and labor costs, and a few accidents of history. These conditions gave rise, perhaps somewhat by chance, to a rather unusual set of corporate structures and strategies.   But once in place, this industrial regime was quite stable.   It was systematically perpetuated, defects included, not only by the larger economic and policy environment, but also through the structure and practices of the merchant industry.   The most striking of these factors were entrepreneurialism, structural instability, short life cycles for firms as well as products, high personnel turnover, wide use of incentive stock options (ISOs) vesting over four year periods, and an extreme emphasis upon short-term, individual optimization.   In short, the stablest feature of the system was the instability and turbulence of its individual elements.

Once corporate instability, high turnover, and the continuous formation of new ventures became accepted facts within the American industry, subsequent activity came to assume and thereby reinforce them. In Silicon Valley, a large infrastructure of venture capitalists, consultants, headhunters, subcontractors, equipment producers, service firms, and leasing companies arose in response to an industry constituted of young, unstable, cash-limited, entrepreneurial firms.   Business practices came to assume instability, discouraging long-term commitments.   Firms paid thousand-dollar rewards to employees who recruited personnel from other firms, including their previous employers. Stock options became essential to the recruiting and retaining of talented employees until a public offering made founders, venture capitalists, and valued employees wealthy. (Thereafter, performance incentives and loyalty often waned considerably, and firms frequently became net victims of headhunting rather than predators.)   Regional concentrations of high-technology firms, factor markets, and infrastructure--such as Silicon Valley--grew rapidly, reinforcing fragmentation by providing locally the ingredients for new ventures.[44] But as the regime reinforced and perpetuated itself, it also crippled the industry's long-run productivity and competitiveness.

IV

THE INSTITUTIONAL SOURCES OF AMERICAN DECLINE

The U.S. industry's counterproductive behavior, and its decline, derived from elements of its strategic regime which encouraged shortsightedness, distributional conflict, and consumption relative to collective, long-run productivity growth. Hence, the industry gradually consumed and wasted rather than reinvested the fruits of its initially-superior technological position and resources. When Japan reached technical parity and entered global competition, these same weaknesses worsened U.S. competitive difficulties. Rather than merging and/or increasing joint domestic R & D efforts, for example, U.S. firms exited markets, reduced long-term R & D, switched to Japanese suppliers, sold technology to foreign competitors, and sought protectionist measures at the expense of their own customers, including the U.S. computer industry. These problems were not incidental; they were deeply rooted in the organizational and strategic patterns of the industry.

Consider first some concomitants of the fact that the industry, particularly in Silicon Valley, consisted of shifting networks of entrepreneurial, small firms. The flexibility, market responsiveness, shared infrastructure, and informational benefits of such networks have been much discussed. However, these benefits are accompanied by costs, one of which is vulnerability to predation. Even if networks of small-scale firms are highly productive, in the long run many of their benefits may accrue primarily to predators, and come at the expense of larger U.S. firms, future productivity gains, and/or the larger economy. Moreover, in the merchant industry's case, instability fed by unchecked entrepreneurialism led to inflationary spirals, shortened corporate planning horizons drastically, and slowed the increases in capital intensity and vertical integration implied by the direction of technological change. So the system was also incompatible with the industry's optimal growth path.

The fragmentation and instability of the industry left its member firms in poor bargaining positions vis-a-vis those with longer time horizons, better information, superior financial or organizational assets, or scarce talents. Hence whatever the system's productivity benefits, a high proportion of them were redistributed to others not likely to reinvest in the long-term welfare of the industry or the nation. If the accounting could ever be done, we might find that among the largest beneficiaries of the merchant industry's growth period were Japanese and South Korean technology buyers, Silicon Valley landholders, and several thousand of the nation's youngest Porsche and Lamborghini owners.[45] And in part because the industry's regime left it open to both external and internal predation, it was also a rather inefficient way to organize semiconductor production.

Consider, for example, the relationships between personnel turnover, firm life cycles, and long run-productivity. Turnover has averaged 20 percent industrywide in American electronics, versus less than 5 percent in the Japanese industry and a few highly stable U.S. firms such as IBM and AT&T. One source of turnover is defection to new ventures; startups are typically founded and populated by experienced defectors from more established firms. Another source of turnover is failure; layoffs without notice have been common in many Silicon Valley firms, and they do not breed employee loyalty.

Excessive turnover through layoffs and defections reduces an industry's long-run productivity.[46]   Major defections severely disrupt important R & D efforts, customer relationships, or organizations. In some cases, entire R & D groups or design teams have defected in the midst of important projects. AT&T, General Electric, Motorola, Fairchild, and Intel, among others, have been the victims of mass defections which have caused severe operational disruptions. More generally, learning effects of several kinds are widely considered critical to competitive advantage in the semiconductor industry. Under conditions of high turnover many learning opportunities are lost.

In the merchant industry the prevalence of defection reduced firms' time horizons, raised their costs, and reduced their propensity to make risky and/or long-payback investments. If training benefits future competitors rather than current employers, firms will rationally decline to invest in their employees.[47] Conversely, they will be motivated to raid other firms to obtain needed skills. Similarly they will be less inclined to invest in long-term R & D likely to diffuse to competitors through turnover. And they will be forced into inflationary bidding spirals, raising compensation for important employees in order to keep turnover to acceptable levels. There is increasing agreement within the industry that these phenomena have major effects upon corporate policy and operational efficiency.[48]

Instability at the industry level--the rapid ascent and decline of firms--both reflected and aggravated high turnover levels, and also produced other large-scale pathologies. Long-term cooperation between semiconductor producers and their customers or suppliers was unsustainable, and therefore was rarely practiced. Instead, leasing, subcontracting, lenient second-sourcing and technology licensing, low-wage offshore assembly, and external sourcing were widely used by merchant firms to maximize cash flow and reduce capital requirements.[49]

These practices symptomized and worsened U.S. firms' inability to manufacture efficiently, to cooperate with suppliers, to trust and invest in their employees, to plan for future technological requirements, and to invest at efficient scale. Successive waves of young merchant and capital equipment firms thus fell victim to new technologies, and later Japanese competitors, because their narrow product lines, insufficient capitalization, and underinvestment in long term R & D left them vulnerable to sudden change in a single technology or market. Worse, this pattern led U.S. firms to undervalue the retention of proprietary technology and the development of managerial skills.

The sale of technology--through second sourcing or similar arrangements--was encouraged by the weakness of legal protection, by the high rate of technology leakage through imitation and personnel turnover, by merchants' inefficiency at manufacturing relative to development, and by the industry's fragmentation. Technology leakage and manufacturing inadequacies lowered the expected, future value to the developer of declining to license a technology. Conversely, instability and cash flow pressure increased the propensity to license widely, since licensing relieved otherwise unacceptable capital requirements and market risk. In a rapidly changing industry, which was fragmented both horizontally and vertically, technology and capital equipment sales seemingly benefited the seller while primarily damaging competitors. Even if the practice damaged the firm in the long run, the combination of executive personnel mobility and the industry's collective growth implied that such damage had little personal relevance to decisionmakers unless it became visible quite rapidly--say, in less than five years.

Moreover, since the Japanese market was effectively closed to direct U.S. penetration in any case, the alternative to royalty revenue was often no revenue at all. Since the diffusion of the technology (through theft, imitation, or licensing by other suppliers) was regarded as inevitable, declining to sell it seemed senseless. But given the different structures, planning horizons, and manufacturing abilities of the Japanese and U.S. industries, such sales constituted gradual industrial suicide.[50]

In part, then, such practices were traceable to real and individually rational, albeit collectively destructive, strategic incentives facing firms and executives as a consequence of their arena's fragmentation, instability, and lack of cooperation. As one senior merchant executive told me, "One does not accumulate vast personal wealth by trying to swim upstream." But such decisions also derived from, and again reinforced, a wider managerial failure to appreciate long-run technology trends, the importance of manufacturing, and the competitive strength of the Japanese industry. The industry was parochial, rather inbred, inexperienced with the large-scale manufacturing and systems considerations emerging as critical to the industry's future, and habituated to both chronic instability and unquestioned collective dominance. Its executives therefore lacked experience with mass manufacturing, failed to monitor Japanese progress, and assumed that merchants could generate new technology faster than Japanese firms could use it against them.[51]

Consequently Intel, Texas Instruments, Motorola, LSI Logic and other merchants neglected their own manufacturing efficiency while repeatedly licensing their technology to Japanese firms. These same Japanese firms then predictably used their manufacturing skills, increasing technical prowess, and vastly superior resources to turn upon their U.S. benefactors, rapidly becoming their strongest global competitors. Although Japanese firms have used exceptionally aggressive and sometimes legally dubious tactics,[52] a large fraction of the merchants' ensuing problems derived from their own faulty decisions. For example, authorized, Japanese second sources hold almost half the world market for Intel microprocessors;[53] Toshiba now competes directly with its contractual technology supplier, LSI Logic;[54] and Hitachi and NEC first licensed, and then reverse-engineered, Motorola and Intel microprocessors, respectively.[55]

This behavior, in combination with the persistent fragmentation of the industry through new venture formation, implies that to a large extent the U.S. merchant sector functions as a laboratory for research, development, and market testing as much as it functions as a productive industry. Unfortunately, the laboratory is globally accessible to all large, integrated firms, while its large strategic and economic costs are borne by the United States alone.

The contrast with the Japanese industry's behavior is instructive, and suggests how it overcame the merchants' first-mover advantages. As in other electronics sectors, large vertically integrated Japanese producers began by purchasing technology and refining their manufacturing skills, but did so with an eye to the future. While in the late 1970s, 80 percent of merchant-produced semiconductors were still assembled in low-wage Asian facilities, nearly 90 percent of Japanese production was assembled domestically.[56] Japanese semiconductor producers were leaders in both developing and using automated assembly technology, a fact which partly accounts for the quality and cost advantages enjoyed by the Japanese industry in commodity markets. Japanese R & D and capital spending grew rapidly, both as a percentage of revenues and in absolute terms, and now exceeds the merchant industry's.[57] And finally, Japanese firms invested heavily in their employees and used highly skilled workers, including many degreed engineers, in their manufacturing operations.[58]

In the Japanese industry, furthermore, independent venture formation and hostile acquisitions are strongly discouraged; industry entry occurs nearly entirely through the internal diversification of large firms;[59] and no organized venture capital market exists.[60] Supplier relations appear to be stable, of long duration, to involve extensive technology interchange, and frequently to include equity holdings.[61] Personnel raiding is rare and considered unethical;[62] defection is also discouraged by the compensation structure (for example its relationships with social life and its dependence upon seniority).[63] Salary costs can be controlled, and investments in R & D, training, and diversification can be made with some assurance that their returns accrue to the employer and parent firm rather than to predators.

The large-scale structure of the Japanese industry also suggests how its partial strategic coordination (e.g., with respect to American imports and abstinence from personnel raiding) can coexist with competitive discipline. First, there exists a significant and efficient central authority (the Japanese government) which provides public goods and prevents undue disruption from imports, predatory startups, and other sources of strategic disarray. Second, Japanese semiconductor producers are highly export dependent--both in the semiconductor market and in their other electronics businesses, for which semiconductors are one major input.[64]   Third, they are both producers and consumers; the internal capacity of each deters others from overcharging.   And finally, their low capital costs, long time horizons, and vertical integration provide incentives for them to continue their pursuit of technological leadership, because potential future rewards in downstream industries are far larger than those obtainable directly from semiconductor markets.

V

CONSEQUENCES

The foregoing analysis suggests that a technologically competitive semiconductor industry is important to the United States, and that conventional policy measures may be inadequate to sustain it.   First, consider the practical matter of what continued decline would mean.

Through the growing use of digital information processing, industrial activity is entering a deep revolution driven in large measure by the remarkable progress of semiconductor technology.   The technical and economic evidence suggests that this progress will continue for another 20 years or more.   Concomitantly the world semiconductor industry will grow from $30 billion currently to perhaps $200 billion by the year 2000. Hence, even if its decline had no effect upon other industries or upon national security, it would merit some concern.   But, to the contrary, semiconductor production is strategically important in virtually every conceivable sense.   Other industries ever more strongly dependent upon competitive semiconductor technology include computers, digital communications, automotive electronics, industrial instruments, numerically controlled machine tools, and aerospace products.   The semiconductor content of these goods now ranges from 3 percent to 10 percent, and is increasing rapidly.

Collectively, these industries will gradually come to represent a substantial fraction of U.S. and world GNP; by the turn of the century, world computer production alone will exceed $500 billion.   Some of these sectors, such as computers and industrial instruments, are among the few remaining net U.S. exporters.[65]   Moreover, they contribute disproportionately to American living standards.   In 1984, for example, U.S. private sector wages averaged $350 per week; manufacturing sector wages were higher, $434 per week.   But weekly wages in the U.S. semiconductor industry were $516; in the computer industry, $552; and in the entire office equipment sector, $546.[66]   Competitive decline in these sectors would therefore reduce U.S. GNP, living standards, and tax receipts by changing the mix of economic activity towards industries with lower growth, skill levels, and productivity gains.   Decline could also cause welfare losses through trade effects, since these sectors are highly competitive.

In short, the strategic importance of semiconductor technology to industrial growth suggests that, quite apart from geopolitical or military issues, Japanese dominance would be cause for concern. The Japanese industry is a vertically-integrated oligopoly of large multinational electronics firms. The four largest Japanese semiconductor producers are also Japan's four largest computer producers, accounting for 80 percent of all computer production by Japan-based firms,[67] and they are major semiconductor capital equipment manufacturers as well. These companies possess close, enduring relationships with their capital equipment suppliers and customers. They, and the national government which supports them, are strongly committed to success in industries dependent upon microelectronics. Additionally, all of these firms have a history of aggressive, legally questionable behavior,[68] and Japanese markets have long been closed or at least restricted to Americans. For all these reasons, it is overwhelmingly likely that if Japanese firms collectively dominate advanced semiconductor technology, they will deny their best technology to their U.S. competitors in order to gain advantage in downstream markets. Indeed, there is some evidence that this process is already under way.[69]

This suggests a troublesome conclusion. The United States industry has locked itself into institutions and strategic practices which generate behavior contrary to its own, and the nation's, long-term interests. These strategic problems imply that market forces alone will not reverse the industry's decline. To the contrary, merchants, capital equipment firms, stockholders, and executives will continue their distributional struggles while the industry collectively disinvests, voluntarily or otherwise. Concomitantly, the Japanese industry will continue its progress in order to penetrate even larger industries, again at American expense.

But, unpleasant as this conclusion may be, it suggests another which is more troubling still. The existing stock of economic theory (even including newer models of strategic international trade) is largely irrelevant to the semiconductor industry's problems and their solution. Conventional economic analysis would not predict that two national sectors would evolve such completely different structures and practices as did the American and Japanese semiconductor industries. Nor would neoclassical economic models predict that such differences would entrench themselves, persisting even in the face of strong technological and competitive forces. Were such structural and strategic divergence to arise, economics would not predict that the highly competitive industry with flexible markets and large initial advantages would prove the less adaptable, and that it would be systematically defeated by the stable, government-protected oligopoly in which capital rationing and strategic coordination limited personnel mobility and market entry. And finally, the traditional economic prescriptions for such a troubled industry would range from laissez faire to a generic infusion of resources (capital, skilled labor, and/or R & D); explicit strategic intervention would be rejected. So would efforts to reduce the pressures of market competition, for example through vertical integration, horizontal coordination, or disincentives to personnel mobility.[70]

Yet it would seem that economic theory accords rather poorly with the semiconductor industry's past behavior. And on the analysis I have suggested, its usual remedial prescriptions would fare little better. For example, support in the form of generic resources alone--e.g., through industrywide R & D funding, tax credits, or guaranteed procurement--would be largely wasted via the strategic processes described above (distributional conflict, inflationary spirals), and indeed might impede necessary structural rationalization by propping up the current system. If resources are to be used effectively, then, policy must focus upon the industry's specific problems, assist in developing efficient public and private institutions, and change the incentives that these institutions both face and generate. The emphasis must be upon lengthening their time horizons and increasing the profitability of productive investment relative to liquidation, consumption, or zero sum conflicts which produce redundant efforts and mutual betrayal. Structural rationalization, vertical coordination, technology sharing, decreased personnel turnover, and increasing governmental responsiveness would necessarily be simultaneously instruments and consequences of these changes.

VI

ECONOMIC ANALYSIS AND SEMICONDUCTOR INDUSTRY POLICY

The inability of contemporary economic theory to illuminate the semiconductor industry's condition or aid in its improvement flows, I believe, from four related issues in economic analysis-- and in economic activity. The first is the significance of learning and institutional performance, relative to competitive markets, as determinants of long-run industrial efficiency. The second is the importance of an industry's norms of strategic interaction--i.e., the industrywide patterns of cooperation, competition, and reciprocity prevailing in the various economic and political markets which make up industrial arenas. (For example, in seeking government assistance firms may compete in seeking individual gains at each other's expense, or agree to cooperate in seeking industrywide support, or reciprocally support each other's requests for individual benefits.) The third issue is the importance of externalities and industry-level public goods in determining economic efficiency. And the fourth issue is that of the time horizons of economic actors, which are affected by the strategic environment and which have a profound effect upon long- run efficiency. Hence the common thread linking these issues is the interplay between strategic choice, the evolution of industrywide behaviors and incentives, and finally their implications for long-run efficiency.

Models combining these considerations are relatively new to economic theory. Such models are not yet fully amenable to the mathematical formalism or stylized assumptions which have come to dominate the discipline of economics. They also, however, cast serious doubt upon the relevance of traditional competitive market theory to actual industrial behavior, and upon its utility as a guide to economic policy. Indeed, the theoretical results thus far obtained for evolutionary and/or strategically driven processes (e.g., through the analyses of Arthur and Axelrod)[71] have inverted or bypassed many of the results of neoclassical economic theory.

But these forces are critical to the actual dynamics of high-technology industries--and quite possibly to other sectors as well. Learning and technological progress are important to long-term industrial efficiency. Often, their maximal exploitation requires the development of effective and enduring institutions; therefore, the forces shaping these institutions are critical. The same can be said of the patterns of cooperation and competition between these institutions.

In economic competition, firms and industries institutionalize themselves and interact (with each other and with governments) in significant measure through successive decisions to cooperate or compete-- in factor markets, inputs, product markets, and in the political markets affecting government policies. These repeated strategic interactions, in the form of other firms' expected and actual responses to each generation of technology, politics, and market behavior, in turn constitute a large fraction of the environmental forces affecting corporate efficiency and strategy. The time horizons of firms, and therefore their long-run productivity growth, will be both a causal force and a consequence of the strategic norms of the various arenas in which they act.

For example, Silicon Valley firms came to feel that they could not appropriate benefits from long term investments, and that they could not trust their employees, their suppliers, or each other. Hence fewer long-term investments were made, fewer public goods were provided, less cooperation was undertaken, mutual betrayal became normal, and future strength received less attention than current profits. Over time, the industry's shortsightedness, internecine warfare, and inefficiency became entrenched in an equilibrium of chronic entrepreneurialism which corroded subsequent decisionmaking and precluded the development of farsighted, effective, efficient-scale institutions.

To the extent that such forces as these are at the core of the industry's behavior, there is no particular reason to suppose that "the market"--i.e., the long-run outcome of these various strategic interactions --will supply a result satisfactory to the U.S. economy-at-large, future generations, domestic semiconductor users, our military allies, or even the semiconductor industry's current employees. There may be efficient markets for many products, but there is no reason to suppose an efficient market for national industrial systems. Nor is there reason to have confidence in the ability of the semiconductor industry itself, in its current state, to use productively any assistance provided to it, unless such assistance is tied to conditions which change incentive structures for the better.

Semiconductor industry policy, therefore, must combine the provision of resources with mechanisms which both encourage long run efficiency and weed out those who cannot or do not practice it. Essential provisions in such a policy would be measures to reduce personnel turnover, dampen current cost growth from professional wage increases, rationalize the industry, encourage technical information exchanges, increase the linkage between compensation and long run success, and support major investment programs by large users of semiconductors and/or capital equipment. Only in the presence of such changes to the U.S. incentive structure would large commitments for engineering education, manufacturing technology development, semiconductor capital investment, and/or government procurement yield enduring productivity gains.

A number of policy instruments are potentially useful in effecting such incentive changes. For example, support programs (such as R & D grants or low interest loans) might disburse aid over long time periods, and might require collateral, long-term commitments by the employees and executives of supported firms. Support might, for example, be restricted to firms which possess pension funds meeting specified criteria in order to maximize incentives for stability. Defaulters, individual and corporate, could be forgiven their debts but then barred from subsequent assistance. Subsidy programs might also impose requirements for long-term profit sharing or equity grants to employees of recipient firms.

Support for small firms might require matching participation by a firm in the downstream industry--say, equity investment obligatorily phased over a five-to-ten-year period. Alternatively, support might be allocated to groups of firms with the requirement that they commit to purchase a portion of each other's output, and of each other's stock. Funding should also be open to foreign firms, perhaps up to some maximum percentage, but all recipients should be required to invest a minimum fraction of their funds within the United States.

Such programs might be administered, and government-provided funds allocated, by boards of directors drawn from industry, relevant government agencies, and universities. If so, their tenure should be sufficiently long, and their terms arranged, so as to insulate the system from disruptions caused by electoral or other political shifts, and their activities should be exempted, statutorily if possible, from operational oversight by Congress and from legal constraints such as the antitrust laws or stockholders' claims. More conventional assistance--educational loans, university grants, national laboratories--could then proceed in parallel with industrial growth oriented towards long-term productivity gains.

In such a policy context, the recommendations of the Defense Science Board and the U.S. industry's attempt to institutionalize joint manufacturing technology development (i.e., Sematech) represent small but encouraging developments in a generally bleak picture. They also represent an opportunity for precisely the forms of institutional change and collective learning required for the future health of American high technology, for the education of American policymakers, and for reassessment of relationships between academic policy analysis and the real economic choices which confront us.

NOTES

1. See, for example, the report of the Defense Science Board Task Force on Foreign Semiconductor Dependency (1987); Charles H. Ferguson, "American Microelectronics in Decline: Evidence, Analysis, and Alternatives," VLSI Memo 85-284, MIT Dept. of Electrical Engineering, 1985; National Academy of Science, "Advanced Processing of Electronic Materials," 1986; and the Japanese Technology Evaluation reports compiled by the Commerce Department and the National Science Foundation.

2. Unless otherwise indicated, semiconductor production and market share estimates are from Dataquest Corporation, Semiconductor Industry Service. Trade data are primarily from the U.S. Commerce Department; some of the principal statistics are summarized in the Commerce Department's annual "U.S. Industrial Outlook." The semiconductor market as defined here excludes "captive" production (i.e., for internal use only) of U.S. firms such as IBM, AT&T, and GM. This exclusion changes absolute statistics somewhat, but not the general picture of American decline. Captive production accounts for roughly 40 percent of U.S. production. It must be emphasized, however, that semiconductor economic statistics should be considered approximate.

3. The Defense Science Board Task Force concluded that the U.S. now maintains a lead in only 3 of more than a dozen technologies it surveyed. Similar conclusions have been reached by a number of other assessments, both public (e.g., National Science Association, Japanese Technology Evaluation) and proprietary. The consensus is that the U.S. leads in design and software, but lags in most other areas, particularly those relating to manufacturing.

4. The long-run growth trend (since the late 1950s) of world semiconductor production is roughly 15 percent annually. Cost performance has improved approximately 40 percent annually. Semiconductor technology improvements account for a significant and growing fraction of the productivity improvements of these other industries, all of whose semiconductor content is growing steadily.

5. As recently as 1980, Japan imported two-thirds of its capital equipment requirements, at a time when imports of semiconductors themselves had already declined to less than a quarter of Japanese consumption.

6. Semiconductor imports were subject to severe formal restrictions until 1975, and are still restricted in practice through a combination of government and industrial practices. Direct foreign investment, once explicitly prohibited, is now increasingly common, though a joint venture with a local producer is usually a practical necessity. Texas Instruments (TI) was granted exceptional permission to establish a wholly-owned Japanese subsidiary, at a time when TI had leverage

through its possession of critical patents. As a condition for entry, TI was required by the Ministry of International Trade and Industry (MITI) to license its patents to the entire Japanese industry, which it did, and to restrict itself to a small fraction of the Japanese market. This latter condition proved very easy for TI to meet.

7. U.S. integrated circuit imports from Japan were less than $50 million in 1977. In 1984, they were over $1.1 billion. Source: U.S. Department of Commerce, U.S. Industrial Outlook (Washington, D.C.: Government Printing Office).

8. Dataquest Corp. For Japanese data, BA Asia Ltd., "The Japanese Semiconductor Industry," 1980 and 1982.

9. The identities and rank order of the principal Japanese semiconductor producers have remained extremely stable. In contrast, market leadership changed hands repeatedly in the U.S. industry. For market share data, see Dataquest and BA Asia Ltd.

10. BA Asia Ltd., op. cit. See also M. Borrus, J. Millstein, and J. Zysman, "Trade and Development in the Semiconductor Industry," in J. Zysman & L. Tyson (eds.), "American Industry in International Competition," Cornell University Press, 1983.

11. Company annual reports; Dodwell, "Industrial Groupings in Japan" and "Key Players in the Japanese Electronics Industry," various years; Japan Company Handbook, various years.

12. Semiconductor industry statistics are notoriously uncertain, and captive production is difficult to estimate precisely because captives rarely disclose production information, and because their production is not sold competitively. However, fairly reliable estimates of captive production have been constructed. IBM is the largest captive by far with worldwide production of $4 billion. Other major captives are AT&T, GM/Delco, Hewlett-Packard, and DEC. Estimates for captive production are those of Dataquest, ICE Corp., and the author. Estimates for merchant production are those of Dataquest.

13. For extended descriptions of U.S. merchant industry behavior, see Ferguson, op. cit., and E. Braun & S. Macdonald, "Revolution in Miniature," 2nd ed., Cambridge University Press, 1984, particularly chap. 10.

14. Dataquest; company annual reports. See also Chase Econometrics, "The U.S. and Japanese Semiconductor Industries: A Financial Comparison," commissioned by the U.S. Semiconductor Industry Association, 1980.

15. For information regarding turnover in the U.S. industry, see: Braun & Macdonald, op. cit., particularly pp. 132 ff.; for industrywide statistics, see the surveys of the American Electronics Association.

The author has also gathered proprietary information from industry sources.

16. For discussion of the U.S. industry's fragmentation and instability, see Braun & Macdonald, op. cit., particularly p. 123 for the evanescence of market leadership; Ferguson, op. cit.; and, for concentration ratios, U.S. Industrial Outlook (1986), pp. 32-3.

17. IBM was among the first, if not the first, to produce semiconductor memories and use memories (of its own manufacture) in computers in the early 1970s, and also developed elaborate testing and packaging technologies in the same decade--for example, Level Sensitive Scan Design (LSSD) and Thermal Conduction Modules. AT&T has been a technology leader throughout the industry's history. And as early as 1971, there existed a public study (J. Tilton, "The International Diffusion of Technology: The Case of Semiconductors," Brookings, 1971) which suggested that the Japanese Industry was rapidly closing on the U.S. industry. By the mid-1970s, Japanese practice was less than a year behind the U.S. industry in most technologies.

18. Statistical data are taken from company reports; Dodwell, op. cit.; VLSI Research Inc., a U.S. market research firm covering the semiconductor equipment industry; the U.S. Dept. of Commerce, "A Competitive Assessment of the U.S. Semiconductor Manufacturing Equipment Industry," 1985. Assessments of supplier--customer relationships and comparative technological strength are derived from confidential industry and government sources. Considerable effort has been devoted to these questions.

19. Sources: Dodwell; company annual reports; VLSI Research.

20. VLSI Research; S.E.M.I.; Dataquest; and company reports.

21. SEMI membership data.

22. SEMI membership data.

23. For example, single-chip microprocessors now available contain 100,000 to 500,000 devices, sell for $100 to $500, and possess more functionality and speed than the largest computer CPUs in existence 25 years ago. Such 1960 machines required thousands of small scale semiconductor devices and cost over $1 million.

24. Dataquest.

25. Source: Dataquest Corp., except for trade data from the U.S. Department of Commerce.

26. VLSI Research; industry and government sources.

27. Confidential industry and government sources; for a public assessment, see the report of the Defense Science Board (DSB) Task Force on Foreign Semiconductor Dependency, 1987.

28. Confidential industry and government sources. One major U.S. firm stated that it now stockpiles certain materials as a consequence of the domination of world supply by a single Japanese firm. It was remarked, however, that stockpiling is of limited utility in high-technology areas because such stockpiles rapidly become obsolete.

29. National Science Foundation, Science Indicators (1985), Appendix table 1-20, p. 205.

30. Damian Saccocio, "Publish Or Perish? An Analysis of Semiconductor Papers in the U.S., Japan, and Europe," unpublished manuscript, MIT Dept. of Political Science, 1986.

31. Confidential industry and government sources.

32. See the DSB Task Force report, as well as the JTECH report on Opto- and Microelectronics, May 1985.

33. See, for example, Braun & Macdonald, op. cit., chaps. 4-6; and Christopher Freeman, "The Economics of Industrial Innovation," 2nd ed., MIT Press, 1982, particularly Table 4.6b, p. 95 of the paperbound edition.

34. See Gerald Brock, "The Telecommunications Industry," Harvard University Press, 1981, chap. 7.

35. See Freeman, op. cit., pp. 96-99; Braun & Macdonald, op. cit., chaps. 6 and 10.

36. See Braun & Macdonald, op. cit., chaps. 6 and 8; Ferguson, op. cit.; D. Okimoto (chap. 4) in D. Okimoto, T. Sugano, and F. Weinstein (eds.), "Competitive Edge: The Semiconductor Industry in the U.S. and Japan," Stanford University Press, 1984.

37. R. Wilson, P. Ashton, and T. Egan, "Innovation, Competition, and Government Policy in the Semiconductor Industry," Charles River Associates, 1980, p. 146.

38. Industry interviews. See also the DSB Task Force report; Okimoto, op. cit., pp. 84-89.

39. Changes in capital gains tax rates have been strongly correlated to the size of venture capital flows into the semiconductor industry. Venture capital flows have in turn been correlated with levels of startup activity, most spectacularly in the early 1980s. See Ferguson, op. cit., p. 53; Braun & Macdonald, op. cit., pp. 132-137. The capital gains differential may also have increased the relative attractiveness of stock offered in initial public offerings (IPOs), since the returns

to these stocks came primarily through capital growth rather than fully taxable dividend income.

40. Incentive stock options (ISOs) can be granted in amounts up to $100,000 per employee. Under pre-1987 tax laws, they offered both lower effective rates (because taxed as capital gains) and income deferral (because taxed at the time of stock sale, not at the time the options are granted or exercised).

41. See the Chase Econometrics report for an analysis specific to the semiconductor industry. For more general treatments, see for example Data Resources, Inc., "The DRI Report on U.S. Manufacturing Industries," McGraw-Hill, 1984, pp. 28-34.

42. For market shares, the source is Dataquest. For quality data, see, for example, U.S. Office of Technology Assessment, "International Competitiveness in Electronics," 1983, pp. 247-249, for data drawn both from Hewlett-Packard and from OTA consultants.

43. Dataquest. See also Ferguson, op. cit., pp. 19-28; and Braun & Macdonald, op. cit., pp. 124-128.

44. See Ferguson, op. cit., chaps. 2 and 3; Braun & Macdonald, chaps. 7, 8, and 10.

45. See Braun & Macdonald, pp. 128-130. I am indebted to an IBM executive and to a Stanford professor for the unusual form of growth accounting exhibited here. Confidential industry interviews have also indicated the significance of inflationary spirals in land, housing, construction, and wage costs.

46. In order to indicate the feelings held by some regarding venture capital based startups and their effect upon turnover, let me quote the CEO of one of the industry's largest firms: "The best thing that could happen to this industry would be if every tenth venture capitalist was arbitrarily shot."

47. See the OTA report, chaps. 6 and 8, for discussion of many of these issues, including the relationship between turnover, training levels, and product quality.

48. Confidential industry interviews.

49. For the use of leasing, see company annual reports. For the absence of long term obligations, company reports and industry interviews. For the absence of long term investments (e.g., equity holdings) in suppliers, company annual reports. For offshore assembly, see BA Asia Ltd., U.S. Dept. of Commerce trade statistics for semifinished versus finished semiconductors; and Dataquest.

50. For a compilation of Japan-U.S. licensing arrangements (without, however, an evaluation of their relative importance) see Carmela S.

Haklisch, "Technical Alliances in the Semiconductor Industry," New York University Graduate School of Business Administration, 1986. For a highly critical account, see Borrus, Millstein, and Zysman. For aggregate Japan-U.S. technology trade balances in technology and license fees versus products, see Science Indicators (1985), p. 15 and tables 1-16 and 1-17, pp. 201-202.

51. Confidential industry interviews. I am particularly indebted to one extended series of interviews, the subject of which was one firm's rationale for technology licensing to Japanese competitors for assisting in my understanding of this issue.

52. For example, alleged dumping and predatory pricing; NEC's alleged violations of copyright law in connection with its reverse engineering of Intel's microprocessors; and alleged patent infringements by several firms.

53. Dataquest; confidential industry sources.

54. Company annual reports and product literature describe the products and technologies made available to Toshiba by LSI Logic, particularly the LDS computer aided design system. Toshiba supplies process technology in return, but not processing hardware or training. Confidential industry interviews have indicated that the competition between the two companies is quite fierce.

55. Company annual reports; Dataquest. Confidential interviews and press reports indicate that the ensuing rivalries have significantly damaged the U.S. firms in question.

56. BA Asia Ltd., various years; OTA Electronics report, p. 136.

57. Dataquest; confidential industry estimates.

58. Industry and government sources. Statistics are difficult to come by, but there is near unanimity in regard to the high educational and skill levels of Japanese plant-floor workers.

59. See Dataquest for ranked listings of Japanese producers over time; Dodwell's for their general financial characteristics.

60. See, for example, M.T. Flaherty and H. Itami, "Finance," in Okimoto, Sugano, and Weinstein, op. cit.

61. Dodwell; BA Asia Ltd., various years; confidential interviews.

62. Industry reviews.

63. Industry reviews. For general accounts, see, for example, Rodney Clark, "The Japanese Company," Yale University Press, 1979. See also the work of Ronald Dore and Ezra Vogel. For aggregate turnover

levels and variation of wages with seniority, see, for example, Japan Statistical Yearbook, 1985.

64. The major semiconductor and electronics firms export from 25 percent to 75 percent of their total output. Usually semiconductor exports are a smaller fraction. Source: Dodwell's and company annual reports.

65. Commerce Department statistics.

66. Source for all U.S. salary statistics is U.S. Bureau of Labor Statistics, 1985.

67. Japan Electronics Almanac, 1986, pp. 85 ff.

68. Such allegedly irregular behavior is not confined to the practices noted above specifically in connection with the semiconductor industry. For example, Fujitsu has allegedly engaged in large scale software piracy; Hitachi employees were found allegedly seeking to bribe IBM employees, and Hitachi reportedly paid IBM $300 million and permitted IBM to inspect its products for five years, in order to prevent litigation.

69. Confidential industry and government interviews. The process is apparently not confined to captive Japanese production of equipment, materials, and semiconductor products, but also seems to extend to major Japanese equipment suppliers with particularly close relationships to their domestic Japanese customers.

70. Such conventional economic thinking has been very much in evidence in recent discussions within the Federal government, though it is not always heeded.

71. W. Brian Arthur, "Competing Technologies and Lock-In by Historical Small Events: The Dynamics of Allocation Under Increasing Returns," Stanford University Center for Economic Policy Research, 1985; Robert Axelrod, "The Evolution of Cooperation," Basic Books, 1984; and Robert Axelrod, "An Evolutionary Approach to Norms," American Political Science Review, December 1986.

TECHNOLOGY, BUSINESS AND AMERICA'S THIRD CENTURY

by Edward Wenk, Jr.

Americans had many reasons to celebrate the recent anniversary of our nation's birth. Two centuries of constitutional democracy amidst substantial change and social, economic and political tensions testify to the strength, vision, and versatility of the charter. The founding fathers wrought a miracle in setting such durable ground rules for the practice of freedom. Yet, we live in an era of uncertainty and anxiety about the future, with declining confidence in our premier institutions, and amidst confusion and repercussions of technological pulses and external surprises. Thus, we have reason to be concerned about our ability to project America's creed to the nation's third century. One of our major concerns should be the challenge posed by technology to our values as a society.

This essay addresses that challenge by focusing attention on technology, its intricate, powerful and often hidden impetus to cultural transformation; its side effects; and the response to it by all our societal institutions. Particular attention is given to ethical as well as functional relationships between technology, business and government, and the implications of those relationships for America's future.

I

LIVING WITH TECHNOLOGY

In contemporary society, the most powerful engine of change is technology. It underpins every aspect of life: national security; the energy supply; industrial productivity; food production; health-care delivery; urban habitation and infrastructure; education; entertainment; and telecommunications. We refer to ourselves as the information society, a condition made feasible only by new advances in computer (that is, technological) virtuosity.

Should there be doubt as to how salient has grown this ingredient of social process, let the reader consider that technology has demonstrated a fabulous capacity to generate new wealth even faster than capital alone, with the conspicuous virtue of enhancing material standards of living. By both developed and developing nations, technology is regarded as a crucible for economic viability. Moreover, it has linked all nations together in one world, with people, commodities, oil, capital, information and waste freely crossing national borders.

Technology has also functioned as a source of treasured freedoms: freedom from the back-breaking labor of chopping wood, pumping water, and carting ice, and from slavery in the mines; freedom from disease and disability; freedom from geographical and cultural isolation and social immobility; freedom to spend more adult years on education; freedom to plan families. Technology has given more people than ever before the freedom to choose; and it has provided more choices: how and where we live; what we work at; what we eat; how we vacation.   In short, technology has vastly enhanced the quality of life.

In World War II, technology became the great equalizer, helping purchase victory with a minimum loss of life through superiority in industrial production and sophisticated weapons. That heyday of science as an endless frontier was further excited by the 1957 Soviet space surprise. We entered the competition with gusto. We adopted technology as our chosen vehicle to global superiority in the race for people's minds.

The Side Effects

Yet, we are not comfortable with all the changes wrought by technology. The paradoxes are all too familiar: we have more arms but less security from military aggression and from threats of a nuclear disaster; indeed, we generate an unprecedented national debt for purchase of weapons that often fail to meet requirements. We take pride in a history of lively innovation and entrepreneurship, but we now seem unequal to commercial threats from abroad; our world-class economic status that was characterized by export surpluses of manufactured goods and agricultural products has been reduced to the export of natural resources and of money in the form of interest to foreign investors. Through research and computer aids we have more knowledge than ever before, but less common understanding. The adoption of more technologies to reduce risk has seemingly spawned new species of risks--not simply in nuclear weapons, but also in dangers of climate modification, of resource depletion, of genetic changes we belatedly discover pernicious, of institutional malfunctioning, and of the possible loss of freedom which is what America is all about.   There are enigmas of having far better technical communications accompanied by a lost sense of community; of wanting fewer taxes and fewer governmental constraints, while expecting greater governmental protection from the unwanted side effects of technology on people and on the environment. Clearly then, heightened technical means to satisfy human needs and wants have not generated consensus on the ends to be served.

There are additional problems. Technology serves as the organizing principle around which are woven most contemporary organizations, public and private. Those organizations use their technology-reinforced wealth and power to strengthen their control of technology itself and the social environment in which they flourish.   Under these conditions, societal interests, as opposed to parochial ones, are at risk.   In the last forty years, technology has also been the main source of growth in government. The irony is striking.   One purpose of more government was to protect the citizen from the excesses of technological delivery systems.   Yet bigger government itself brings its own substantial problems, including more technology. For example, television now plays a key role in political campaigning and the selection of candidates, debasing the process.

The indirect side effects may be subtle but, in the long run, even more potent: technology has profoundly altered human institutions, lifestyles, and basic values. Consider, for example, how the products of a technological society entice exuberant consumerism, further stimulated by technological leverage in advertising. Or witness the impact of the automobile and the pill on sexual mores. Because the pace of technology evolves more swiftly than the social institutions that husband it, technology has sparked enduring disharmony of purpose between, for example, the economy and ecology. The result--economic and social instability. Indeed, the number and magnitude of problems engendered by technology are unprecedented.

To some extent, our situation arises because we had been asking only, "Can we do it?" In the 1960s, suddenly aware of untoward impacts, we began asking, "Ought we to do it?" In the 1980s, exemplified by disasters such as Challenger and Chernobyl, and by issues such as medical care and gene splicing, we wrestle with a different challenge concerning technology: "Can we manage it?" What we are concerned with is the social performance of technological delivery systems. We need a stronger focus on the broader consequences of technology and on the broader participation of society as a whole in critical management choices regarding that technology.

Coping with predicaments about the way ahead means coping with unparalled complexity. It is not simply that technical facts, and artifacts, lie beyond common understanding. There is also heightened social complexity. To deliver technologically based goods and services now requires elaborate networks of more numerous and more diverse organizations, private and public. Independently, each is subject to change; therefore the webs of relationships are also so transient as to depress understanding.

We also encounter a whole new taxonomy of ethical dilemmas dealing with life, with death and with being human. The next American century surely will be subject to severe and unprecedented stresses. If we cherish the values made possible by our capitalist democracy, we are obliged to face salient realities of contemporary life so as to diagnose pathological trends and create the future that we want.

Whoever controls technology controls our future. In attributing such weight to this phenomenon in modern life, we must recognize that in the United States the delivery of technologically enhanced goods and services has been largely the province of the private sector. Hence, any examination of the role of technology in human affairs must take into account the institutional structures and processes by which the necessary intellectual, fiscal, and natural resources are mobilized and modulated by business to meet demands of the market. Exploration of our technological future, then, must comprise the role, the behavior and the ethical principles of business, including trends that may signal changes ahead which pose threats to our creed. President Calvin Coolidge said that the business of America is business. He was wrong. The business of America is technology and its impact on our values.

To understand the influence of modern technology, there are four major premises to keep in mind. First, we should define technology as social process, not just technique. Second, the grand issues of our time involving technology are made by public policy rather than at the market place. Third, the delivery of technically enhanced goods and services is the province of the private sector, thus the latter's relationship to government is of special interest. Fourth, the hazards and the opportunities that lie ahead demand greater exercise of foresight and of integrity.

Technology as Social Process

People have two fundamental misconceptions about technology. In the first place, many think that technology is hardware--ubiquitous automobiles, 747s, telephones, Polaroid cameras, VCRs, and home refrigerators. We forget that technology is also software, or perhaps squishyware; people and their institutions must furnish instructions as to its use. So, at its root, technology is more than technique.

The second misconception arises because we forget that everyone is also directly involved in technology. That is obvious for the mechanic, the industrial manager, the scientist, or the engineer. But we neglect the bankers who decide on investment capital for plant expansion, or policy officials who make choices and allocate resources for weapon systems, or who set standards for water quality. And we disregard just plain citizens. They are involved as consumers of technological products; as voters on referenda for nuclear power; as investors in high-tech enterprises; and as unknowing victims of unfavorable impacts. Technology is not a spectator sport.

Almost all contemporary organizations, both corporate and public, are engaged in technology. GM produces cars; Sony markets consumer electronics. Government agencies deal with armaments, medical research, toxic waste disposal, and so on. Virtually all governmental agencies created since World War II are rooted in some aspect of technology.

In the social process, we also discover that technology acts as a mobilizing agent for institutions to concentrate wealth and power. It then plays a political role in every society, developed and developing, capitalist and socialist. It starkly accentuates distinctions between who wins and who loses, and how much. Indeed, technology tends to discriminate against the unrepresented and the disadvantaged and to support the elitist establishment. Technology, at least in its impacts, is not neutral. Because of the choices involved regarding beneficiaries, technology has become more political. Conversely, through TV campaigning and computerized voter lists, politics has become more technological.

Tomorrow, we should expect more technology, not less. To shape that future, we need to acquire this broader image of technology as more than technique or products. It entails a tangled skein of familiar social processes, communication networks, and institutions, along with natural processes and technical facilities, and a blend of science and human values. And while the technologically laden future isn't what it used to be, human nature is. No matter the degree of technical virtuosity, we must contend with people and their vulnerability to ignorance, error, folly, blunder, mischief, avarice, and pride.

II

THE ROLE OF GOVERNMENT

In the social management of technology, we find that the grand decisions are no longer made in the marketplace. They are made by public policy. Choosing those goals to which a technology is directed, creating an atmosphere for industrial innovation, setting priorities for research, making tradeoffs between employment and environmental protection, committing funds for massive civil projects or expensive weapon systems-- these are today's salient choices. And the major actors in this process are not scientists and engineers. They are elected officials at all levels of government.

The Government-Technology Connection

In the United States, government today is involved with technology in five ways. First, private entrepreneurship and investment are directly assisted by a galaxy of land grants, subsidies, tax incentives, import quotas, and market guarantees. These inducements to stimulate technological activity go back almost to the nation's birth, so that over the intervening years, almost every sector has become a special pleader for handouts.

Second, the private sector is indirectly assisted by government funding of social overhead. Included in this notion are supports for higher education, specialized training, and research and development; fiscal aids such as the Export-Import Bank; services such as space shuttle launching of communication satellites; and assistance to companies seeking business overseas.

Third, by its deficit borrowing and its fiscal and tax policies, government heavily influences the capital market and economic infrastructure. Such manipulation impinges on interest rates, balance of payments, and on industry's ability to compete overseas.

Fourth, the government has been obliged to intervene through the regulatory process when technological activities of the private sector have been inimical to the public interest. Antitrust legislation and other measures to monitor the securities market were put in place over a long period. Following World War II, when technological momentum increased sharply, government interceded in a myriad of problems threatening health and safety, ignited by freewheeling industries mediating new and powerful technologies. In the public interest, government is expected to manage risk.

Finally, government is itself a major customer of technology, especially of weapons systems for national security. Indeed, with defense expenditures growing so swiftly, the nation tacitly adopted a permanent war economy with a new and virulent strain of pork barrel politics.

The vehicle for these five classes of decisions is public policy, which defines both what governments do and what they may not do. Once issues are dramatized so as to focus political energies on the choices ahead, public processes theoretically afford citizens the right of petition to explain how prospective action may affect them. Whatever emerges in the way of policies constitutes the primary guidance signals by which separate parties in our pluralistic society can then steer collectively and coherently toward common goals. Public policies now set the course and the strategies for the most potent of our technologies. We must be concerned, therefore, with the art of technological choice, which unfortunately seems primarily characterized by a grappling for influence by special interests.

Technology and New Exposures to Risk

We live with the sober truth that, at any level of technology, there is no such thing as zero risk. Under these circumstances, we have to ask how society's institutions, including business, respond to the craving for safety. First, we must recognize that in terms of acceptable risk, safety is a social judgment. No number expressing acceptable risk can be derived analytically. Investigating how safe is safe involves two considerations. The first is a technical matter of estimating the two components of risk-- the probabilities of occurrence and the severity of harm. These can be based on what we know. The second consideration is based on what we believe: the cultural and ethical factors that revolve around norms in valuation of human life, or of property, or of the natural environment. At stake are tradeoffs, say, between life and the cost of measures for its protection and extension, or between one risk and another. Salient are perceptions as to whether those at risk are the source of risk or the unconsenting victims of initiatives by others, and whether these exposures are subject to human control.

For society to judge how safe is safe enough, there must first be simple awareness. Although the general public has always been an affected party in technological enterprise, it has often been unaware of imminent decisions and possible hazards. Moreover, the general public was seldom represented in the bargaining. Until activists such as Ralph Nader courageously publicized the fact that GM's Corvair was "unsafe at any speed," and until the subsequent formation of organizations representing consumer and environmental interests and the work of few investigative reporters, most people even lacked access to information essential to realizing their exposure to risk and strategies for its mitigation. Those commercial enterprises which generated risk never advertised the situation, and many sought to conceal it. Johns-Manville's knowledge of lethal asbestos hazards four decades before judicial intervention is a case in point.

In effect, we had an age of technological innocence. To some extent, we still have one. Only after the 1985 chemical disaster in Bhopal, India, did residents of Institute, West Virginia, learn that they had been exposed to similar risks at the nearby Union Carbide plant, where safety reporting requirements had been violated. No small wonder that government has grown at about the same pace as the influence of technology.

Government: Power Broker or Steering System?

For all five purposes mentioned earlier, it is important to distinguish between government as a power broker and as a steering system. As a broker, government serves as umpire between contenders for power and the public purse. The brokerage process revolves around political bargaining, with the relative influence of different parties weighing as heavily as, or heavier than, the merits of their cases. Moreover, each group almost always argues from its parochial short-term interests. In whatever compromises are negotiated, accommodations are usually made between different immediate benefits. These pressures tilt the legislative process to favor what is urgent rather than what may be important. Normally overlooked, therefore, is the reality that today's technological decisions cast a long shadow ahead. Hence, policy resulting from political bargaining becomes an uncertain bridge between the present and future.

On the other hand, steering is a process that heavily seasons decisions with information about the way ahead: opportunities, forks in the road, obstacles, dangers of hostile competitors, and need for course correction. If nothing else, such steering is the counterpoint to defensive driving on dangerous freeways. It becomes crucial to survival in a high-tech dangerous world.

This appeal to foresight does not mean divination. Rather, it is a form of sagacity driven by an awareness that looking ahead is not a matter of predicting the future. Rather, it is anticipating plausible future repercussions of today's decisions. As much as anything, it means anticipating the behavior of the deciders.

That behavior, however, is deeply influenced by the manifest tilt in our culture towards the short run. Given this orientation of the broader culture, it is not surprising that government--an integral part of that culture--tends to act more as power broker than helmsman. This tendency is reinforced by the condition that most issues seem propelled by either crisis or pressure. This being so, policies tend to be reactive rather than anticipatory. Further reinforcing this already clear orientation towards brokering is the fact that political steering of the disjointed socio-technical system by public policy is becoming ever more demanding. Yet brokering may not meet the emerging needs of what Zbigniew Brzezinski in 1970 called "the technetronic era." Government must stand for something. It cannot simply be a referee at a technological ball game. It must learn to steer by collective wishes of the polity. And all parties, not only those with influential connections, must have powerful information by which to steer.

Pathologies of the Short Run

Whatever relationship we assume between technology and the future, we must admit, in the face of latent threats to human survival, that leadership is viscous in response. It is almost as though the policy apparatus were deaf to signals about the future. Examples abound. When nuclear energy was being pushed thirty years ago as a cheap source of electricity, the safe disposal of the inevitable radioactive waste was ignored; so was decommissioning of aging reactors. When subsidies were adopted for crops, no one inquired as to the aggregated annual costs or as to the inadvertent incentives to expand production with exorbitantly priced land. When feasibility of artificial kidneys was demonstrated, no one calculated the costs of their distribution. As the nuclear arms race continued unabated, people still failed to recognize that more arms, at a cost in six years of two trillion dollars, did not purchase more security. With personal computers proliferating in the home, inquiries have yet to be started on whether this may create a new social division of the information-rich and the information-poor.

There seems to be little desire, much less the capacity, to look before we leap. However, notwithstanding the uncertainties of forecasting, we must engage in it. Why, then, is there so little inclination to look ahead? Why is there uncritical dedication to the here and now? Why do we knowingly ignore the bills that are sure to come due tomorrow when opting for benefits today? What lies beneath our social pathology of the short run?

First among causes of this disease is the familiar reward structure in politics. An incumbent's quest for votes to remain in office is always a factor in political choice. Short-term benefits are more certain and more tangible to constituents; so for the policymaker, they are more admired. Also, political leadership receives little encouragement from the bureaucracy for dealing with the longer run. Most large organizations, private as well as public, resist looking ahead because doing so opens up the possibility of change, and change is threatening. While all organizations begin life as the embodiment of a new idea, some mature only to invest their creative energies in combatting forces inimical to their congealed beliefs. Policymakers thus become captives of their entrenched bureaucracies and think twice before investing the energy required for internal reform.

In private enterprise, as in politics, the reward structure places a premium on the short run. Pressures for immediate performance are intense, measured by Monday's stock quotation, or the quarterly statement of profit and loss, or an impatience for rapid return on investments, especially when interest rates climb. Executive promotions and bonuses are based on accomplishments visible this year. Indeed, officials are not moved to contemplate a future that they are not in: success that accrues too far ahead may only bring credit to a successor. There is little motivation even to contemplate the future, much less to act on that foresight.

To load all the blame on the self-serving traits of business and policy executives, however, is wrong. To a significant degree, the entire culture is at fault. Excessive zeal for the short run has many sources. As Walter Lippman said, modern men are predominantly isolationists, preoccupied with the more immediate events which may help or hurt them. They are marked by a vast indifference to the big issues, especially those about which they feel they can do nothing. Indeed, many people are so buffeted by daily crises in simply trying to survive day-to-day that it may be expecting too much for any but an especially attentive sector of the general public to engage these tormenting questions of the day. Suffice it to be entertained, not informed, by the evening TV news.

Then there is frustration over uncertainty; the way ahead is always obscured. Even when there are danger signals, pundits and experts disagree, and warnings may be weak, ambiguous, or worn out from shrill repetition. Doubt and perplexity sow seeds of anxiety, and that leads to bald denial.

Coping with uncertainty means coping with complexity. As noted earlier, it is not simply that the technical artifacts may be beyond common understanding. Rather, it is the social complexity induced by technology that is heightened. More and more diverse organizations must be wired together in every delivery system. Given the intricacy, fragmentation, transiency, and opacity of these networks, people discover that they are so imbedded in a maze of constraints, and so dependent upon the uncertain initiatives of others, that they feel pulled and pushed by forces over which, in the long run, they have no control. In trying to solve these riddles, we stumble over the threshold of exhaustion. So we dismiss the challenge. Finally, neglect of the future is prompted by a feeling of bliss through selective ignorance and by the cultural imperative for immediate satisfaction.

III

TECHNOLOGY AND BUSINESS

Concentrating Energy, Capital, and Information

These, then, are the broad contours of our dilemmas. We now focus on the particular problem of the relationship between business and technology. In Western society, the discovery of the iron boiler meant that steam could be fed to mechanical engines to do work. Because these devices could be installed wherever energy was needed, critical limitations of human or animal labor, and especially of water power, were overcome.

As engineering invention progressed, the limits to applications were not technical; they were institutional. Organizations were thus formed to concentrate capital, for only with ample funds could industrial firms expand operations with intricate and expensive machines.

The next requirement was planning: firms had to organize the separate tasks involved and identify the essential specialized skills and their functional interconnections. Thus emerged the familiar organization chart. Planning was also necessary to deal with the external world: to sense the market and tune products to its signals; to assure formation of capital in phase with anticipated expansion; and to obtain sufficient credit to pay wages before products were sold. When sales became sluggish, market demand had to be manipulated through advertising, timed so that output would not pile up unsold in warehouses.

Finally, management had to deal with the economic risk associated with uncertainties, domestic and foreign, including the growing encroachment of government in a previously laissez faire atmosphere. In its primitive beginnings, industrial management of risk often meant employing political tactics, coercion, or brute force to contain adverse external influences that interfered with the hallowed free market. Such was the first furious and violent reaction to unionization--a response that later had to be outlawed.

In recent decades, the industrial firm has encountered a new challenge. In addition to the concentration of energy and capital, and the planning associated with that task, a concentration of information is now required. To be sure, specialized proprietary information on product design and manufacturing processes has always been at the heart of successful enterprise in a competitive atmosphere. But with manufacturing techniques becoming so complex and so changeable, a considerable investment is now represented by the research and development enterprise associated with the more vigorous industries. Here, information is property; indeed in rapidly evolving firms engaged in high tech, it may be far more important than the land, bricks, mortar and machines that ordinarily define capital assets. So companies must nourish, conserve, and guard their information resources: the professionals who constitute the walking libraries; highly skilled personnel with empirical talent, the pipelines to knowledge in the scholarly community and the files.

Apart from narrowly technical information, broader knowledge is essential for decision-making. Reports are required about the internal workings of the organization, and about how to measure and maximize productivity. Intelligence is needed concerning the uncertainties in the external world referred to earlier, including quivers and spasms in global events regarding markets, research breakthroughs, commodities, competition, economic and political stability, terrorism, and government policies.

Objectives of the Firm

The historic goal of profit remains, but maximizing earnings on investment is not the only goal. Contemporary enterprises also seek the confidence of Wall Street, which can lead to increases in the price of stock and greater attractiveness to investors generally. They angle for the ability to control their economic and political environment, at least to effect stability. They try to minimize a large portfolio of risks. They seek growth in size through acquisitions as well as in their slice of the market. They hope for respect within the business community through their innovativeness and recruitment of high talent, and by their ability to attract venture capital. As the goals of private enterprise have changed, so have the recipients of the benefits. At one time, these accrued to individual owners. Now, corporate profits go to stockholders.

The crux of the matter is that corporations having a suite of goals are obliged to make tradeoffs among them as they plan their strategies. Overt greed does not kindle public esteem. Neither does overzealous intrusion into politics.

Business Isn't What It Used to Be

Today, President Coolidge's dictum notwithstanding, the business of America is technology. While some believe that America's business is human freedom and dignity, the reality of the 1980s is that technology drives the business machine.

In a sense, the internal creed of business has changed. At one time, the individual owner-manager looked forward to providing his heirs a legacy of identity, investment, permanence, and reputation. There was an intrinsic longer-term view that the company would continue forever in the family.

Today, the chief executive officer is likely to be a workaholic with a single-minded focus on the job because of the hypnotic lure of continually solving problems, and the career rewards of success. But noneconomic achievements are also important: virtuosity in responding to surprise in markets or to uncontrollable, external events; the provision of safety and conviviality in the workplace; and finally, evidence of social responsibility that earns esteem from the general public.

Processes have also changed. The classical entrepreneur focused sharply on the play of the marketplace. And the owner-manager fashioned the necessary internal organization and planning mechanisms for production--mechanisms that affected both short- and long-term company strategies.

However, in the firm, as in society, the past is not prologue, because now the knowledge base that undergirds the enterprise changes so swiftly. New discoveries hasten technological obsolescence in both product and production methods. The corporation is far more vulnerable to foreign events including terrorism; to the vagaries of domestic conditions, such as inflation; and to whims in popular fashions, including what is considered sexy in the stock market. There is a greater demand for public accountability, and a zealous press is ready to pounce on blunders or neglect of social responsibility.

There has been a surge of laws for human rights. These concern child labor, labor relations, affirmative action and occupational health and safety. Indeed, the broader implications of human rights were recently connected to the health and safety of the general public. At issue is a wide range of possibly adverse effects: poisons that escape to air and water during manufacture; toxic waste disposal; and hazards to consumers in the use or misuse of products. Moreover, a heightened concern for the natural environment has elicited a network of regulations to protect it.

Such drastic increases in constraints on business reflect major changes in the culture itself. There is a greater social awareness of three things: technology's impact on human affairs; the traditional concentration by most private enterprises on making a profit, with studied indifference to external effects on the public; and the corresponding need for greater accountability.

At the same time, there have been other cultural shifts highly favorable to business. Postwar prosperity in the Western world brought with it a bottomless appetite for material goods. In the 1980s, this thrust was accompanied by a new popular wave to reduce taxes and the influence of government.

Indeed, the pecuniary interest of the business sector and the values of society were in resonance in yet another and salient way. Both focused on the short term at the expense of the future. People have enthusiastically adopted a credit-card economy; they want their investments to rise swiftly. In general, people have become willing to defer or even ignore the longer-term effects, whether beneficial or harmful.

What Will Industry Do When Government Gets Off Its Back?

Every society cherishes myths. One simplistic image is so congenial to American private industry that it is pleased to propagate the notion vigorously. This popular economic model casts the private sector as the swashbuckling, imaginative, risk-taking generator of abundant jobs for workers, income for investors, and the good life for everyone else. A corollary is that business is at its best when completely unfettered. Government spoils the fun. So industry reinforces its mystique (of free enterprise) by loudly complaining at each and every governmental step to tax or to regulate. Because the nation was built on premises of capitalism, any government interference in a laissez faire environment is argued by Chambers of Commerce as a step toward inhibited productivity, socialism, or worse. To these protagonists, government is the enemy. No wonder they cry, "Let's get government off our backs," and offer enthusiastic support for politicians exalting that rhetorical theme.

In truth, government and industry need each other. The government requires a vigorous economy to foster material progress, minimize social discontent, and provide an affluent base from which to siphon off taxes. Industry needs protection from unfair competition, domestic and foreign, and from excessive risk in projects of unprecedented scale. It also needs protection against vulnerability to lawsuits for damages stemming from the failure of unprecedented technologies.

Both government and industry crave security, economic predictability, and relaxed tensions among confrontational interest groups. And both seek stability in world affairs. Both parties seek national eminence, now mostly through powerful technical means rather than through the force of ideas or ideals. With so many identical goals, both are quietly willing to trade off ideological precepts of separation for that nirvana of their common objectives, although in the United States, neither willingly parades the essential compromises in public.

As a result, government has been a willing partner in stimulating the private economy when it flags. One by one, almost every industry and agricultural sector has quietly sought and received government benefits. These include fast tax writeoffs for oil exploration wildcatters, subsidies to tobacco farmers, lower interest rates for overseas sales of Boeing aircraft through the Export-Import Bank; tax credits for purchase of capital equipment; direct subsidies for construction of merchant ships to counter lower-cost foreign shipyards; protection of steel producers by quotas on foreign sources; import taxes on textiles; aid to wheat sales to the Soviet Union; and weapons sales to dozens of countries, not all friendly. At times, government has been called upon for a complete bailout, as with Chrysler and Lockheed. Then there have been such illogical incentives as permitting tax write-offs to companies purchasing bankrupt concerns, or contributing other goodies to firms diversifying by acquisition, even if such strategies contributed nothing to enhance productivity.

Government support has not been accompanied by inordinate regulation. Government has always been an unwilling regulator. Most governmental initiatives to protect the public interest by controlling the private sector have occurred only after excessive abuses were detected. Monopolistic price-gouging, violent union-busting, occulted disposal of toxic waste at midnight, or unmitigated exposure of workers to hazardous coal dust or asbestos initially passed the threshold of ethical tolerance unnoticed by the entire culture. Now and then muckraking initiatives by investigative reporters or by public interest organizations exposed areas where the pecuniary interest of business collided with public interest. Government requirements for safer cars can be traced to heroic initiatives of Ralph Nader in exposing the unsafe GM Corvair. Pressure for environmental protection was mobilized only after the public read and reacted to Rachel Carson's Silent Spring.

So what would industry do if government backed off, both with its assistance as well as with its regulation? It is not at all certain that industry and agriculture sincerely want the free market for which they clamor. Many industries might not survive without artificial government supports. This is especially true in the international marketplace, where many foreign dealers are subsidized by their governments.

Also, notwithstanding the macho legend, most mature industries prefer stability to competition. They strongly dislike uncertainties about inflation and the costs of energy, capital or labor. The private sector wants the Securities Exchange Commission to regulate the morals of Wall Street. Judging by industry's ultimate acceptance of a national environmental policy, it may even prefer the imposition of uniform regulations regarding environmental and occupational health and safety so that everyone plays by the same rules, rather than be exposed to lawsuits for damages.

Business especially abhors uncertainty in world order, the wallow and lurch of third-world governments. This partly explains the uncritical support most non-defense industry lends to military expenditures. In the business culture, there is widespread belief that foreign policy is best practiced with gunboat diplomacy. It is thought that we need to display our technological muscle, rather than ideas and ideals, to assure the viability of U.S. bank loans to foreign creditors.

So there is quiet recognition by industry that excessive independence may be dangerous to its health. This is all the more true in light of the need to compete on the world market, where most if not all other industrialized nations have been systematic and public about their government-industry partnerships. As one manifestation, the free market has virtually disappeared in international trade. Japan, Inc. is often trotted out as a model, it being suggested that the comfortable relationships adopted there, in keeping with Japanese culture, are worth studying even if not emulating. However, characteristics long a part of one culture are not necessarily instructive for another society. We tend to forget that the Japanese Ministry of International Trade and Industry relied on state-sponsored cartels to achieve developmental goals as far back as the 1920s.

Putting the Japanese model aside, we turn to the issue of social responsibility in the American context. Industry focuses on profits with a corollary of minimizing financial costs. The economist would say there is little if any spontaneous incentive for industry to include externalities within its initiatives. Indeed, there are no methods, much less rewards, for individual firms to estimate unwanted side effects, to say nothing of acting voluntarily to reduce them in the public interest. Government's intervention, therefore, may be the only major mechanism by which these costs can be identified and fairly mitigated.

By the rules of incorporation, the state released those owning and managing the firm from individual risk. These firms are regulated by requirements for extensive financial reports in internal operations, but they are not required to issue corresponding reports on external impacts.

There is no required social accountability.   Perhaps there cannot be. Nonetheless, the large publicly held firm today is sensitive to public criticism.   As voters, the public cannot be ignored.   As investors, the public holds a similar power, but only when there is enough momentum for investors concerned about corporate responsibility to exert their sovereignty.   By putting a premium on securities that have been vetted to confirm that business practices accord well with the public interest, investors can influence the corporate boardroom.   This was done in 1985 regarding firms doing business with South Africa.   Industry might thus exert foresight as to the social impact of its initiatives, in advance of consequences inimical to its own long-run self-interest.

Industry's preoccupation with tracing its disabilities to government leads many industrialists to believe their own rhetoric.   What is then overlooked are the devils of mismanagement within the firm itself.   With economies of scale favoring massive size, flexibility is lost.   With excessive "top-down" hierarchical management, skilled subordinates are not consulted, the biases of top management are perpetuated, and at all levels resistance to change increases.   With the owners of capital not directly in control, there is a serious loss in entrepreneurial risk-taking; corporate officials may put personal economic security ahead of the firm's.   Accompanying this condition is the tendency to seek stability at any cost, and with it, artificial protection against competition.   With the intensive focus on new production technology, there is further isolation of labor from the decision opportunities and loss in worker productivity.   With excessive compartmentalization of tasks comes weak quality control.   With dependence on the apparatus of persuasion to counter market weaknesses, there is reduced attention to improve products and to lower cost.

Externalizing blame only inhibits any internal search for true sources of disability or for new ideas--including those inimical to top management's biases.   In the early 1970s and the 1980s, expos s published by General Motors' insiders confirmed this disability.   On the other hand, many firms have adopted a more candid as well as more sophisticated view of themselves and the world in which they operate.

Nonetheless, parochialism abounds, and nowhere is it more evident than with the tax laws.   With these introduced under pressure of industrial advocates, there has emerged a new phenomenon, what policy analyst Robert Reich calls "paper entrepreneurship."   Profits have been made by the manipulation of rules and money, not by innovation to reduce costs, attack new markets, or improve productivity.   Shrewd maneuvering to finesse tax laws puts a premium on an entirely different type of manager, one more familiar with accounting than with engineering.   Business schools tout their courses on efficient administration, using communication technologies and a personal secretary.   But managers lose touch with the real world of people, and they may have extreme difficulty performing in the spirit of free enterprise that they espouse.   Meanwhile, capital employed for acquisitions soaks up capital that might otherwise be employed to enhance technology.   As Reich has said, "We have changed from a nation of traders to a nation of brokers."   If government were completely off industry's back, there is a major question as to how many firms would survive.

The Question of Partnership

Hence, the issue is not whether there should be a government-business partnership, but what should be its nature. Since the myth has been perpetuated that the effective management of technology is largely the responsibility of private enterprise, it is argued that government and business should be as separate as church and state. Any intimate union of industry and government is considered, curiously enough by both liberal and conservative factions, to be a deviant sin, although for completely opposite reasons. What is not widely recognized is that government and industry have increasingly become silent partners in the business of technology. Entrepreneurs do not want to advertise this reality because it destroys the romantic image of freewheeling, rugged individualists of eras past. They would like to conceal both their dependency on government and their initiatives to keep their own hands on the steering wheel. Likewise, government officials hide these relationships, mostly because they hope to avoid accusations of undue meddling in economic processes, and sometimes simply to head off implications of collusion. Along with this increase in partnership has come a relatively invisible struggle for power between people and vested interests.

Thus, the problem is the hidden nature of the partnership between business and government. Because both sides treat this intimate relationship as illicit, there is denial of the necessary cultural legitimacy witnessed in other industrial nations. One result may be the unwitting preservation of outmoded and counterproductive industrial management. However, as the U.S. trade balance tilted alarmingly in the mid-1980s, pressures were reawakened for a reindustrialization of America. That is indeed a responsibility of an open partnership that can withstand tests of public as well as private interests.

First Sputnik, Now Toyota

In 1957, the Soviet Union's successful launch of Sputnik was perceived as an unprecedented threat to U.S. national security because other nations might interpret this success as proof of the U.S.S.R.'s technical superiority. In the midst of a cold war atmosphere of military confrontation, that potential loss in technological prestige galvanized the nation into action. In the 1980s, another external threat to national security has developed. This time, it comes from Japan, and it is economic.

It began with expanded imports of automobiles, first from Germany and then from Japan. Soon, there were steel nails, steel girders, and even plywood manufactured from trees grown in America. Then came the flood of consumer electronics, followed by such professional electronic gear as TV cameras. By 1985, there was scarcely any consumer product not being manufactured abroad, with a corresponding loss in American sales throughout the world. As American firms found the price competition too intense, there were cries for protection. But the American consumer not only found the lower prices of imports attractive, the quality and style were often superior.

Toyota's continuing threat is tangible. It is most conspicuously distinguished by an unfavorable trade balance that soared from $30 billion in 1980 to $200 billion by 1986. Meanwhile, the American dollar in the past continued to be so strong that price competition from foreign goods continued to embarrass American suppliers. As this enigma grew, and as it became apparent that import taxes and quotas could backfire on U.S. manufacturers who sought to market abroad, the quest for answers intensified. For a while, it became chic to analyze the Japanese production culture and advocate imitation.

While the limitations of any witless transfer of Japan, Inc. to the United States were recognized, one feature was readily apparent: in Japan, industry and government had a far more harmonious partnership than they had in America. The Japanese government joins in researching and choosing which world markets Japanese firms will seek to penetrate; provides venture capital under favorable circumstances without expecting instant return; helps nourish fledgling industries of high promise, rather than propping up the obsolete or inefficient; assists with licensing of foreign patents; controls debilitating internal competition among domestic rivals; protects certain domestic markets from serious foreign competition; and encourages firms to meet changing market conditions without repeated firing and hiring of employees. Aging industries, on the other hand, are left to expire.

No one expects the U.S. response to Toyota to resemble the muscular response to Sputnik. Nor should the U.S. government alone be expected to take the leadership. Nonetheless, the consequences of uneven industrial vitality are extremely grave. Perhaps half of our 6-7 percent unemployment can be traced to jobs lost to foreign competition. And these are jobs which have not yielded to governmental or industrial palliatives.

Meanwhile, talk goes on of governmental policy for "reindustrialization." Not much flesh is wrapped around the bare bones of that slogan; nor does the concept have vigorous adherents. The President's Commission on Industrial Competitiveness developed proposals in 1984: changing antitrust laws to permit joint ventures in research; offering permanent tax credits for research and development; making government data on trade more accessible; increasing protection of proprietary information; restoring patent life lost during the long government-approval process; streamlining patent law; and making trademark counterfeiting a criminal offense. These seem like weak tea for a very sick patient.

Gradually, therefore, there has been an awakening to the stubborn fact that countermeasures must depend on major initiatives within the private sector. The weakening of the technological infrastructure needs reversing, along with a recognition that more is at stake than mixing technical innovation with venture capital.

IV

TOWARD ENLIGHTENMENT

Business and the Next Century

What can industry do? First, it can examine more carefully the relationships of management style to productivity and, where indicated, reform archaic practices in dealing with the work force. Second, it can improve its salesmanship in marketing abroad, especially by countering ignorance of the sales territory and provincialism of attitude. Third, the private sector--manufacturing and banking alike--can reexamine its propensities towards the short run, giving up those tax breaks which afford instant profits but contribute not one whit to productivity; and it can try to exercise patience in expecting payoffs from investments. Next, the civilian sector of industry should recognize the existence of powerful tradeoffs and, thus, rethink its uncritical support of defense expenditures. Our mammoth defense budgets divert capital and top-quality manpower from more productive civilian endeavors, for the sake of what may be illusions of national power and prestige in a world that cannot be controlled by economic colonialism or big-stick diplomacy. Business should lead the way to making peace profitable.

Fifth, industry should reexamine its obligations to exercise social responsibility. It might ascertain the costs entailed by government constraints and lawsuits because of failure to exercise due diligence and to patrol its own membership. With Johns- Manville having concealed the known hazard of asbestos, and Union Carbide having ignored what The New York Times discovered in the way of documented defects in the Bhopal chemical plant, it is understandable that the public lacks confidence in the industrial giants.

Sixth, industry should reexamine its traditional characterization of government as enemy, its demeaning of the civil service, and its attempts to corrupt by using political channels to place ideological clones in the bureaucracy and the regulatory agencies without reference to competence. Most of all, industry must recognize that when the state confers the privilege of corporate status on a firm, permitting it to trade as an individual but protecting its officers from legal responsibility, there should be an unspoken quid pro quo. The firm must be expected to follow the same principles of ethics and accountability to society that are the noblesse oblige of a nation's elite. Insider trading scandals should be exorcised by the sector that now leads the way in fostering practices centered on "me, now."

Organized labor also has a key role and responsibility in "rebuilding America," as even the International Association of Machinists and Aerospace Workers notes. Over the past three decades, widespread pressures to increase wages and fringe benefits were not accompanied by increases in productivity; and costs were simply shuffled to consumers without recognition that other nations had entered the game. The year 1985 saw many firms forcing wage reductions to stay in business. If the unions are to recapture the respect and support of citizens and a balance of power, they will have to demonstrate a different, unselfish commitment in a high-tech world, one in which they can contribute to social as well as economic progress.

Finally, the nation as a whole may have to reexamine its attitude toward the bittersweet relationship between industry and government. It may have to accept new rules based on an open partnership. Heightened visibility of industry-government alliances would help to head off collusion. At the same time, their acceptance need not undercut the government's role as steward of both the public interest and the firm's social accountability.

Trends Toward a Corporate State?

Legitimate relationships between business and government date to the origins of this nation. There has been repeated federal assistance to entrepreneurs, with the expectation of mutual benefit: strengthening our merchant marine; building barge canals; extending railroad arteries westward; enhancing agricultural productivity. In the technological age, that symbiosis has grown further. Indeed, arguments spun previously imply stronger ties. Even with heightened visibility, however, there are risks of such relationships inadvertently undermining constitutional principles.

To trace implications, we can examine futures studies using scenarios to portray alternative paths ahead. One such analysis suggests five possibilities. First, there could be a return to the liberal precepts and practices of the 1930s through the 1960s. Second is a society that finds strength and stability through more spiritual means--what could be called the conservation ethics. Third is dependence on technological "fixes" to remedy side effects or overcome limits to growth that engender strife. A fourth alternative is deterioration of the social environment, with unending debilitating conflict. And fifth, there is an evolution to what can be called a corporate state.

In the fifth scenario, industry and government are merged, not so much in organization as in goals, creed, commitment to similar management strategies and interchangeable managers. Many analysts think we have already begun such an era, demonstrated by government-industry linkages for military security. If that is our most probable future, examination of its impacts is crucial to illuminate what America's third century might be like.

Evidence of this trend can be sought through behavior of major political sectors. The Reagan Administration, for example, is unabashedly and unequivocally pro business. It has touted "privatization" of traditional public functions. In the Iran-Contra affair, it has even moved to privatization of foreign policy. While such proposals are rationalized on the basis of higher private-sector efficiency, such transformations would also ease the unprecedented budget and deficit crunch that contradicts the Administration's campaign promises of frugality. Anticipating another avenue toward corporate purposes, business clearly applauds this privatization philosophy, also entering with gusto such arenas as health care and prisons that were the province of nonprofits or government.

The Administration has filled presidential appointments and positions exempt from civil service with candidates more distinguished by their political loyalty and economic conservatism than by talent. And their number forced to leave government because of indictments or other legal actions bearing on lack of integrity has grown well above that of any prior administration. It would appear that many individuals coming from the business community so fasten on the profit motive, and are so inclined to measure people by their net worth, that they seem indifferent to social concerns and norms of ethical behavior in government.

Meanwhile, the private sector intensifies lobbying at every level of government, both to solicit preferential treatment in taxes and to maim regulatory constraints. Of considerable importance is the growth in influence of the military-industrial complex that aggravated President Eisenhower in 1960. Today, it appears sufficiently potent that Congress has great difficulty cutting any weapons systems, even those that do not work under battle conditions and that duplicate armaments among the three services. Meanwhile, the military-industrial-complex extracts outrageous profits from a return on investment in defense contracting that is roughly three times higher than that in the civilian sector.

But as was said before, blame for shortsightedness or indifference to these trends cannot be loaded only on government and business leadership. It stems to a significant degree from society's current values and obsessions. From polling of popular sentiments, we find:

1. Our society seems caught up in the web of materialism, with concern for self-fulfillment rather than social commitment. And given the concern with economic status, jobs, control over inflation and low interest rates, there is an uncritical dependency on promises of prosperity through leaving business alone to do its thing.

2. With this public fixation on the glory of wealth, books on its accumulation become best sellers. College seniors justify their higher education solely on the basis of career earnings, rather than on the development of a personal philosophy and understanding of society that attracted many students to the university in the past. Along with this enticement, there seems to be little sensitivity to unruly behavior--say on Wall Street, witness

insider trading and takeovers that reward players in the economic game.

3. People want less government. They want an escape from paperwork, zealous bureaucracies, excessive rules and constraints. Many have completely abandoned confidence in accountability and competence in government, with lowered expectations also as to honesty. Conspicuously lacking, for example, is any public rage at the constitutional crisis created by the Iran-Contra shenanigans.

4. Meanwhile issues which seized public attention in the 1960s- disenfranchisement, disservice, disamenities and demands for environmental and consumer protection--seem to have faded. Now we find a new set of conflicts based on narrow issues amenable, according to some, to simplistic solutions and elemental political action. Even anxieties in the 1970s over an unstable energy supply seem extinguished. To some degree, this apathy stems from beliefs that the grand issues are too complex to be understood, except by the expert and the elite establishment.

5. In an escapist mood, people accept a peace of mind through claims of military security purchased by arms.

Overall, the capacity to exercise critical judgment seems crippled. So, exposed to a steady drumbeat of hyperbole in the merchandizing of commercial products, and seduced by a user-friendly TV, people seem vulnerable to the same techniques in merchandizing political candidates and policies.

The technology of politics may be as important as the politics of technology. Less discrimination or demand for the truth projects a condition that George Orwell assumed led to his pathological 1984.

When all of these social indicators are tested against the five alternative futures projected earlier, we find the vectors well aligned. A strong current is running toward the corporate state. If we continue to drift in that direction, the existing salutary tension between private initiatives potentially inimical to the commonweal in the long run and the government's role as trustee of the future may atrophy. We may then discern that a major shift will have occurred in our social arrangements. That, in itself, might be an early warning.

Taming the Wild Computer Chip

The potential danger to a democratic society inherent in the corporate state is exacerbated by technology. To uncloak fully the interaction of technology with politics is to lay bare the anatomy of power, which concerns not the energy that drives machines, nor even the goading of society by what has been termed technological determinism. Rather, it is to recognize that those who control technology control the future.

That reality stings. Most people shudder at the notion of slavery, whether by technology and its controllers according to Orwell's model or by uncongenial side effects triggered by the actions of strangers in remote districts at an earlier time. One such outcome is simply feeling isolated by a techno-culture that has left people thrashing alone in its wake.

Equally troublesome are the side effects of power. For as old-fashioned as power may be, it acquired fresh potency from having been conferred on the interlocking owners and managers of newly minted technology in a manner that is seemingly inaccessible to the people who both benefit from it and bear its risks. The cleavage between the information-rich and the information-poor has also increased. Apart from reinforcing a cultural polarity in our society between those infatuated with technology and those alienated by it, that gulf in knowledge and understanding serves to confirm the trickling away of control that engenders feelings of vulnerability and impotence.

In the early 1980s, as in the 1950s, society as a whole was enthusiastic about technology's exotic developments. Judging not by what people said but by how they acted, people loved the festival of commerce; they seemed quite unwilling to unplug what has been termed the Christmas Machine. TV ads for beer and autos chanted, "You can have it all!" "All" generally involved something tangible. It was almost as though consumption was a hallmark of patriotism, of being a good, worthy, and fulfilled person who is also invulnerable to the nuclear Sword of Damocles. Thus began the age of the personal computer.

Now, technology has became more explicitly connected with the future, and we have to bite the bullet of choice. Society can no longer afford to "have it all," especially both guns and butter. The ambiguous love-hate relationship of the 1960s regarding technology seems to have returned. Anxieties about potentially devastating threats to survival that had centered on bombs and mushroom clouds, chemical plants and noxious fluids have now shifted to economic confrontations involving Toyotas and jobs, deficits and defense spending. Along with the attention-getting headlines is a quiet awakening to the fact that the computer has sharply changed our lives, but in ways not clearly seen or understood. Notwithstanding the appeal of an advertising campaign by IBM with a clone of Charlie Chaplain, the more thoughtful are not so sure that computers are all that user-friendly.

If increased utilization of the computer for management and control of industrial processes and of information is a symbol of this bewildering high-tech era, it may also serve to represent what is at stake regarding the human experience. Not only computer literacy is involved in using the machine or its robotic application to the uses of power. Values are at risk. Thus emerges the notion of taming the wild computer chip.

This notion has nothing to do with the hardware of technology, with circuit design, or even with computer software. Rather, it concerns the institutions associated with technological delivery and their behavior, along with the information networks that lace them together, the systems that have spun the golden webs. Going beyond questions of <u>what</u> we should think about, we need to ponder the far more perplexing question, "<u>How</u> do we think about technology and power?"

In taming the computer chip, therefore, perhaps we need to look again at the notion of a fourth arm of government, an independent, information network. If citizens were aided by new and untainted sources of information as to issues, options, and tradeoffs, they would be aware of the critical importance of the choices facing us as a nation. Under those circumstances, more of them might participate effectively in the political process. First, however, people must understand how vital and sensitive is this act of civic responsibility in <u>setting</u> the course for the future, not simply <u>staying</u> the course.

Technology and the Third Century

The role of business in America's third century, and its purposes and practices, will be strongly conditioned by the social, economic and political context; that is, by circumstances that reflect powerful subterranean currents of an evolving culture. Thus, the future in a democracy will reflect acts of institutional and political choice far more than it will reflect the elegance, novelty or virtuosity of technical hardware. To comprehend this situation, consider certain realities of a high-tech world.

First, we should expect more technology, not less. Second, the artifacts will continue to be delivered by the private sector, but the key choices will be made by public policy. Third, all of the crucial decisions involve tradeoffs, particularly on the question of risks, their origin, their distribution and their management. Fourth, because technology acts as an organizing force around which are mobilized massive resources, institutional behavior will increasingly intensify to influence the political environment. Next, because there will be winners and losers associated with technological initiatives, we should expect more, not less, conflict.

The quality of decisions regarding these issues, measured in terms of compatibility with constitutional principles, depends heavily on the quality of information available to all parties. Optimally, it should be timely, complete, comprehensible to the nonspecialist, uncontaminated by self-interest, and packaged so as to reveal uncertainties, options, benefits and side effects of each. The maxim "Knowledge is power" will be truer than ever, especially with its technology-aided concentration. Impulses to control information should be expected to grow, while access to its custodians, especially at top levels of government and business, will shrink. Jefferson's epigram that "people cannot be safe without information" has a special poignancy today.

Unfortunately, the more advanced an investment in technology, be it a chemical plant, a nuclear reactor, or a weapons system, the more determined are advocates to hide data on undesirable impacts, alternatives and possibilities of a shutdown. Thus originates, through parochial institutional behavior, a widespread form of technological determinism.

The art of technological choice thus requires an imaginative search for options and the consequences of each, expressed in long-as well as short-term impacts, differentiating effects on different interested parties, including innocent bystanders. That process requires an unprecedented degree of vision and foresight.

America's third century might thus be characterized neither by new rules nor by rigid and blind adherence to old ones that have become obsolete. The best protection of the creed we cherish, of freedom, social justice, peace, individual dignity and opportunity, lies in a commitment to look ahead more self-consciously than before at unwanted consequences of technology: social, economic, ecological, legal and political.

We should address three questions about technology: "Can we do it?" "Ought we do it?" and "Can we manage it?" Answers should be sought in the most open of forums so as to incorporate multiple perspectives, not simply those represented by groups bargaining from their narrow, short-range interests, infected by institutional bias, group-think, prejudices and provincialism. In America, we must be committed to the social, not just industrial, management of technology.

This may suggest new constitutional, or at least statutory, mechanisms through which those affected by technologies have a legal right to know what is planned. If legally as well as philosophically the future were considered common property in which all share rights and responsibilities, we might establish more systematic efforts to look before we leap. Our inheritance of resources and a nurturing social and natural environment would then be regarded as a loan from our progeny, rather than as an inheritance to be squandered for instant gratification. Government would be more clearly a steward, exercising fiduciary responsibilities for all our assets, tangible and intangible.

Every salient technology raises ethical questions. Thus, the most important principle in the social management of technology is the exercise of moral vision. That process is not a matter of law but of fundamental commitment to a backdrop of tradeoffs people make between their selfish, short-term interests and society as a whole, including future generations.

In looking ahead, this may mean a sharp change in education and homework for the next century. For what is needed is more than scientific literacy. It is a civic competence for the steering of technology to produce socially satisfactory outcomes. The two most influential activities toward that end are the media and education.

The mass media, electronic and print, are the most powerful transmitters of technological information linking all participants. Investigative reporting unfettered by any pernicious influence from business and government must be depended upon not only to elucidate the wonders of science, but also to alert the public to social repercussions. Without such a lacework, the social functioning of a democracy would be impaired. If the public is ignorant of the issues and of a calendar for their resolution, decisions will be left to an elite or a junta operating through private networks. And no institutions will be accountable.

Direct or indirect constraints on the freedom of the press may signal the erosion of the entire democratic process. With editorial control over the national news media so centralized (and such media are themselves businesses, it should be remembered), our high-tech information system is vulnerable to subversion. In a technological society, where control of information linkages becomes easier, the public needs a press that will report when the government lies. At a more subtle level, if we are not careful with television, we may lose the knack of critical judgment, healthy skepticism, and demand for evidence before making up our mind.

Our educational establishment, especially our business schools, should strive to graduate students distinguished by breadth rather than specialization. Graduates will need to be: versatile; schooled in the technologically induced processes of change; sensitive to the key role of values that underpin individual, political and institutional behavior; capable of self-discovery; able to distinguish truth from hyperbole and huckster's techniques of persuasion; and eager to participate in governance with an understanding of the social contract--a balance between getting and giving.

In short, the best guarantees for preservation of our constitutional principles in a complex and interdependent world are an open acknowledgement of the partnership between government and industry, integrity, strengthening of information, reform in education and foresight. American business has a responsibility to take initiatives in all of these areas, and to nurture them to fruition.

BIBLIOGRAPHY

Janis, Irving L., and Leon Mann.   Decision Making. New York: Free Press, 1977.

Johnson, Chalmers. MITI and the Japanese Miracle. Stanford: Stanford University Press, 1982.

Linder, Steffan B. The Harried Leisure Class. New York: Columbia University Press, 1970.

Miller, Jon. The American People and Science Policy: The Role of Public Attitudes in the Policy Process. New York: Pergamon, 1983.

Reich, Robert. The Next American Frontier. New York: Penguin, 1982.

Vickers, Geoffrey.   Value Systems and Social Process.   New York: Tavistock, 1968.

Wenk, Edward, Jr.   Tradeoffs: Imperatives of Choice in a High-Tech World. Baltimore: The Johns Hopkins University Press, 1986.

Will, George F.   Statecraft as Soulcraft. New York: Simon & Schuster, 1983.

LINKING THE WHOLE HUMAN RACE:
THE WORLD AS A COMMUNICATIONS SYSTEM

by Alex Inkeles

The nations and people of the world have become and continue to
become interconnected and interdependent to a degree totally different
from the level which prevailed through most of human history. We are all
becoming part of a totally new type of global social structure. A single
worldwide social system is emerging, one loosely organized and still
continuously evolving, but with enough shape and form already developed
to make the effort to delineate it meaningful and practical. Two of the
main elements of that new system are greatly expanded world trade and
the reorganization of production on a global basis. Our focus here is on
another element, communication--the transmission and exchange between
and among individuals and institutions of information, ideas, techniques,
art forms, tastes, values and sentiments. Of particular interest to us are
those messages which cross national boundaries and thus contribute to the
linkages which increasingly make the world a single social system.[1]

I

THE GREAT TRANSFORMATION

Throughout most of human history the vast majority of individuals
could know of and have significant contact with only a relatively small
circle of people, and generally those had to live physically in close
proximity as members of the same band or as residents of the same village
or similar primary community. Contacts with individuals outside this
narrow circle were rare and limited, and mobility was so restricted as to
ensure that these contacts would bring the outsider--say an official or a
trader--to the individual, and not the reverse. Modern methods of
transportation and communication have totally transformed these
historically dominant patterns. The ties linking individuals across national
boundaries and over great distances which initially grew rapidly have
recently begun to expand at rates which can only adequately be
characterized as phenomenal.

Postal Services

The first great transformation in interpersonal communication both
within and across national boundaries was effected by the development of
national postal systems. For example, in the United Kingdom rising
literacy and the stimulus of an expanding business community yielded a
more than ten-fold increase in mail within a thirty-year period, from a
total of 82 million items in 1839 to 933 million by 1869. Steady growth
over the next century brought the total amount of domestic mail in the
U.K. to over 11,000 million items in 1983.[2] As national postal systems

came to be to linked through the Universal Postal Union, there was a comparable rapid rise in the exchange of mail across national borders. Thus, by 1981 some 6.5 billion letters and postcards were sent across national borders, equal to about 4 percent of the volume of comparable domestic mail worldwide.[3]   However, the importance of international relative to domestic mail has actually been decreasing in recent decades, at least in the case of the more developed countries, as newer technologies have come to provide vastly more rapid and often more reliable means for communicating across national boundaries.[4]

The Telephone

In contrast to the situation in the post offices, telephone exchanges are experiencing a much more rapid rate of increase in international traffic than in domestic, at least in the case of the more developed countries. In the period from 1966 to 1984 the median rate of increase in international calls for West Germany was about 15 percent, while the domestic increased at only 8 percent per year. In Japan, reporting only for 1967 to 1979, international telephoning grew as a rate of over 20 percent per year, the domestic only about 3 percent.[5]

In the 1950s telephone calls which crossed the boundaries of the United States increased in frequency at 7 percent per year, a rate sufficient to double the number of international calls every decade, but between 1966 and 1984 the median increase rose to 24 percent per year, which would double the number of such calls about every three years. Consequently, over the 34-year period from 1950 to 1984 the number of such calls outgoing from the U.S. evidently increased an astounding 540 times.[6]

By 1984 the number of international phone calls originating in West Germany was more than 369 million, and in the United States 419 million.[7] Assuming that incoming calls match the outgoing on a one-to-one basis, it is likely that by 1988 the number of international phone "conversations" in which U.S. residents participate will reach one billion.[8]   In 1986 the AT&T, which controlled all but a small part of the U.S. market for international telecommunications, grossed over $6 billion in revenues from this one source alone, some half of which it then had to share with the national Post Telegraph and Telephone Administrations with which it is linked overseas.   It is another sign of the growing importance of cross-national communication that income from international calls rose at a rate more than double the increase in income from domestic services.[9]

Although it is by now a century old mode of communication, the telephone continues to enhance its ability to cover great distances efficiently by continuous improvements in the technology developed to carry its messages over land and sea.   Indeed the leaps are often staggering.   The great advance of the early 1930 period was the coaxial cable which could carry 24 telephone channels. Currently a standard cable can carry 8,000 telephone channels simultaneously, but with the use of optical fibers it is anticipated that cables will be developed to carry 500,000 telephone calls or their equivalent in other services.[10]

As for crossing the seas, the current standard submarine cable can carry up to 4,200 voice channels. Because earlier cables had less capacity, the 30 odd international underwater cables which had been laid up to 1980 were collectively capable of carrying only 17,000 circuits. Currently this capacity is being greatly increased by the laying of an optical fiber cable, expected to be operational in 1988, which will carry 40,000 voice circuits at the speed of light under the Atlantic. Under a new technical standard, of which practical testing began in 1986, such cables will allow the transmission of voice to be supplemented by video and data moving along the same channel.

Satellite Services

Meantime, satellites had been launched with many thousands of additional telephone circuits to carry messages across borders and over seas. And here again the pace of technological advance was dazzling. As a result of these surges in technology, and the associated cost reductions, satellites could claim, as of 1986, to be carrying half of all international telecommunications and two-thirds of the traffic specifically identified as international telephonic communication.[11]

By 1984 the number of commercial satellites in orbit had risen to 150, the greatest part of these having been launched in the previous five years. At the end of 1987 more than 100 communication satellites were in a queue awaiting the availability of launch vehicles, whose shortage was made acute by the delays forced on the industry by the space shuttle disaster in 1986. Indeed, it is estimated that over the next ten years some 200 commercial satellites must be orbited to replace worn-out equipment and to provide expanded services. To take advantage of this window of opportunity both the Soviet Union and China are offering to use their rockets on a commercial basis to launch satellites, although so far they have few takers. Greater success has been enjoyed by Arianspace, the commercial arm of the European Space Agency. Following their start-up in 1979, they enjoyed 14 completed launchings by 1986, but they also experienced 4 failures. Then, after redesigning their rocket, they again achieved a completed launch in September of 1987. How great the demand is may be judged from the fact that Arianspace reports having a backlog of orders from 46 customers prepared to pay a total of $2.5 billion for launchings through 1991, and that is only about one-third of the backlog of the launching business.[12]

Only a portion of these satellites are for truly international communication, in which the key actor is INTELSAT, the International Telecommunications Satellite Organization. Intelsat is the product of international agreements and reports to the United Nations, but unlike most elements of that body it is an operating company designed to provide channels in space for international telecommunications on a commercial and nondiscriminatory basis. It achieves its purpose by maintaining communication satellites in geostationary orbit over the earth's main oceans, of which technology its seer, Arthur C. Clark, had predicted that "it will link together the whole human race, for better or worse, in a unity which no earlier age could have imagined."[13]

By a recent count INTELSAT sold its services to 170 countries, 109 of which were actual members of the Organization. As of 1984 INTELSAT had 15 satellites in orbit, collectively providing some 50,000 circuits, with the latest model, INTELSAT VI, supposed to be launched in 1987, making a great leap up to 80,000 voice channels on a single satellite. INTELSAT'S satellites are connected to some 300 earth stations located in more than 130 different nations. These stations are, in turn, linked through a network of 1,600 earth level pathways, or more than 100 per satellite. INTERSPUTNIK was designed to serve the Eastern bloc and some Soviet satrapies elsewhere, but it carries only about 1 percent of the world's space traffic because its members actually rely mainly on Intelsat.[14] When this INTELSAT system is joined to the international cable network, and both in turn are linked to the various national systems for telecommunications, the result is effectively to link every one of the 600 million phones on earth with every other anywhere on the globe. It is then no wonder that this incredible web has been dubbed "the largest integrated machine ever built."[15]

Press Services

Over the last century, first wire services, then radio, followed by television made immediate and real to billions of people certain events and personalities. In the case of the press, four great Western news agencies each day gather and disseminate a vast amount of news and features. For example, the U.S. agency United Press International (UPI) serves 92 countries, where it provides its services to over 2,200 newspapers plus 36 national news agencies, while the French agency AFP is subscribed to by 69 national news agencies and through other arrangements simultaneously gets its material into 152 countries.[16] These and other Western news services, if supplemented by Tass, the Soviet news agency, could put across the desk of a subscribing newspaper in Bombay or Buenos Aires a flow of some half million words a day. And if these sources seemed culturally too confining the editors could turn to reports from some 40 news agencies from the less developed countries organized in the News Agencies Pool of Non-aligned Countries, or to Interpress, which is a UNESCO sponsored third world news service. Through their elaborate chain of wire and satellite connections these sets of international news agencies have the potential of focussing the attention of a large part of the literate world on a single event, issue, or personality.[17]

Radio and Television Services

Newspapers can, of course, reach only the literate. The radio overcomes that barrier. Even in the less developed world, at least outside the poorest countries, the great majority now can listen to the radio, and their stations have access to the same news services as does the press. Music, moreover, requires no translation and so the same popular song can be almost universally diffused by the radio. And for those who have the greater means required, television adds the dimension of the visual, so that distant persons, places and events may be simultaneously observed. By 1983 there were still 25 countries in Asia and Africa without TV, but more than 100 nations, including the majority of the less developed, had television at least in their major urban areas. New countries were coming on stream rapidly, and all systems were expanding considerably.

For television the analogues of the international news agencies are VISNEWS and UPITN. The scale of their global reach is reflected in the fact that the second of these two organizations alone sends films, tapes, and programs by satellite to more than 200 stations in over 70 countries.[18] Wealth and technology inevitably influence a nation's chance to participate in this new method of diffusing communications. Thus, as of 1985 only 9 low-income countries versus 45 middle-income countries participated in satellite networks. Nevertheless, many third world countries were a considerable presence in this business. India and Brazil were early possessors of national communication satellites, and Mexico expected to join the club in 1985. Moreover, some of the less developed countries have themselves become centers of diffusion to other nations. Indonesia, for example, uses its satellite to link and provide materials to countries throughout Southeast Asia, and ARABSAT serves some 22 members in the Middle East and North Africa.[19]

As the reach of these and related systems becomes wider and wider, more and more of the people who were previously outside the world network of communication linkages are drawn into it. Thus, the Communist China which Chairman Mao so long kept tightly compartmentalized and almost hermetically sealed against the outside world, now has television in all 29 of its provinces, and is building more than 7 million new sets each year. As a result, 80 percent or more of the households in the major cities have television sets. Countrywide, of course, the figure was much lower, at 20 percent of households, but even in areas with very few sets, the location of receivers in public places and the gathering of viewers in the homes of those with sets brings the percent of individuals who watch regularly up to 60 and even 80 percent, depending on the region.[20] Over millennia the millions of China could never know the face of their local Governor, let alone that of their Emperor, but for their contemporary descendants the face and voice not only of their own Premier but as well of an American or a North Korean President has become a familiar and even commonplace experience.

When they can be induced to act in concert all these media have the power to create a truly worldwide audience, one which can simultaneously focus the attention of vast audiences on the same actors in the same time and space. Elihu Katz has suggested we call these "media events" and has nominated as examples of international and even global significance the coronation of the Queen of England, the funeral of President Kennedy, some of the visits of the Pope to sites outside Rome, and the Olympic Games.[21] We may surely add the 1987 Reagan-Gorbachev summit in

Washington. Of these, the Olympic Games are clearly of most universal appeal, and this is reflected in the estimates that via all the media combined the Los Angeles Olympic Games of 1984 garnered a total audience of 2.5 billion persons. That means that half the human race was more or less simultaneously linked as observers of this greatest media event of all time, something not only physically impossible in earlier times, but unimaginable as well.

Business Communication

Within this worldwide audience there are, of course, many distinctive subgroups and special interests. For example, the geophysical exploration industry has hundreds of thousands of detectors scattered over the earth's surface and in its seas, and in a single year they will record one quadrillion (10^{15}) bits of geophysical data.[22] One of the most important, and rapidly growing, of the special interest communicators is the world of production, commerce, and finance, that is, the world of business. Thus, of 121 million telephone access lines available in the U.S. about 18 percent are devoted to business organizations, and if one adds the lines devoted to data transmission, then business commands about one in four of the available lines. Moreover, this proportion has been steadily rising. Indeed, business communication may be the most rapidly growing sector in both domestic and international telecommunications.

Data transmission represented about 15 percent to the world's telecommunications market in 1985, but near the end of the decade of the 1990s it is expected to account for as much as 40 percent.[23] Characteristic of this trend are the newly developing international Value Added Networks (VANS), largely used for business, which were expected to grow at a rate of 40 percent per year in 1987.[24] In recognition of the growing importance of such communication INTELSAT launched a special International Business Service (IBS) in 1983, configured as one of the newest integrated digital networks and specifically designed to serve the needs of the international business community. It has experienced phenomenal growth, going from a mere 7 circuits at the end of 1984 to 161 full-time (64 kbps equivalent) circuits by the end of 1985.[25]

Although this rapid rise in the use of satellites reflects the general increase in the volume of business communication, a crucial element in the shift to satellites are the factors of cost and time. Thus, a large corporation may in one day of business transactions accumulate a record equal to 30 megabits on a disk. To send the information coast to coast by land-based facilities would require almost 14 hours, whereas by satellite at 3.0 megabytes per second it would take only seven minutes.[26]

Such great savings in sheer time on the line would, of course, not mean so much if the seven minutes of satellite time were enormously expensive. But the main story has been one of extraordinary and continuous reductions in the cost of satellite channels as improvements have been made in each subsequently launched unit. Expressed in constant 1984 dollars, the cost of a single voice channel went from $57,000 on

INTELSAT I in 1965 to a mere $370 on INTELSAT V-A/V-B in 1984.[27] This reduction was made possible by the fact that launching costs increased only modestly, whereas the number of circuits carried by each satellite increased enormously, going from 480 live channels in the first satellite sent aloft in 1965 to 30,000 on those launched in 1984, with a further rise to 80,000 planned for those to be launched in 1986-87, an increase in capacity of 166 times in little over twenty years.

Communications as Big Business

Just as business is a big communicator, so communication is big business. The investment made in the infrastructure for telecommunications alone currently accounts for one-tenth of the gross fixed-capital formation in the United States and Europe. When one adds the fixed-capital formation for other forms of communication, and then augments that with the current expenditures for communication services, it becomes evident that communications in all its aspects probably represents at least 15 and possibly 20 percent of any modern economy. Unfortunately, different sources and analysts may use different conventions in aggregating and disaggregating these vast expenditures. In addition, the pace of technological and related organizational change tends to blur what were once important contrasts, such as the one between data transmission and data processing. Consequently, it is difficult to present a definitive picture of the details of worldwide expenditures on communication, but some of the most salient facts are suggestive of the magnitude of this operation.

In 1985 U.S. factories alone shipped an estimated $52 billion of communications equipment. About 29 percent was spent for telephone and telegraph equipment, of which the U.S. generally absorbs about half of the total world production. The rest of the $52 billion went for broadcast, studio, communications, navigation, and other equipment. All this was largely independent of the market for computers and software, the separate worldwide sales of which were expected to reach $155 billion in 1987.[28] Revenue from the services provided by all this equipment must be distinguished from the cost of the physical infrastructure. Thus, the operating revenues from telephone and telegraph services in the U.S. in 1985 was $105 billion, which required the employment of some 950,000 persons.[29]

When we add to telecommunications the radio and television, the film, newspapers, book and journal publishing, it becomes evident what a vast, complex, and costly enterprise is involved. A narrow definition of the communication industry, which we have been following, would show it to account for some $217 billion in the U.S., or about 4.5 percent of the country's GNP in 1987, and a broad definition would credit it with well over 10 percent of GNP.[30]

The printing and publishing industry exemplifies the magnitudes involved. In the U.S. alone the industry encompasses 53,000 establishments employing 1.3 million, and in 1986 they shipped products valued at almost

$100 billion, of which about one-third was accounted for by purely commercial printing. This market was not solely domestic. Because English is so widespread and American textbooks and technical works are so much in demand, the U.S. in 1986 was able to export books valued at $610 million. Even Communist China, which carefully husbands its very scarce foreign exchange, paid out $20 million in 1986 to purchase books printed in the U.S.[31]

As sources of information books, and the great libraries which have been their traditional repositories, are increasingly in competition with information stored and retrieved electronically. From a modest beginning in the 1970s this industry has recently grown at about 40 percent each year, and by 1985 there were some 2,800 data bases available on-line worldwide, with the U.S. having a commanding but declining lead. Although the greatest share of the activity involves business, finance, industry and econometrics, there are vast data bases serving law, science, and medicine.[32]

A significant proportion of personal income goes into purchasing objects and services for communication. To select but one small item we may note that the worldwide market for records totalled $12 billion in 1983, nearly one-third of it spent in the United States.[33]   Beyond recordings, in 1987 the U.S. consumer spent some $83 billion of personal income on mass communication, somewhat over half of it on radio and television sets and services, another 30 odd percent of it on newspapers, books, magazines and other print media, and a residue of about 15 percent of his media budget for film, theaters, sports, and other admissions.[34]

Meantime, through these same media a different kind of communication, namely advertising, drew some $114 billion from U.S. business establishments in 1987, and those expenditures have been rising at a rate of 11 to 12 percent per year. In recent years the U.S. expenditure for advertising has been about half the world total. But the habit of advertising, stimulated in good part by efforts of the multinational corporations to advance their name and product, has been spreading rapidly throughout the world often producing purely local elaborations and inventions of considerable ingenuity. So powerful is this tide of activity that it is predicted that by the time the 21st century arrives the global advertising bill will be some $780 billion per year.[35]

II

THE CONTENT OF WORLDWIDE COMMUNICATION

Channels of communication across national boundaries have no significance unless they can carry mutually intelligible messages. For that to happen there must be mutually comprehended symbol systems available. Of all human systems of communication, language, in particular the verbal or oral, is arguably the most ubiquitous. Some might press a claim for gesture as the most common, and it surely could claim second place. Sign language occupies a special niche, combining the elements of both verbal language and gesture, although it is, of course, used by only a very limited and particular population. In that it perhaps shares its position with a whole set of specialized media of communication which, collectively, may be designated professional-technical symbol systems.

This set includes the notation systems used in mathematics, music and chemistry, on topographic and cartographic maps, and in electronic wiring diagrams. Rules of the game, as in chess, might well be thought of as falling in the same group, but I prefer to treat them as a transition to a third category, which I call the popular or mundane symbol systems. As the designation of this category suggests, these are the symbols used in the course of conducting the everyday business of living. Included in this category are the signs by which the prices of goods at given quantities are indicated. For those living in the more affluent world, road signs are a good example, the most obvious being the red light symbolizing "stop" and the green "go," a distinction which in China survived unchanged even the efforts of the Red Guards to reverse the order during the height of the Cultural Revolution. Religious symbols fall in this set, as for example in the special form of the cross which indicates the Russian Orthodox Church, or the lamb and the fish representing Jesus in Christian iconography.

Logos to identify the nature of the business conducted in different locations may also be placed in this set. Thus, a large pair of eyeglasses hung over the door of a shop will tell its story, just as a knife and fork will tell another, although perhaps less unambiguously. In its modern form the commercial logo comes to be distinctively identified with the products of the large multinational companies. Coca-Cola and Pepsi-Cola signs are perhaps the best known--they can be "read" or decoded correctly virtually anywhere in the world regardless of the local language. Political symbols may be thought of as similar to the commercial logo, or as more akin to the religious symbols and therefore as deserving treatment as a separate category. The Union Jack, the Stars and Stripes, and the Hammer and Sickle serve to represent this genre. In sports the signals by which the officials--designated as umpire or referee or the like--indicate whether there has been a score, a legitimate play, or a foul, and of what kind, make up yet another subset of common-man everyday symbols.

Symbols may be abstract, as I conceive the blinking red light to be, or they may be very concrete and pictorial, as in a painting of Christ's descent from the cross or a sculpture of the birth of the Buddha showing him emerge from his mother's rib cage. Any set of symbols may have a quite small and highly specialized vocabulary, as in the case of road signs, or it may be vast and indeed virtually unlimited, as in the case of the vocabulary of a modern language.[36] The symbols may be highly discrete and largely unrelated, as in the case of commercial logos, or they may be heavily dependent on context for meaning, as is the case for a letter in an alphabet which generally has meaning only when linked with other letters in a word.

Similarly, the order in which symbols appear may be unimportant, or at least set minimal constraints on meaningful communication, or there may be quite hard and fast rules governing the ordering of the elements of a symbol system, as in the case of the syntax for most languages. Vocabulary and grammar also set limits to the ability of a symbol system to communicate the interrelations of and sequencing of events so as to tell a story. An appropriate road sign may be able to tell you that there has been an accident in the road ahead of you, but it can communicate little or nothing of the circumstances surrounding the accident or of the sequence of events before and after the event. In sports, the right sequence of signs from the referee can tell you that there has been a foul, that team A was offside, that they are being given a five yard penalty, and that play will resume on the forty yard line. While thus being potentially coherent and informative, the official's repertoire is quite inadequate for describing the rich details of actual play which the language of the sports announcer permits him to communicate.

The ability of individuals to understand each other's communications is no guarantee of good fellowship, especially if the signals being sent are hostile or threatening. If shared symbol systems were sufficient to create brotherhood, we would not have had the long history of civil wars which has characterized human experience since Cain slew Abel. Nevertheless, community and communication go together. Indeed, one way of defining a community is to assess the degree to which individuals share a common language and a set of other symbols which have more or less the same meaning for all. Even with communication in mutually intelligible symbol systems, understanding is always problematic and sympathetic understanding even more so, but without such communication there is virtually no hope of expanding the circle of those who in some degree can act together to achieve common and mutually rewarding social goals. Across ethnic and cultural divisions within nations, and across boundaries between and among nations, the degree to which symbol systems are shared is a key factor in shaping prospects for common action to advance welfare and to insure peace.

Despite the obvious advantage which would accrue to humanity from having them, we are almost totally lacking in symbol systems which permit near universal, to say nothing of truly universal, communication. There are, however, some developments which move us closer to that goal. The widespread diffusion of the physical channels of communication already described, although far from completely linking everyone on earth into the same network, has gone very far in that direction and involves a process which will surely see such linkages established worldwide early in the next century.

The achievement of the goal of universal physical linkage is not very problematic. What is problematic is our ability to develop the means for mutually intelligible communication over the physical channels which will soon be established universally. Great investment in translation will of necessity be a major part of that process. It must begin within the internal structure of the machinery of communication itself. As we stand now analogue systems of telephonic communication, are in effect speaking a different language from digital systems, and as many discover to their dismay, computers made by different manufacturers have a great deal of difficulty communicating with each other. With larger systems of telecommunications and data transmission, switching and interface problems are the central issues. One major step in achieving mutual intelligibility in the signals sent by different national telecommunications industries was achieved in the early 1980s through the adoption of a standard switching interface called X.25. Although the U.S. TELENET system took the lead, the complexity of such operations was reflected in the fact that it required sharing the initiative with Trans-Canada Telephone System, the French Post and Telegraph Organization, Nippon Telegraph and Telephone, and the United Kingdom Post Office.

Beyond the elimination of such barriers, within the architecture of the technical components of our systems of communication, it will also be critical to develop languages and other symbol systems which permit mutually intelligible communication over the now more open physical channels without the costs and other limitations of translation. There are many ways in which this goal can be achieved. Organized sports, and particularly international competitions such as the Olympics, may play a special role in increasing our limited repertoire of universally comprehensible symbol systems. But for the foreseeable future, translation will continue to be an indispensable aid to cross-national and cross-cultural communication.

Translation as a Path to Communication: The Printed Word

The inability to understand each other's languages is the greatest barrier to sharing the culture of other people. The solution is, of course, to attempt translation of the works of other cultures into one's own language. From ancient times, great works of philosophy, science, religion and literature have been made available to wide segments of humankind by this means. Thus, Roman civilization depended heavily on translations of the great works of Greek composition, as later Islam drew heavily on the contributions of both of these predecessors. In turn much of what medieval Europe knew of science came to it from Islamic sources. Of course, when few could read, and books had to be laboriously transcribed by hand, those who could be reached directly by these translations were very few in number, however important they were individually in the courts of great rulers or in the councils of major religious centers.

Books in Translation

With the spread of literacy and the aid of rapid mechanical printing, the prospects for wide sharing of the written work of other cultures are enormously expanded. The more recent growth has been notable. Thus, for 1932 the INDEX TRANSLATIONUM noted only some 3,200 translated titles published in 6 countries, but by 1978 UNESCO found translations published in 74 countries and the number of titles translated showed an 18-fold increase over the period. This reported increase may give too sanguine a picture because the first listings in the INDEX may have been underreported. The more complete records for recent periods indicate that the number of titles being translated increased by about 25 percent in the decade from the 1960s to the early 1970s. This is a considerably more modest rate of increase than that manifested by many other forms of international communication, especially the electronic channels. Moreover, the latest reports available indicate that the number of translations may actually be declining. Nevertheless, the translation of over 53,000 titles reported for the latest available year, 1980, indicates a quite wide diffusion of this part of the world's cultural property.[37]

Unfortunately, as is often true in the realm of world communication, nations do not participate equally in the cross-national diffusion of literature. Germany, France, Spain, and the USSR are very active in translating books, each accounting for between 6,000 and 8,000 titles per year, according to the latest data available in 1985. Quite small countries such as the Netherlands and Denmark translated some 2,000 or 3,000 books each year. By contrast, the less developed countries, in general, are not very active in book translation. Contributing to this situation are shortages of foreign currency, scarcity of paper, and limits on the size of the available local audience. In addition, ethnic and religious interests and sensitivities in many third world countries, especially when combined with great powers of political censorship, also act to inhibit book translations. In any event, there are objective grounds for concluding that the slowdown and even decline in book translations may be disproportionately determined by the action of less developed countries, while the more advanced continue to surge ahead.[38]

The sources contributing to the translation flow are also not equal. Almost half of all the titles translated are literary works rather than books on social and political issues or those dealing with practical matters, and so on. Equally concentrated is the original language of the books. English is overwhelmingly more important a source than any other language. Thus, of some 53,000 titles translated about 1980, about 23,000, more than 40 percent, were books originally in English. French, German, and Russian contributed about 6,000 titles each, so that collectively they contributed less than English alone. With these four languages so dominant, all the rest of the 100 or so major languages in the world had to divide up the honor of contributing the remaining 20 percent of the titles.[39]

This process of translation has made it possible for some books to achieve extraordinarily wide geographic distribution. Probably the all-time record is held by the Bible. Since 1815 it has been made wholly available in close to 300 major languages, while the New Testament has been translated into over 600 languages. Portions of the Scriptures are available in an additional 1,500 less important languages, and there are 555 new translation projects underway. This means these texts are available in a very large proportion of the estimated world total of living languages. Indeed, only some 4 percent of the world's population is left without having at least some part of the Scriptures available to it in its native language. Together the numerous editions of the Bible yielded some two-and-a-half billion copies between 1815 and 1975. Despite this enormous backup supply, the printings get larger each year, with current (1987) output running at about 46 million complete Bibles and 67 million New Testament copies a year. These great numbers become much larger if one includes printings of portions and selections along with the entire Bible. On that basis the total printing goes to over 600 million items for 1986, and to a total of almost 8 billion for the period 1947 through 1986.[40] The distribution of the Koran in translation has over time also been geographically great and numerically surely vast.

Works of politics compete in being widely distributed in great numbers. Copies of The Communist Manifesto have appeared in many dozens of languages in untold numbers. The writings of Lenin are perhaps the leading example of the worldwide distribution of political literature. His works have been translated into 222 languages, and in the early 1980s there were about 450 translations of his works each year, a number greater by far than those credited to any other author. These great distributions no doubt owe much to the special concern of different interest groups, religious, political and other, but such considerations cannot explain the extraordinary diffusion of works of literature. It is thus heartening to find Tolstoi almost number one amongst all cited, with 1,063 translations in 22 countries in the decade 1961-1970. In a lighter vein stand the novels of Agatha Christie, whose 87 books have been printed in over 300 million copies in more than 100 languages. Children too share in this experience of translation. Indeed, Walt Disney Productions holds the record for the decade 1961-1970, with 1,102 translations to its credit.[41] Clearly, very large and diverse audiences are being linked worldwide by a common interest, and are sharing a common experience through their exposure to these written works.

Magazines and Newspapers

Of course books are not the only form of print entering into translation. Indeed some magazines achieve an international distribution which puts them equal to or ahead of the giants of international book publishing such as the Bible. Foremost among these is The Reader's Digest. In recent times each monthly issue has appeared in 15 languages, plus braille, organized in some 25 national editions, with a total distribution of some 28 million copies per month.[42] In some regions of the world, notably in Asia, it is the largest circulation magazine regardless of type.[43]

Limitations set by low levels of literacy and widespread poverty mean that books in translation and world circulation magazines can hope to reach only a small share of the world's population, so small as to merit for them the designation elite communication. To reach the great masses of the literate population requires turning to the world's 60,000 newspapers, and especially to the 8,000 dailies, which together enjoy a circulation of some 500 million. Again these are unequally distributed, with about one-third in North America, and another third in Europe-- including the USSR--leaving all the rest of the world with the remaining third. That means that there are still a few countries, as in Africa, with no daily newspaper at all. Further, in most of the remaining countries on that continent the papers, generally weak in resources and poor in quality, can print only some 20 per thousand persons as against the 200 to 300 per thousand population in the more developed countries. Still, worldwide, the ratio for dailies is about 110 to 120 copies per thousand population.[44] Dailies are of course supplemented by newspapers which come out less often, most commonly as weeklies. In some advanced countries these will outnumber the dailies three or even five times in number. And while generally focussed overwhelmingly on local affairs, they often carry national and international news as well.[45]

Making allowances for the age distribution of the population and for multiple use of the same copy, including its being read aloud, it is not unlikely that a billion people get at least some exposure to a newspaper each week. We may then wonder how this multitude, some one in five of the total of humanity and close to one in three of its adult population, may be linked by its newspaper exposure to the rest of the world living outside the boundaries of the individual nations in which they reside.

Few papers are wealthy enough to support their own foreign correspondents. To report what is happening in the world they must rely on international news services or agencies. According to a count published by UNESCO such agencies are together pouring out some 32 million words a day. Jonathan Fenby is not alone in calling this number "awesome," but he is in a better position than most to help us recognize some limits on these numbers not evident to all. He points out, for example, that the same 1,000 word story sent out by a single agency, say Reuters, through some 20 different subscriber services and regional desks belonging to that agency, will end up being counted as a 20,000 word output by the UNESCO method of tabulation.[46]

In actuality a much more controlled and limited flow of news results from the practice of the wire services to select and package material for different regions, say Latin America or Asia, along the known lines of interest in each part of the world. Consequently, the flow of foreign news to any given national agency will be both more limited and more comprehensible than is suggested by the huge totals described by UNESCO.

At the upper end of the scale, the Japanese agency Kyodo will each day receive some 600,000 words of foreign news, only some modest part coming from its own correspondents abroad, while the great majority come from some 50 agencies to which Kyodo subscribes. This is, of course, still a formidable flow. At the other end of the scale a poor country in Africa might subscribe to no more than three or four agencies, and if it received some 20,000 words from each, the total flow would at most be 80,000 words. These are, moreover, figures applying at the equivalent of the wholesale level, since national agencies like Kyodo further select and repackage the news in smaller batches sent out to the individual newspapers (and radio stations) which buy Kyodo's services and through which those papers and stations are linked to the outside world. After eliminating the duplication of stories on the same event from different agencies, selecting those of interest for Japan, and then cutting even those down to usable size, Kyodo sends out only some 12,000 words of foreign news daily to its subscriber newspapers.[47]   Whatever the significance of these numbers, of course, they are less important than knowing the content of the messages they carry.

Newspaper Content

A study of the distribution of news sent out by five major agencies to Europe, Africa, and the Middle East in 1980 showed by far the most important focus to be international politics and relations, with about one-third of the news items dealing with that theme.   Economics, and domestic politics, came next, each accounting for about 13 percent of the stories.   Stories about sports ran a close third with about 12 percent of the items.   After that the categories dropped off rapidly, with social life involved in only some 2 percent and art, culture, and science together accounting for less than 2 percent of the stories.[48]   Other studies indicate that approximately the same pattern has persisted for some time and applies to different news services.[49]

Inevitably, U.S. agencies such as the Associated Press, carry more news about the U.S., and European agencies, such as Reuters, carry more news about Europe, in a ratio of about 2-1 in favor of the home territory of the sending agency.   The content of what goes out from the services also varies by the nature of the region receiving the material.   Thus, in some services to Latin America more than 20 percent of the stories would deal with sports, no doubt reflecting the South American infatuation with soccer competitions, whereas some Reuters services to the Middle East seemed to contain no sports news at all.[50]

After all the selection by the international services, and subsequent screening by the national agencies, it is in the end the individual newspaper editor who decides what his readers will learn of world events through their newspaper.   That editor may, of course, operate relatively freely, or he may be under tight control from owners, government officials, political party bosses, religious leaders, or other forms of censorship.   Tightly controlled or not, editors and their papers will adapt the content they present to the character of the audience they are trying to reach.   Thus, in the United Kingdom the so-called "quality" newspapers such as The Guardian typically turn over almost one quarter of their space to external events, including sports abroad, whereas the more popular newspapers such as Daily Mirror manage to devote only one-tenth or less of their space to events abroad.[51]   The pattern is similar in less developed countries.   Thus, in Brazil, O Estado de Sao Paulo, generally considered to be the most distinguished and influential newspaper in the country, regularly devotes at least 8 of its 48 odd pages to foreign news, whereas the more popular O Globo, with about the same overall size, will give considerably less space to foreign affairs while using those pages for fuller coverage of sports events.[52]

As a rough rule of thumb we may expect a central city newspaper which is of the elite or so-called "prestige" variety to devote at least 15 percent, and more likely 25 percent or even 30 percent, of its news space to foreign news.[53] In the case of more popular central city newspapers, and the main paper in more provincial cities, the proportion of material reporting on developments abroad will be from 10 to 20 percent. In both cases, of course, we must allow for exceptions in particular countries and specific newspapers.[54]

Within the limits of whatever foreign news they do carry, most editors evidently assume that their readers will be strongly interested in news from the region in which their country is located. Some 40 to 50 percent of the foreign news published in newspapers in the countries of Asia, Africa, Latin America and even Europe was, in each case, focussed on other countries in the respective region.[55] Nevertheless, this left room for the remaining half or more of the foreign news stories to convey information about people and events in parts of the world outside the region in question. A large part of that remainder inevitably focussed on the U.S., the USSR, and other world leaders whose actions impinge most powerfully on the condition of other nations. It is, however, easy to exaggerate the prominence of these main actors on the international scene in the news reports in typical papers around the world, an impression which some studies done in the 1960s strongly fostered.[56]   The overwhelming weight of the evidence for more recent times leads to the surprising conclusion that in most newspapers, "third world" countries are paid more attention than "first world" countries in the ratio of about 2 to 1. Thus, in the newspapers of sixteen representative less developed countries studies in 1978, the third world accounted for some 30 percent of the foreign news items, whereas the first world netted only 15 percent.[57]   But this pattern is not limited to the press of the less developed nations. In Great Britain, for example, material about North America, meaning mainly the U.S., made up 18 percent of the foreign news items in the 1970s, whereas the third world areas combined captured 36 percent, again a 2 to 1 ratio.[58]   The situation was much the same in a study of the four leading newspapers in the U.S.[59]

It is, of course, important to know what is being communicated about foreign areas in whatever fraction of the newspaper is devoted to them. A rough division would assign 40 to 50 percent of the stories to the category of international relations, including military matters; economic issues will account for 15 to 20 percent; and the domestic affairs of the foreign countries for some 10 to 15 percent. It is apparent, then, that this division leaves little room for material on cultural developments abroad nor for descriptions of how people live their daily lives.[60]   Here again there is variation depending on the country involved and whether or not the newspaper in question is part of the elite press or is oriented more to the mass public. Thus, the breakdown for newspapers in the Arab world did not include a separate category for sports, and such stories were presumably incorporated in the 5 percent classified as human interest stories, whereas in Asian newspapers 12 percent of news about third world countries dealt with sports events, an amount of attention twice that given to military affairs and equal to the space given to all other news about domestic affairs in the foreign countries.[61]   In Great Britain the more popular newspapers stick to the current news events abroad, whereas the "quality" newspapers carry many feature stories about foreign regions and personalities.   In The Guardian such features made up 13 percent of all foreign news, but in the mass circulation Daily Mirror such stories accounted for less than 1 percent.[62]

Communication by Radio

Wire services send their foreign news not only to newspapers, but to radio and television stations as well.   Reuters, for example, sends its material directly to over 400 radio and TV stations, many of which are abroad.   In addition, the local radio stations worldwide can get news of foreign events by subscribing to their respective national news agencies, which, in turn, are linked to the international wire services.

Although radio does not escape the problem of linguistic specificity and the necessity for translation, it does escape the limitations set by low levels of literacy.   In addition, the development of the mass-produced hand-held transistor radio brings the cost down so low that all but the most destitute households may have one.   Moreover, the low cost of the set and the ease of sharing it reduces the cost of each exposure to a level far below that of a single issue of a newspaper.   Equally impressive is the ability of radio to overcome the obstacles of distance and other challenges to the distribution of newspapers in isolated places with difficult access.   One can go to the remotest village in India or to the settlements on the greatest heights in Latin America and find peasants at work in their fields with a transistor radio hanging from a nearby branch or pole, thus potentially tying their owners almost instantly into events occurring anywhere in the world.

No nation is without its broadcasting station, and, of course, the larger countries have many to blanket their territory.   Consequently, the less developed countries alone have more than 8,000 stations, broadcasting mostly on medium waves, and worldwide there are just over 30,000 stations.[63]   These numbers are exclusive of China.   With more than 50 million net receivers added to the supply each year, the world total reached a billion sets by 1976, and the 1987 total should have reached 1.6 billion sets extant.   That would yield a ratio of close to one set for every three persons, or one for every two above the childhood years.[64]

If these receivers and stations were distributed uniformly worldwide, then by   multiple use of the sets in families virtually everyone in the world capable of understanding the radio could be within listening range of one.   Alas, the distribution is far from equal.   Thus, the less developed world has only one-fifth of the broadcasting stations to serve some three-fourths of the world's population.   When it comes to the sets themselves, the advanced countries are more or less saturated, generally having almost 800 sets per thousand of population.   In the United States there are almost two sets per person, and in most developed countries an average of one set per person.   By contrast the low income countries, were reported to enjoy but a fraction of that level, providing one set for approximately every 10 persons in the population.[65]

It is probable, however, that these figures reported to and by UNESCO under-enumerate the availability of the small and inexpensive transistor radio. Moreover, growth in the number of sets available has been very great, with Africa, the poorest continent, increasing its supply of radios seven-fold in the fifteen years from 1960 to 1975,[66] while in the following decade many of the African countries further doubled the number of radio receivers in the hands of their citizens.[67] Moreover, as ownership diffuses, it becomes physically easier for those not owning a radio themselves to have the opportunity to hear one. Thus, in Kenya a 1980 survey showed that only 35 percent of the rural people owned a radio, but almost double that number, 69 percent, claimed to listen to the radio.[68] Given these patterns, it seems likely that by the end of the 20th century everyone will be brought within the range of a radio to which they can listen regularly. This would make radio the first truly universal channel of communication.

It apparently has not proved simple or easy to assess in detail just what goes out over the air waves in different nations, but a study of 10 representative countries in the less developed world indicated that typically about 40 percent of the broadcast time went to what the researchers considered to be "serious programs" as against "entertainment." They classified as serious programs those which gave news and commentary, as well as materials on religion, school programs and adult education.[69] Given that the proportion which was explicitly news, commentary, or description of matters foreign was likely only a modest part of this "serious" programming, one must reach the sobering conclusion that for the typical citizen in most developing countries the flow of international news and commentary via radio may occupy but a very few minutes each day. Thus, a review of the role of the news in the broadcast day in 7 typical less developed countries found that in the worst case only 6 percent of broadcast time went to news, while the average was 20 percent--against an average of 40 percent for music. About 30 percent of the news items broadcast were international in nature, and 13 percent regional. Surprisingly, this gave foreign matters about the same weight as national news, the remainder being purely local. Despite the oft repeated claims that the news agencies of the advanced countries dominate the selection of news in less developed countries, less than 20 percent of the radio news stories broadcast was taken from them.[70] Of course, limits of time are not a sure indicator of the focus of individual attention nor of the extent of impact. Moreover, newscasts are not the only point of access through radio for things international. That flow may be supplemented on the "entertainment" portion of the broadcasting day by reports on international sports events and the transcription of foreign music. Compared to a simple transistor radio a television set is quite expensive. It also makes stringent demands with regard to electricity, and it has a decidedly restricted range. All this largely limits it to urban centers and their environs, at least in the case of developing countries. It too may not escape the necessity for translation when it uses language. Yet it has the towering advantage of making the enormous leap over the limits of verbal communication by entering into the realm of the visual, or pictorial. With that leap one attains the possibility of direct and universal communication without the necessity for translation.

The TV camera brought the battlefield in Vietnam not only into the living rooms of the Unites States, but of Europe as well. Shots of the police clubbing the blacks in Soweto, South Africa, or of the poor in the shantytowns of Santiago, Chile, tell a story which can be read equally easily by viewers in Athens, Greece and in Athens, Georgia. Moreover, television's coverage of extra-national material is not limited to the news. Through special features it can widely disseminate knowledge of the physical characteristics of foreign countries, their regions and their cities, and spread knowledge of how people abroad live, work, and recreate.

Because of its relatively high cost and its technical limitations, television, in contrast with the radio, will be found for sure only in the high- and middle-income countries. As late as 1979, 17 of 45 low-income countries did have television broadcasting. A later report for 1983, using a broader definition of geopolitical units which included dependent territories, found that 45 out of a total of 216 such entities did not have any TV broadcasting.[71] In addition, in many of the middle-income countries only a few main cities had such broadcasting, again a contrast with the relatively blanket coverage of the radio stations. On the other hand, televisions's growth has been phenomenal. The number of transmitters worldwide more than doubled between 1970 and 1980, and currently there are well above 50,000 in operation. Their distribution is, however, highly unequal, with less than a tenth of the transmitters located in the developing countries.[72] Technical considerations, plus the substantial barrier of higher costs, have kept both the number of receivers and the equality of their distribution at lower levels than is the case for the radio. The latest data from UNESCO (for 1983) report a worldwide distribution of 131 sets per thousand of population, with the developed countries at 437 and the less developed at a mere 26 per thousand. In the case of the less developed that works out to one set for every 38 persons, so that even with the communal group watching common in those countries, a very large part of the population would be left outside the circle drawn around any set.[73]

TV Programming

Cost and technical factors also play a distinctive role in shaping the broadcast content of TV as contrasted with the radio. For many countries, perhaps even for most, it proves much less expensive to purchase material from abroad for rebroadcast at home rather than to attempt local production. In addition to being less costly the imported material, at least in most less developed countries, is likely to be of higher technical quality than what can be produced domestically. For news which is to be read aloud by a "talking head" not supplemented by pictures, TV stations can rely on the same wire services which supply the nation's newspapers. However, since the main advantage of television is the pictorial, TV producers seek, wherever possible, to have pictures accompany the voice presentations of the news. For this purpose all but a few must rely on an international agency such as VISNEWS which provides videocassettes in a matter of days, and more or less instantaneous transmission of pictures by satellite to stations all around the world.[74] Nevertheless, TV news and information programs seem to be less dominated by foreign sources than some imagine. A worldwide study done in 1983 showed the largest foreign influence in TV news and information programs to be in Asia, where 30 percent of such material came from outside the broadcasting country. The comparable figure for Latin America was 20 percent. For Africa the figure was only 8 and for Europe 5 percent. The explanation, of course, lies not only in the cost of foreign services, but as well in the fact that people are more likely to be interested in local or national news than in what happens in far away places.[75]

Similar pressures of cost and limits of technology influence TV stations, especially in the less developed countries, to fill their subscribers' screens with non-news programs made abroad and subsequently sold on the world market. In 10 representative less developed countries studied by Katz and Wedell for the year 1973-74 the lowest proportion of imported programming was 30 percent, in the case of the Nigerian Broadcasting Corporation, while the figure ranged up to 60 percent in Peru and 65 percent in Cyprus.[76] This yielded the seemingly anomalous situation that in the evening of July 15, 1975 viewers in Bangkok could choose between three American programs called "Manhunt," "The FBI," and "Get Christie Love." Also widely, one might say ubiquitously, shown in this and other less developed country capitals were "Hawaii Five-O" and "Kojak." Of course, not all of the imported programs thus shown came from the U.S. The U.K. contributed its share as did France and Japan.[77]

All of this might well have been taken as positive evidence of the internationalization of communication. However, it could also be, and was, described as subverting local cultural traditions, and as being a form of cultural imperialism.[78] In addition, it meant a drain on foreign currency reserves. Many nations, therefore, responded by trying to restrict the inflow of foreign programming while building up the supply of those locally made. Thus, as part of its 1968 Revolution, the new Junta governing Peru called for increasing the proportion of locally produced material shown on TV to 60 percent from the less than 40 percent then their norm. That such efforts were only partially successful, however, was demonstrated in a large follow-up study for 1983. It showed 70 percent of prime time broadcasting in Ecuador to be from foreign sources, 55 percent in Algeria, and 61 percent in Zimbabwe. Moreover, this deficiency, if such it be, was not limited to less developed countries. Prime time in Austria was 61 percent foreign origin, and in New Zealand 65 percent. Even the nominally "closed" socialist countries of Eastern Europe imported a fourth or more of their television fare, and of that part a surprisingly large proportion, close to 60 percent, came from nonsocialist countries. The U.S., the source of so much of everyone else's imports, took only 2 percent of its broadcast material from abroad, against a general average of about one-third.[79]

By contrast, some less developed countries managed to reduce significantly the proportion of their TV programs which they imported, while others were able to keep the waves of foreign material at a low level. Between 1973 and 1984 Brazil reduced its importing from 60 to 39 percent of all programs, and Venezuela from 50 to 33 percent.[80] India limited foreign material, even at prime time, to below 10 percent, Pakistan to 12 percent, and the Philippines, despite American influence, to 20 percent. The combination of a large internal market and ideological controls enabled the Soviet Union and China to produce all but 8 percent of their programming locally.

There is also some evidence of a fuller internationalization of the worldwide TV programming market, reducing the overwhelming dominance of American exports. For example, cartoons made in Japan have begun to replace those from the U.S., and Brazilian programs now go out to 90 nations. Mexican programs, especially their telenovelas, have become a major ingredient in the broadcasting of most Latin American countries, and Mexican broadcasting into the United States, targeted on its Spanish speaking population, gives it the fourth largest network audience in the country.[81]

Communicating Through Film

The moving picture considerably preceded television as a medium based on the visual. It played this role with regard to disseminating the news as well. For many years, throughout the decades from the 1930s through the 1950s, no movie program in the U.S. was complete without its introductory newsreel. As is the case with television, the film generally cannot rely on the visual alone, but must combine its presentation of pictures with language, spoken, or written, in the form of titles. Yet the film has certain distinctive advantages over television as a form of communication. Its large screen gives it greater interest and impact; its use of a special segregated setting focuses attention and increases concentration; and its ability to command more extended blocks of the viewers' time enables it to develop longer and more complex stories. All these contribute to making it a powerful medium of communication. Although its audience has been partly cut into and absorbed by television, the film continues to have enormous attraction, drawing to itself a vast audience throughout the world.

The high cost of making moving pictures in the style of the elaborate Hollywood spectacle makes it compelling that each film be brought to as large an audience as possible, which in most cases means having it widely disseminated beyond the country in which it is made. However, the technology of making films is such that, unlike something like a satellite, it cannot easily be monopolized by the wealthiest countries. Taking advantage of that fact, and understanding the possibilities of the low budget movie, makes it possible for less developed countries to produce entertainment films on a large scale. Thus, it comes as a great surprise to many that the U.S. production of feature films, numbering close to 400 in 1983, is far exceeded by that of India. India's production of over 700 films made it the world's leader, as it has been for many years by annually producing about one fifth of the total world production. Hong Kong, Mexico, and Brazil are also significant producers, each having generated over 100 films in 1983. As a result of such efforts, the less developed countries managed to produce more than half the world total of 3,690 feature films made in 1983.[82] Moreover, many of the films made in the less developed countries are suitable for export, and some get extensively distributed beyond their respective national borders.

The widest foreign distribution, and almost certainly the greatest impact in spreading non-native ideas and experiences, is commanded by the smaller production of the United States, and, to a lesser degree, that of the U.K. and France. Virtually all the countries reporting to UNESCO imported some films from the U.S., and in 74 of the 87 reporting nations films from the U.S. constituted 10 percent or more of their imports. Moreover, in many cases, such as Nigeria and Gibraltar, U.S. films were 80 percent or more of the imports. Nevertheless, the films produced by the studios of some of the less developed countries also enjoy very wide circulation. Thus, Indian films constituted 10 percent or more of the imported films in 32 of the 87 countries, accounting for as much as 90 percent of the imports in the Maldives, 60 percent in Kuwait, and 50 percent in Somalia. In turn, the films produced in tiny Hong Kong managed to win 10 percent or more of the import market in 23 countries, in some years capturing up to 80 percent of the import market in Ghana, 60 percent in Thailand, and 45 percent in Brunei.[83] These figures suggest that the full length movie is the leading instance, perhaps the sole one, in which the less developed countries play a truly major role, even if not the predominant one, in the worldwide exchange of communications material.

The Movie Audience

Once made, a moving picture can be disseminated without the need for the complex technology required to disseminate TV programs, but this may be offset by the fixed capital costs of maintaining the buildings to house the 20 to 40 theater seats per thousand of population which most countries provide. Of course, there is always the alternative of converting other space, such as a gymnasium or meeting hall, for use as a theater, and ultimately one can turn to the out-of-doors. In the latter case, however, the need for a power source is an obstacle, as it is likely to be even indoors in undeveloped or remote regions. Some nations have attempted to meet this challenge by stressing self-contained mobile units. Cuba, for example, has more mobile units than fixed cinema locations, and reports annual attendance at these mobile projector showings almost equal to that in the regular theaters.[84]

UNESCO sources indicate that the rate of movie attendance per inhabitant in the more developed countries is under 8 times per year, whereas in the less developed countries it is under 3 visits.[85] Of course, leaving out the smallest children would raise those numbers. Moreover, when one multiplies the rates by population, the size of the resultant audience becomes quite substantial. Thus, Korea's 300 cinemas show to 44 million per year, Mexico's 3,000 theaters to 300 million, and the 16,000 movie houses in the U.S. to over 1 billion annually. Worldwide, the number of attendances is approximately 16 or 17 billion per year, a number which has been relatively stable for a decade.[86]

Large as some of these numbers sound, one should be aware that the total instances of exposure to the screened film each year are not great when compared with the frequency of radio listening or TV watching, which are not only everyday affairs but which may also occupy many hours in a single day. Of course, television vastly increases the audience for films by reproducing them on the tube, and VCRs have further widened their circulation. Nevertheless, the big screen continues to play a critical role. What the screened film lacks in frequency of contact, it may make up in strength of impact, since in surveys people often report that, of all the media with which they have had contact, the films they have seen had the greatest effect. Certainly the film is a powerful medium for introducing people to the physical form of distant places and to the social arrangements and patterns of personal interaction in foreign cultures. It is precisely for this reason that governments and religious organizations are so often moved to censor films, to restrict their audiences to select groups, or to forbid their showing altogether. Films depicting sporting events, by contrast, tend to be viewed as ideologically neutral, and their distribution across national boundaries is relatively uninhibited.

Overcoming the Translation Barrier and Communicating Without Words

The obvious advantages to humankind of being able to communicate without the burden of always translating our mutually incomprehensible languages has led many to urge us the adoption or development of a universal language. The impulse to find such a language is strengthened by awareness of numerous languages which have achieved the status of lingua franca over wide geographical areas having many different local languages in use. Examples include Arabic for a long period after the 8th century in the Near East and Africa; Latin in medieval Europe; French throughout the Western world's diplomatic and aristocratic circles in the 18th and 19th century; Swahili in most of East Africa in the 19th and 20th century. In each instance, however, the language widely used served special purposes or social strata--as in trade, diplomacy, or religion.

Today English, despite its extremely wide utilization, suffers from a similar limitation by being the language of science, preeminently, and to some extent of diplomacy and commerce. Despite its wide adoption, therefore, it is far from satisfying the criterion of a universally used language. Indeed, by the simple criterion of the number of different nations in which it serves more or less the entire population, Spanish may be argued to be more universal than English. And neither English nor Spanish can claim to be understood by as many people as can understand Chinese, although this applies to its written form rather than to the spoken language with its mutually unintelligible dialects. In any event, neither Spanish nor Chinese seem destined to become a language known to all humankind. Meantime, Esperanto, constructed explicitly to give the world a language which would be understood by everyone, everywhere, seems unable to secure adoption in any but the narrowest circle of adherents to its great idea.

A Language of Gesture

While we are unlikely to escape the necessity for translation to insure worldwide communication so long as we remain in the realm of spoken language, there are forms which have great potential for the direct communication of meaning universally comprehended. These are the language of gesture, the pictorial, and sports. And of these three I believe the prospects for universalization of the language of sport are the greatest.

Some gestures do seem to be universally understood. Thus, both a smile and a frown will be recognized as such everywhere. A sharp blow may be a universal communicator. One of the grimmest exemplifications of this truth was in the polyglot Mauthausen concentration camp where the rubber truncheon used by the guards was called der Dolmetcher, meaning "the interpreter: the one who made himself understood to everybody."[87] But the list of gestures which are unambiguous across cultures is actually quite limited. The same nod of the head can mean "yes" in one culture and "no" in another, as Europeans discover to their dismay when visiting India. And anyone who has been to southern Italy, to name but one region of many one could cite, quickly discovers that being part of European culture is alone not sufficient to insure any understanding of the vast repertoire of highly expressive local gestures in use there.

It is challenging to confront the fact that in the period just after World War I the silent films made in Hollywood constituted almost 90 percent of those shown all over the world. Although they did use occasional written titles, their communication depended predominantly on pantomime. Indeed, there have been geniuses in the language of gesture, who have managed solely through that means to communicate to people of quite diverse cultures rather complex ideas and sequences of action and meaning. Charlie Chaplin was the greatest of these, and he surely came close to developing a universal language of gesture. Marcel Marceau too has displayed a similar capacity. However, such genius seems to be extremely rare, and its character always idiosyncratic. Thus, there seems to be little prospect that, on the basis of the genius of these men, we could construct and introduce into use a generally understood language of gesture.

Looking to the various forms of sign language in use does not offer a solution, because they are tied to existing national languages. The experience of working with national sign languages has certainly provided a basis for creating a universal and systematic version. Indeed, the World Federation of the Deaf has developed and published such an international sign language, called GESTUNO. Whatever its value for the deaf, however, such a language would seem to be considerably less advantageous than a constructed oral language, and it seems likely to fall short of even the limited success Esperanto has enjoyed.

The Role of the Pictorial

Much of the pictorial also needs no translation. Culturally specific qualities of painting, such as the Western use of perspective, or the Chinese convention of building a painting in linear vertical fashion, certainly require some adjustment on the part of viewers coming from other cultures which follow different conventions. Nevertheless, a nature scene in these styles, or in any other basically representational tradition of painting, is highly accessible to viewers from very diverse cultural backgrounds. The same will be true for a still-life, or a portrait, that is, cultural boundaries will not prevent correct identification of the objects portrayed. It is for this reason that paintings such as those in the Lascaux caves speak to us so directly today regardless of how many millennia separate us in time from their painters, and no matter how great the contrast in the conditions of our lives and those of the original cave-dwelling artists.

Some forms of sculpture are closely related to the pictorial, and like the Lascaux paintings can speak directly to people sharing no other language. Certainly this is true of the sculptural analogue of the still-life, that is in sculptures which represent common animals or basic human relations, as in the case of the female with a baby at her breast. Nonrepresentational painting is not so immediately accessible, but the barriers to understanding seem to be more matter of level of education or modernization rather than of linguistic difference. The same transcendence of the limits of spoken language can be achieved by abstract sculpture. It is interesting to note, in this connection, that in 1987 a great collection of the sculptures of Henry Moore was put on permanent display in an outdoor museum in Hakone, Japan, and apparently communicated exceedingly well to the numerous Japanese who have been flocking to view the pieces.

The challenge to communication through the pictorial increases sharply, however, when we go beyond simple identification of objects, persons, and primal relationships and move to communicate more complex ideas and interrelated sequences of meaning. As ever larger numbers from different cultures lacking a common language come to interact more and more closely in new types of shared space such as highways, airports, elevators, hotels and swimming pools, it becomes imperative that a language of signs be available which does not require translation for effective communication. Quite apart from the literacy issue, this becomes necessary as a consideration of efficiency. Often there simply is not enough space available to write out all the appropriate languages, and even if there were, the time required for people to locate their own language in a long list may be prohibitive under the given circumstances, as is the case of instructions meant for persons in fast-moving automobiles, or of those for turning on a fire alarm. To meet this challenge the world is increasingly developing universal signs. The smoking cigarette with a large red X across it comes gradually to be understood everywhere as meaning "No Smoking." An entire vocabulary of road signs to indicate no parking, no passing, left turn only, and so on has been devised and is being disseminated throughout the world.

Road signs use the pictorial to express quite simple ideas, but they are not well developed for communicating sequential and interrelated messages. The cartoon is better suited to such purposes. Its virtues for telling stories to those unable to follow a written language has been recognized for centuries. Thus, when Christianity sought to impress on the minds of the uninitiated the events of the creation, or to tell the stories of its saints and martyrs, it covered the walls of its monasteries and churches with cartoons. In the modern world, the effectiveness of the cartoon is dramatically demonstrated in the impact which the more talented political cartoonists have made. The cartoon's universality was clearly demonstrated by Walt Disney, first with Mickey and Minny Mouse, and then with a host of other characters. As they become increasingly complex, however, these efforts at universal communication through the cartoon come to depend increasingly on the verbal as a supplement to the underlying pictorial structure, and hence once again require the services of translators. Thus, one of the most popular comic strips in Brazil's largest newspaper O Globo is only the American "Beetle Bailey" renamed "Recruta Zero," with the translation substituting references to the Brazilian army for those originally applying uniquely to the U.S. army.[88]

Music as Transnational Communication

Music has high potential as a universal language, although through most of human history its transportability has been limited, especially when it had to cross the great regional cultural divide which separated the musical traditions of East and West. Modern cultural exchange programs bring Peking Opera and gamelan orchestras to the United States and Europe, but their audiences are very limited. A much more widespread diffusion is evidently granted to the corpus of so-called "classical" music of the West, which can be heard continuously played in hundreds of coffee houses in the major cities of Japan. This is one of the few instances where the balance of trade currently favors the West, indeed it much favors Europe over the United States. Thus, in 1985 Europe sent the U.S. some 14.3 million long-playing records, whereas U.S. exports to the European Community totalled only about 2.5 million recordings.[89]

The success of this genre is, however, dwarfed by the appeal of the music of mass culture, perhaps best exemplified by the worldwide popularity of the group which generated such a special fervor that it was given its own distinctive name as "Beetlemania." Since the Beetles communicated not only through musical scores but equally through the words of their English language songs, the geographical spread of their popularity becomes even more impressive. More recently, comparable success in reaching into virtually all corners of the world seems to have been won by new popular idols. Madonna has the power to draw to her young fans from all over Japan to pack themselves 35,000 deep in Tokyo's

Korakuen Stadium, part of an audience of some 2 million spectators before whom she will perform on a single tour covering three continents.[90] Meantime, Michael Jackson's record "Thriller" followed up its 1983 sales of $16 million by reaching an unprecedented $38 million in 1984, with a surprising 40 percent of those sales outside the United States. Currently, his 1987 recording of "Bad" is expected to achieve sales of 100 million copies worldwide, helping to make him not only a very big name, but very big business as well.[91]   In recognition of this sort of appeal a special program called "Music Box" is now broadcast by satellite specifically targeted at the youth of Europe living in sixteen countries. Despite the many different languages these young people speak, the network is convinced that "our type of programming has a universal appeal which transcends national cultures."[92]

Sports as a Universal Language

Many sports are confined to a single country or its offshoots. Thus, football, in the American version, is largely limited to the United States, and cricket to Great Britain and a few of its former colonies. Some other sports have become much more widely played and are followed by audiences across a considerable range of countries. Tennis is one of these, golf perhaps another. Ping-pong would qualify, as certainly would volleyball, while soccer likely is the most widely diffused and probably enjoys the greatest mass following.

If any sport is to be played in more than one country, those who propose the engagement must confront an inexorable fact. It is not possible for teams to play with each other unless they both know, accept, and follow, the same rules. It is not sufficient to translate the rules followed by one set of players into the language of the other team. The rules must be identical. In another sense, therefore, the players must be able to speak the same language. This also applies to the referee, and not only with regard to his understanding of the rules, but equally as concerns the signals he will give to express his decisions. The same condition applies to the audiences. They must all know the same set of rules and understand their application in the same way. In a sense then, once they have mastered the rules of the game, in whatever original language that was done, the spectators now, with this mastery of the rules, have come to share a common language. Whatever ordinary language he or she speaks, each person watching the game can read it just as they could a story or a play, although the elements are pictorial and gestural rather than verbal. A game has a beginning, middle, and end; it unfolds in a given sequence; it involves an equivalent of vocabulary, syntax and grammar; every element has meaning, as does the game and its performance as a whole.

Through the sports event, therefore, it becomes possible for vast audiences simultaneously to "read" the same game as it occurs, and thus in effect to share the same experience, without the necessity of translation from one language to another. There is, admittedly, a limitation on this sharing of experience, in that what is common is the ability to understand the story as it unfolds, but not to communicate it. If the several national audiences which easily followed every nuance of a game as they watched it were afterwards obliged to tell each other what had gone on during the game, they would once more be thrown back on their individual national languages and be able to communicate, again, only through translation.

It is worth remembering, however, that notational systems have been and are still being evolved which permit each play of a game to be described in sequence, so that ordinary language is not required to give a complete account of a game as it was played. Those used to describe chess games are perhaps best known, but they exist for soccer and football as well. These are truly non-national universal languages. It may not be expected, however, that they will be much used by those who follow sports, even in the case of the most dedicated, and their use by mass audiences seems improbable in the extreme. For them, the meaning of sports events depends overwhelmingly on seeing them "live," as they happen. Their meaning also depends in good part on elements not intrinsically part of the play, but rather part of the setting for the play--the size of the audience and the brilliance of the color scheme it creates, the flow of the crowd, the blare of the announcements, the ritual of the players coming on the field, the shaping of the first formations. These are elements of communication mostly outside of ordinary language. They require us to approach major sports events as having a special character and requiring for their analysis the tools used to understand ceremony and ritual. But in this respect international sports events, which include the Wimbledon Tennis Championships and preeminently the Olympics, have a special status because their ritual cannot be local or parochial. It must speak to and be understood by people of all nations and cultures. And it has distinctive potential for uniting or dividing the world's inhabitants.

III

SUMMARY AND CONCLUSION

The remarkable recent expansion of the scope and speed of communication lends itself to hyperbole and, unfortunately, even to hype. It is therefore very appropriate for critics to dampen the overly enthusiastic by calling attention to the fact that the world is still far from being a global village, that most people still spend most of their lives in familiar and narrow circles communicating only with those close to them in physical and social space. The acknowledgement of this condition, however, does not contradict the fact that we have recently lived through and continue to experience a profound transformation in how, with whom, and about what we communicate. Our own view is more in accord with that of Asa Briggs, who listed the "communications revolution" among the eight most important developments by which history will judge the 20th century, characterizing it as "a basic technological revolution comparable to the Industrial Revolution and to earlier eras of radical change in human history that involved the mind as well as the body."[93]

We conclude by briefly sketching seven salient features of this new communications environment: its scope and immediacy; its unprecedented rapid rates of change; its marked technological breakthroughs and the associated dramatic reductions in costs; its particular pattern of persistent inequality; its generation of tighter linkages and greater interdependence; its fostering of an emergent world culture; and the fear and hostility which that development mobilizes.

In the past an entire island could disappear beneath the Pacific without anyone knowing of it, and a great city could be covered by ash with only its inhabitants and those in sight of the volcano as witnesses. Today, minutes after an earthquake shakes Tokyo we learn of it on our radios in New York and London, and almost immediately after can see the shaking buildings on our TV sets. They place us visually, aurally, and almost tactilely in the midst of a battlefield in Vietnam, in the eye of a hurricane off Florida, and in the center of a race riot in South Africa as these events unfold. Virtually everyone has become one end point in an extraordinarily complex network which makes it possible for any person in the world to be linked to any other, and for all to be involved simultaneously in the same communication process. In addition to all our other attributes, characteristics, statuses and roles, we all have a new identity as a part of a continuously changing but permanently present world audience.

The scope and immediacy of these connections has grown and continues to grow at exceptionally high, indeed often unprecedented rates. Africa triples the number of television receivers in operation in one decade; Brazil does the same with its telephones; within a few years of their introduction VCRs are found in half the homes of some rich nations, and even a poor country like India reports 700,000 units already in place by 1987; Japan increases the number of calls placed to overseas destinations by some 21 percent per year; and the demand for satellite circuits doubles every three years.

The pace of these developments is both driven by and acts as stimulus to technological breakthroughs and the associated dramatic reductions in the cost of communicating any bit of information. In twenty years the power generated by a communications satellite increases by 32 times, and its circuits by 62 times, and the next unit on line will in one stroke double these capacities. Even more remarkable, the per bit cost incurred in storing information with the aid of programmable memory chips decreases by 1,000 times in ten years as a result of compressing 300,000 transistors onto a single chip. Such developments make it possible for a company which previously required 13 hours to transmit its day's business record to now send it all out in a 7-minute burst. These are, of course, among the more dramatic advances, but they are approximated at many levels and in diverse forms of communication.

The speed of technological advance and the associated dramatic reductions in cost play a considerable role in shaping the distinctive pattern of inequality which characterizes the field of communications. On the one hand, the fact that high technology is fundamental to advances in communication tends to exclude the poor nations, and indeed a large number of the relatively advanced, from any significant role in shaping the course of future events. This condition is epitomized by the U.S. control of some 80 percent of the computer market, Japan's even greater dominance of the market for VCRs, and their almost total joint monopoly on the development of fiber optical communication. On the other hand, bringing down the cost of transistors and chips means we are very close to having a transistor radio in every household on earth. Consequently, their governments permitting, the poorest individuals in the least developed countries can hear the same news at the same moment delivered by the same international wire services as are available to the richest citizen in the most advanced country.

As a result of such technological developments we are more tightly linked, more interdependent, more vulnerable to the consequences of each other's action. There is no way to erect barriers which can prevent a crash in the New York stock market from having almost instantaneous repercussions in all the other markets of the world, and ultimately cascading its effects downward to damage the livelihood of a cacao farmer in Nigeria or the coffee grower in Columbia. Moreover, we are vulnerable not only to the actual actions of each other but to the ghosts in our machines, so that the failure to interpret correctly the track of a flock of geese on the radar screen, or the action of one malfunctioning miracle chip, can trigger an alert, sending squadrons of atomic armed bombers aloft, and put us all within minutes of the possibility of annihilation.

This general vulnerability is but one element of a much larger set of experiences and activities which our common linkage to the modern means of communication permits us to share, and which become elements in the emergence, for the first time in human history, of a truly universal world culture. We come increasingly to share the same movies, television programs, music, and sports events. Our clothing becomes more alike and our cooking and ways of eating more internationalized at every turn. Interpersonal relations, patterns of marriage, birth, and death become increasingly homogenized. Of course, endless and profound differences persist from society to society, as well as within the same nation or community. A single world culture is not a fact, but rather is only an emergent of which only a few elements are firmly established. Nevertheless, the process is clearly well underway, and there is not much reason to believe that it can readily be reversed.[94]

Those more moved by an ecumenical spirit are not only comfortable with this trend, they are eager to promote it as the presumed precondition of a world of peace and plenty which they believe must be based on world citizenship and universal brotherhood. For others these trends are anathema, and they generate fear and revulsion at the prospect of a loss of distinctiveness, the erosion of ethnic and religious diversity, the abandonment of tradition, and the insidious diffusion of modernity.

Khomeni's Islamic Revolution is one manifestation of this reaction. But the expression of such fears is not limited to the less developed countries, nor is the tendency to express them in extreme language. Thus, Helmut Schmidt, former Chancellor of the Federal Republic of Germany, seriously argued that if commercial TV programming via a Pan-European satellite were allowed to reach within the Federal Republic, that programming "could ultimately pose a greater peril for German society than any danger inherent in nuclear technology."[95]

Running counter to these tendencies to build Berlin walls around local cultures are the recent moves of two nations which previously followed a policy of cultural isolation longer and more absolutely than any others in modern history. Communist China's official policy is now one of "openness to the world," and Gorbachev's slogan of glasnost carries a similar message. How far these policies will be implemented, and how long they will be maintained, is inherently uncertain. But their simultaneous and independent adoption, and in the case of China their considerable implementation, is surely an important indicator of the direction in which the world will ultimately go.

NOTES

1. Our definition excludes the activities which create knowledge, symbols and values, such as science, religion and art. It also excludes transportation, in the usual sense of moving goods physically. Much of electronic communication is, in a sense, a form of transport, but it is nevertheless included in, indeed it is central to, our inquiry.

2. B. R. Mitchell, European Historical Statistics, 1750-1970 (London: The Macmillan Press, Ltd., 1975), p. 652. uromonitor Publications Ltd., European Marketing Data and Statistics, 1987/88 (London: Euromonitor Publications, Ltd.; Detroit: Gale Research Co., 1987), p. 346.

3. Universal Postal Union, 1984, T. XIV and XVIII. Worldwide data for later years was not available as of 1987. ewspaper and small packet mail, not included in our figures, euals the volume of letter and postcard mail, but involves less international traffic.

4. For the period 1977-81 we calculated the share which international mail constituted of all mail worldwide, letters and packages combined, and found the role of the international fell off steadily, with the percentages being, respectively: 2.78, 2.74, 2.70, 2.65, 2.58. This decline was, however, accounted for almost entirely by a sharp decrease in the flow of international mail from the more developed countries. Over this same period the less developed countries, not so able to acquire electronic means of communication, were increasing their international mailings at a steady rate of about 7 percent each year. See Universal Postal Union, 1984, pp. 200-205.

5.   Calculated from data given in International Telecommunication Union, 1977 and 1986. Despite their more rapid rate of growth, international calls were still a modest proportion of domestic calls. For example, in Germany in 1984 cals going abroad equalled less than 1.5 percent of domestic calls.

6.   The International Telecommunications Union credited the U.S. with placing 773,000 foreign calls in 1950, as reported in MacBride p. 55, and with 419.7 million such calls in 1984, as reported in ITU 1986, p. 138. One should note, however, that there was a tremendous surge in the report of such calls between 1981 and 1982. As reported by the ITU, in that one year the calls escalated from 127 to 310 million. It may be that much of this traffic was not in the form of conversations, but rather reflected the increasing tendency to send computer and other electronic information along phone lines.

7.   ITU Yearbook, 1986, pp. 38, 138. The seeming anomaly that Germany, with one-fourth the population of the U.S. might account for almost as many international calls appears in a different light if one allows that in respect of geography the nation states of the European Community are analogues to the several states of the U.S. A call from New York to San Francisco conducted in a foreign language counts as a domestic call; one from Paris to Brussels carried on in French, or from Milan to Lugano spoken in Italian, will be scored as international. The conventions for defining different types of calls, which vary considerably from country to country, also play a role in confusing efforts to compare the phone traffic of nations.

8.   The World's Telephones: A Statistical Compilation as of January 1982, published by AT&T, reports on the basis of total international "conversations," thus taking account of incoming as well as outgoing calls. As of 1982 they credited the U.S. with 530 million international conversations, presumably for the calendar year 1981. In that year the Federal Communications Commission reported to the ITU only 127 million outgoing calls, but as noted above, the figure was revised sharply upwards for 1982.

9.   U.S. Industrial Outlook, United States Department of Commerce, 1987, pp. 31-1, 8.

10.   Ploman, 1984, p. 31.

11.   MacBride, p. 55; Firestone, 1985, pp. 146-150; Mosteshar, 1986, p. 1; Martinez, 1985, pp. 1-2. Not all the telephone circuits available on a satellite are used for strictly international communication. National telephone systems may also rent satellite channels to use for communication within a single country. However, the dominant mode for carrying telecommunications overland, and within nation, is by point to point microwave transmission, which accounts for as much as 80 percent of all long distance traffic revenue. 1986 Edition Electronic Market Data Book, Electronic Industries Association, 1986.

12. Demac, 1985, p. 7; U.S. Industrial Outlook, 1987, pp. 31-39;   New York Times, September 16, 1987; Business Week, November 9, 1987.

13. Quoted in Martinez, p. xvii.

14. INTELSAT Annual, 1975-76, p. 198-8; Martinez, 1985, pp. 3-4.

15. McBride, pp. 54-55. The figure for the number of phones is our estimate for 1988. Calculating the world's stock of phones is made problematic by national differences in how phones as against phone lines are counted, and by the imprecision of many of underlying national surveys. The latest estimate of the worldwide total we could find was for 1984, at which time AT&T placed the number just under 500 million. U.S. Industrial Outlook, 1987, credited the U.S. alone with 220 million phones. Since in recent times the U.S. has consistently had close to 40 percent of the world's phones, it seem highly likely that in 1988 there will be 600 million sets in the world.

16. Smith, p. 5.

17. Merrill, pp. 14-15.

18. Merrill, p. 48.

19. Demac, p .7.

20. Gertner, p. 639.

21. Katz, 1981.

22. Savit, pp. 19-22.

23. Electronic Industries Association, 1986, p. 56.

24. Electronic Industries Association, 1986, p. 55. VANS are private data networks which, while transmitting data, offer related services beyond what the regular long-distance carriers normally provide. Their market was estimated to be $310 million in 1985, expected to rise to $1.5 billion in 1988 and $2.25 billion in 1993.

25. U.S. Department of Commerce, 1987, no. 31, pp. 1-9. Just a year before this business service was established another went into operation under the name INMARSAT to link all vessels at sea with each other and the land. In this case the Soviet Union actually became a member, indeed it took a share, at 14 percent, second only to that paid by the U.S., the rest divided among some 40 maritime nations. See Martinez, pp. 1-2.

26. Hudson, p. 36.

27. Firestone, 1985, p. 37. Of course, such cost reductions at the macro level depend in good part on reductions effected at the micro level.

Thus, the Intel Corporation reported in Business Week, November 9, 1987, that in ten years it had brought the cost of programmable memory chips down from 1,000 millicents per bit to a mere 1 millicent per bit.

28. Much of what was incorporated in this equipment was, of course, a product of the electronic components industry, which in that same year made shipments valued at over $43 billion. We should also note that a significant portion of the communications equipment shipped was meant for use by the military. See Electronic Industries Association, 1986, pp. 35-39; U.S. Department of Commerce, 1986, pp. 32-2, 28-7.

29. U.S. Department of Commerce, 1986, p. 31-1; Electronic Industries Association, 1986, pp. 35, 57. To arrive at these totals only four media were considered: telephone, data communication, mobile radio and paging, and satellite and broadband communications. For an earlier period, approximately 1980, Loomis, p. 175, put the total "information market" at $250 billion, and the telecommunication element within that market at $100 billion, with an annual growth rate of 20 percent, which would cause it to double every 3.5 years. She did not, however, indicate what subcategories were combined to arrive at this estimate.

30. The 1987 figures are estimates based on data for earlier years given in Survey of Current Business, March 1986, and National Income and Product Accounts, September 1986, T. 6.1. The narrow definition includes only the industries designated printing and publishing, telephone and telegraph, radio and television broadcasting, and motion pictures, being lines 32, 47, 48, and 66 in Table 6.1. A broad definition would include some fraction of electronic equipment manufacture (line 21), but more important, it would take account of education, which is mainly based on communication, and which alone accounts for some 6 percent of GNP.

31. U.S. Department of Commerce, 1986, p. 27-10, and 1987, p. 27-10.

32. Sauvant, p. 82.

33. Mondo Economico, 14 March, 1985, p. 53.

34. The latest data on consumer expenditures available to us was for 1984, as reported in Survey of Current Business, March 1986, p. 71. To arrive at the total for mass communication expenditures we followed the convention of combining expenditures in five categories and lines as follows: book, etc. (83); magazines, etc. (84); radio and television receivers (87); radio and television services (88); admissions (90). The total for 1984 was $64.7 billion, and to reach the 1987 figure we assumed an annual increase of 8.5 percent which has been characteristic for recent years.

35. Haigh, p. 218; H. Schiller in Haigh, p. 183, quoting a prediction made in Advertising Age. U.S. Department of Commerce, 1986, p. 59-4, put the total U.S. advertising expenditures at $66.5 billion for 1982, the latest date available, and I arrived at the 1987 estimate by applying a compound growth rate of 11.5 percent.

36. This points to one of the limits on sign language, since its international form has only some 2,500 signs, at least as of 1975. See British Deaf Association, 1975.

37. UNESCO Statistical Yearbook, 1965, 1975, 1985. The totals for the latest years reported were: 1978, 57,000; 1979, 54,000; 1980, 53,000. The books translated in recent years equal approximately 7 percent of all titles published worldwide in any given year.

38. For example, the number of translations in 1971 versus 1980 was: for the Federal Republic of Germany 4,200 vs. 6,700; for France 1,900 vs. 5,600; and for the U.K. 727 vs. 1,300. By contrast Israel went from 579 down to 330; Turkey from 801 to 694; India from 739 to 655. Of course, some more advanced countries also slowed down or declined, and some less developed countries increased their translations, but there does seem to be a clear trend. UNESCO Statistical Yearbook, 1975, T. 11.9, and 1985, T. 7.13.

39. UNESCO Statistical Yearbook 1985 T. 7.15.

40. Barrett, 1987, and information provided by the American Bible Society, November 16, 1987. Also see Guiness, 1986.

41. Guiness, 1986; UNESCO Statistical Yearbook, 1985, VIII, pp. 130-132.

42. This information can be found reproduced in many editions of The Reader's Digest.

43. Merrill, p. 142.

44. Smith, T. 2; Merrill, pp. 36-37; UNESCO Statistical Yearbook, 1985, T. 6.2 and 7.18.

45. UNESCO Statistical Yearbook, 1985, T. 7.19 compared with T. 7.18.

46. Fenby, pp. 90-91.

47. Fenby, pp. 91-92.

48. Fenby, pp. 97-101. The five agencies covered were: Reuters Europe North; Reuters West Africa; AP Europe; AP Middle East/Africa; and UPI Europe. The survey covered three days in May and dealt with 2,459 news items totalling 574,530 words.

49. See, for example, Rachty, 1978 on the wire services input to nine Arab countries, and Scrhamm, et. al., 1978, on the wire services in Asia.

50. Fenby, p. 94.

51. McQuail, pp. 29, 248. Variations in such estimates result from the different conventions and rules about how to calculate both the base and the subject matter which is part of it. McQuail took as his base only "news" space, which meant he excluded financial and business news and feature stories. If those had been included the observed proportions might have been different.

52. Merrill, p. 277.

53. For explication of the concept of the "prestige" newspaper, and a discussion of their performance, see Pool, 1970.

54. Pinch, 1978, analyzed four leading U.S. newspapers in 1978 and found them to give about 25 percent of their space to foreign news, without much variation. The sixteen newspapers from less developed countries he examined gave an average of 35 percent of their space to events abroad. There was, however, very great variation from country to country. For example, The Indian Express gave only 12 percent of its news space to matters foreign, whereas the Singapore Straits Times turned over an astonishing 62 percent to such material. The most frequent pattern, however, was to give about 25 percent to this realm.

55. Fenby, p. 96.

56. In the classic study of the newspapers of thirteen representative countries, reported in Schramm 1964, Figure 1, p. 60, the share of the space dealing with the U.S. was generally 30 to 40 percent of that given to all foreign countries. France and the Soviet Union each captured 15 to 20 percent of the attention. Obviously that left little room for other countries to be featured.

57. Pinch, 1978, T. 1. Rachty 1978, p. 8, working with eight Arab countries, found a similar ratio, assigning 60 percent of foreign news to the third world and only 34 to the first world.

58. McQuail, 1977, p. 254. In evaluating these results it should be kept in mind that events in the third world may more often get attention because of great power involvement in their affairs, as would be the case for Nicaragua as it confronts U.S. Policy.

59. Seventy-seven percent of the space in these newspapers was given over to the home country, much as is the custom worldwide. Beyond that, they gave 17 percent of their space to the third world and under 10 percent to the first world, something less than, but close to, the 2 to 1 ratio. Pinch, p. 5.

60. For relevant breakdowns see McQuail, for Great Britain; Rachty, for the Arab press; and Schramm, 1978, for newspapers in Asia.

61. On the Arab countries see Rachty, and on the Asian countries, Schramm, 1978. Note that in the Arab countries all foreign news items were scored, whereas in the Asian press study only the items dealing with the third world were further classified by subject.

62. McQuail, T. E1, p. 248.

63. UNESCO Statistical Yearbook, 1986, VI-19; Katz-Wedell, p. 59; also Smith, 1980, T. 2.

64. UNESCO Statistical Yearbook, 1986, VI-20; Katz-Wedell, p. 59; also Smith, 1980, T. 2.

65. UNESCO Statistical Yearbook, 1986, T. 6-9, reported for 1983 the developed countries had 835 sets per thousand of population, and less developed countries 113. Also see MacBride, p. 128.

66. MacBride, p. 132.

67. UNESCO Statistical Yearbook, 1985, T. 10.2.

68. Merrill, p. 222.

69. Katz and Wedell, T. 5.1.

70. Cowlan and Love. The stations surveyed were located in: Egypt; Argentina and Columbia; Ghana and Nigeria; India; and Jamaica.

71. As reported in Head, whose source was evidently World Radio-TV Handbook. The 1987 edition of the Handbook lists 174 "countries" as having television, but many of those listed are territories or dependencies, such as the Virgin Islands and the Galapagos Islands.

72. UNESCO Statistical Yearbook, 1986, T. 6.10 gave the number of transmitters as of 1983 as 45,370, and extrapolating on the basis of recent rates of growth would have yielded almost 52,000 as early as 1986.

73. UNESCO Statistical Yearbook, 1986, T. 6.11. Also see MacBride, 1980, p. 128.

74. Merrill, p. 48.

75. Varis, Table 2.

76. Katz and Wedell, p. 156.

77. Katz and Wedell, pp. 161-62.

78. See Smith, 1980, whose book is subtitled "How Western Culture Dominates the World." A succinct and moderate summary of the argument about cultural imperialism will be found in MacBride, especially in Part III. The perceptive comments of Elie Abel, appended to the report, serve as a useful critical challenge to some of the main assumptions on which this argument rests.

79. Varis, p. 273 and Table 2.

80. Antola and Rogers, p. 186.

81. Antola and Rogers, p. 186; Wirth, 1984, p. 157.

82. UNESCO Statistical Yearbook, 1985, T. 6.5 and 9.1.

83. Calculated from T. 9.2 in UNESCO Statistical Yearbook, 1985.

84. According to the latest reports, applying to 1983, Cuba had 880 mobile film units as against 525 fixed locations, and the attendance at the mobile showings was 41.6 million compared to 44.7 million in the regular cinemas. UNESCO Statistical Yearbook, 1985, T. 9.3.

85. MacBride, p. 128; UNESCO Statistical Yearbook, 1985, T. 9.3.

86. UNESCO Statistical Yearbook, 1985, T. 9.3 and 6.7. UNESCO set the total for 1983 at just over 14 billion, exclusive of China. If we assume a billion Chinese go to the cinema on average only twice a year that brings the world total to at least 16 billion attendances.

87. Based on information from Marsalek and reported by Primo Levi in The Drowned and the Saved, New York: (Summit Books, 1988), p. 92.

88. Merrill, p. 258.

89. Inside Recording, 1986. This source did not explicitly distinguish classical from other forms of recorded music, but we may assume that the greater part of what the E.E.C. exported to the U.S. was of that type.

90. Rolling Stone, September 10, 1987.

91. Rolling Stone, September 24, 1987.

92. Rolling Stone, September 10, 1987.

93. Briggs in Haigh, p. 208.

94. On the emerging structure of world society see Inkeles, 1975.

95. Quoted in Firestone, 1985, p. 299.

BIBLIOGRAPHY

Antola, Livia, and Everett M. Rogers. "Television Flows in Latin America." Communication Research, vol. 11, no. 2: 183-202. New York: Sage Publications, April 1984.

Astrain, Santiago. "'Early Bird' to INTELSAT IV-A (A Decade of Growth)." Telecommunications Journal, vol. 42: no. XI., 1975.

AT&T Communications Overseas Marketing Department. The World's Telephones: A Statistical Compilation as of January 1982. Atlanta, GA: R. H. Donnelley, 1982.

Barrett, David B. "Status of the Global Mission, 1987, in context of the Twentieth Century." International Bulletin of Missionary Research, January 1987.

Briggs, Asa. "Looking Back from the Twenty-First Century," in Communications in the Twenty-First Century. Robert W. Haigh, George Gerbner, and Richard B. Byrne, eds., New York: John Wiley & Sons., 1981.

The British Deaf Association. Gestuno - International Sign Language of the Deaf. Carlisle, England, 1975.

Cowlan, Bert, with Lee M. Love. A Look at the World's Radio News. Medford, MA: Tufts University: Edward R. Murrow Center of Public Diplomacy, The Fletcher School of Law and Diplomacy, March 1978.

Demac, Donna A., et al. "Equity in Orbit: The 1985 ITU Space WARC." A Background Paper, World Administrative Radio Conference on the Use of the Geostationary Satellite Orbit and the Planning of Space Services Utilizing It. London: International Institute of Communications, June 1985.

Electronic Industries Association. 1986 Edition Electronic Market Data Book. Washington, DC: Electronic Industries Association, 1986.

Elias, Norbert, and Eric Dunning. Quest for Excitement: Sport and Leisure in the Civilizing Process. Oxford: Basil Blackwell, Ltd., 1986.

Euromonitor Publications Ltd. European Marketing Data and Statistics, 1987/88. London: Euromonitor Publications, Ltd., Detroit: Gale Research Co., 1987.

Fenby, Jonathan. The International News Services: A Twentieth Century Fund Report. New York: Schocken Books, 1986.

Firestone, Charles M., ed. International Satellite and Cable Television: Resource Manual for the Fourth Biennial Communications Law Symposium. Los Angeles: University of California Regents, 1985.

Gertner, Richard, and William Pay, eds. International Television and Video Almanac. 32nd ed. New York: Quigley Publishing Company, Inc., 1987.

Head, Sydney W. World Broadcasting Systems: A Comparative Analysis. Belmont, CA: Wadsworth Publishing Co., 1985.

Haigh, Robert W., George Gerbner, and Richard B. Byrne, eds. Communications in the Twenty-First Century. New York: John Wiley & Sons, 1981.

Hudson, Heather E., ed. New Directions in Satellite Communications, Challenges for North and South. Dedham, MA: Artech House, Inc., 1985.

Inkeles, Alex. "The Emerging Social Structure of the World." World Politics, vol. XXVII, no. 4: 467-495, July 1975.

INTELSAT. Annual Report to the Secretary General of the United Nations by the Executive Organ of INTELSAT. Washington, DC: INTELSAT, 1977.

International Telecommunication Union. Yearbook of Common Carrier Telecommunications Statistics (Chronological Series 1966-1975) and Radiocommunication Statistics (Year 1975). Geneva: ITU Press, 1977.

_____. Yearbook of Common Carrier Telecommunication Statistics (11th ed., Chronological Series 1973-1982). Geneva: ITU Press, 1982.

_____. Yearbook of Common Carrier Telecommunication Statistics (13th ed., Chronological Series 1975-1984). Geneva: ITU Press, 1986.

Katz, Elihu, with Daniel Dayan, and Pierre Motyl. "In Defense of Media Events." Communications in the Twenty-First Century. Robert W., Haigh, George Berbner, and Richard B. Byrne, eds. New York: John Wiley & Sons, 1981.

Katz, Elihu, and George Wedell, with Michael Pilsworth, and Dov Shinar. Broadcasting in the Third World: Promise and Performance. Cambridge, MA: Harvard University Press, 1977.

Loomis, Mary E. S. Data Communications. Englewood Cliffs, NJ: Prentice-Hall, Inc., 1983.

MacBride, Sean, et. al. Many Voices, One World Communication and Society Today and Tomorrow. Report by the International Commission for the Study of Communication Problems. New York: Unipub., 1980.

Martinez, Larry. Communication Satellites: Power Politics in Space. Dedham, MA: Artech House, Inc., 1985.

McQuail, Denis. Analysis of Newspaper Content. Royal Commission on the Press Research Series No. 4. London: Her Majesty's Stationery Office, 1977.

McWhirter, Norris D., ed. The Guinness Book of Records. Suffolk: William Clowes Ltd., 1986.

Merrill, John C., ed. Global Journalism: A Survey of the World's Mass Media. New York: Longman, 1983.

Mitchell, B. R. European Historical Statistics, 1750-1970. London: The Macmillan Press, Ltd., 1975.

Mondo Economico. Milan: Instituto per gli studi de economia, March 28, 1987.

Mosteshar, S. Alexander. Satellite Communications. London: Longman, 1986.

Pinch, Edward T. "A Brief Study on News Patterns in Sixteen Third World Countries." Murrow Reports: Occasional Papers of the Edward R. Murrow Center of Public Diplomacy. Medford, MA: The Fletcher School of Law and Diplomacy, Tufts University, April 1978.

Ploman, Edward W. Space, Earth and Communication. Westport, CT: Quorum Books, 1984.

Pool, Ithiel de Sola, et. al. The Prestige Press: A Comparative Study of Political Symbols. Cambridge, MA: The M.I.T. Press, 1970.

Rachty, Gehan. "Foreign News in Nine Arab Countries." Murrow Reports: Occasional Papers of the Edward R. Murrow Center of Public Diplomacy. Commissioned by The Fletcher School of Law and Diplomacy, Tufts University, Medford MA, and the Faculty of Mass Communication, Cairo University, Cairo, Egypt, 1978.

Sauvant, Karl P. International Transactions in Services: The Politics of Transborder Data Flows. Boulder, CO: Westview Press, 1986.

Savit, Carl H. "A Quadrillion Geophysical Data Bits Per Year." Madeline M. Henderson, and Marcia J. Macaughton, eds. Electronic Communication: Technology and Impacts. AAAS Selected Symposium. Boulder, CO: Westview Press, Inc., 1980, 19-27.

Schramm, Wilbur. Mass Media and National Development: The Role of Information in the Developing Countries. Stanford, CA: Stanford University Press, 1964.

_____. "International News Wires and Third World News in Asia." Murrow Reports: Occasional Papers of the Edward R. Murrow Center of Public Diplomacy. Medford, MA: Tufts University Press:; Hong Kong: Chinese University of Hong Kong Centre for Communications Studies, June 1978.

Sennitt, Andew G., ed. World Radio TV Handbook. New York: Billboard Publications, Inc., 1987.

Smith, Anthony.   The Geopolitics of Information: How Western Culture Dominates the World. London: Faber and Faber, 1980.

United Nations Educational, Scientific and Culural Organization. Statistical Yearbook. Paris: UNESCO., 1985.

United States Department of Commerce.   U.S. Industrial Outlook 1987. Washington, DC: Dept. of Commerce, 1986.

_____. U.S. Industrial Outlook. Washington, DC.: Dept. of Commerce, 1987.

Universal Postal Union.   Five-yearly Report on the Development of the Postal Services, 1977-1981.   Berne: International Bureau of the Universal Postal Union, 1984.

_____.   Postal Service Statistics.   Berne: International Bureau of the Universal Postal Union, 1985.

Varis, Tapio. "The International Flow of Television Programs." Journal of Communication (1984): 269-278. (Reproduced in Firestone, 1985.)

Wirth, John.   "Preface."   Communication Research, vol. 11, no. 2.   New York: Sage Publishing, Inc., April 1984.

THE SULLIVAN PRINCIPLES AND CHANGE IN SOUTH AFRICA

by Leon H. Sullivan

South Africa is a social enigma wrapped in an economic and political dilemma that must be solved with more than "all deliberate speed." If apartheid is not soon eradicated, there is a real possibility that the current level of violence within South Africa will escalate to a race war into which the superpowers would be drawn. Hence, corporate America, the United States Government and the entire world community must shoulder their responsibilities by pressuring the South African Government to eliminate the abomination of apartheid.

This article focuses on: (1) the origins and development of the Sullivan Principles, a code of conduct designed to encourage U.S. business corporations operating in South Africa to help ameliorate the abysmal economic, social and political conditions under which blacks in that country live; (2) some positive effects of the Sullivan Principles; (3) the increasingly reactionary response of the South African Government to the demands for black rights in South Africa; (4) my own recent call for the withdrawal of all U.S. corporations from South Africa and for U.S. economic and political sanctions against that country; and (5) the danger, including the potential of racial war, to the interests of multinational corporations and to the entire free-enterprise system if apartheid is not abolished.

I

The South African problem must be resolved soon. At stake is peace in South Africa, in the southern region of the African continent, and in the world in general. The global community has failed to address effectively the profoundly dangerous problem of apartheid. The world continues its ineffective mumblings and turns away, while the greatest of atrocities are perpetrated against human beings. The system of apartheid systematically, blatantly, routinely, and constitutionally continues to be practiced in the Republic of South Africa. And the world community, by its acquiescence, demonstrates the breadth and depth of international racism.

We must work until the evils of apartheid are totally eradicated, because in this challenge lie not only the issue of peace but also questions of morality, justice and man's inhumanity to man. We must take actions, either violent or nonviolent, to bring these terrible practices to an end.

Much has been written about the history of evil perpetrated against black people in South Africa. Thus, it is sufficient that I only summarize some of the conditions.

Racial discrimination has long been a part of South Africa. Since 1660, less than a decade after the Dutch settled there, when a wild almond hedge was planted on a hill above Capetown, and a pole fence extended from it beyond which no black was to venture, South Africa has had its color bar. From that time, blacks in South Africa have been constantly subjugated, and their labor ruthlessly exploited. David Livingston wrote about inland South Africa in the 1840s, and about the widespread use of unpaid labor by the white farmers. The premise was that "the people should work for 'us,' in consideration of allowing them to live in our country."

Racism took its worse and most dehumanizing form in 1948, when South Africa officially adopted apartheid, thereby making racial segregation the law of the land. Unjust laws were passed, and indignity after indignity was heaped upon black and other nonwhite peoples. Apartheid and its policy of separate development, and all the laws and regulations that have followed, have made South Africa the most oppressive government in today's world:

- black labor has been bureaucratically controlled and brutally exploited for the growth of an economy dominated by whites;

- the gap between white and black wages is huge;

- blacks and other nonwhites have been legally and systematically relegated to racially concentrated areas;

- families in vast numbers have been broken up, as segregation laws have restricted family life;

- medical and natal care is so poor in black reserves that half of the children who do not die at birth die before they are five years of age;

- schools, where they exist, are glaring symbols of inequality;

- blacks and other nonwhites have no political power;

- there is no due process of law for nonwhites;

- they are assumed guilty until proof of innocence is provided; indefinite detention of suspects or potential witnesses is permitted;

- half-a-million people are imprisoned each year; in proportion to its size, South Africa has the highest prison population in the world, and has recorded half of the world's reported judicial executions;

- and protests against apartheid have been systematically crushed: leaders and supporters of change have been banned, suppressed, jailed, exiled, and in many cases killed.

The total fabric of black existence in South Africa is affected by all of the foregoing, as well as by many other outrages. The roots of 300 years of racism go down so deep, one wonders whether ultimately the only answer to ending apartheid might have to be a military one. I hope not. The costs, especially in terms of human misery and death, would be horrendous. Means must be found for all to live together in harmony and peace in that beautiful country. A way must be found to build a bridge between the white and black populations before havoc overtakes all. The Sullivan Statement of Principles was an attempt to help build that bridge of peaceful conciliation.

Before my deep involvement in South Africa, I had established Opportunities Industrialization Centers in 100 U.S. cities. The purpose of these centers was to develop self-help training programs for poor, unskilled and unemployed people. Subsequently, during twenty years of travel throughout southern Africa, I established similar programs for poor, unskilled and unemployed people. Those travels introduced me to South Africa's system of apartheid. They also resulted in my becoming acquainted with leaders of various African nations, as well as with representatives of the Organization of African Unity. Through those relationships, I came to understand the deeply insidious nature of apartheid.

My first real confrontation with apartheid, however, occurred in 1971. After I had become a member of the Board of General Motors, a resolution was presented at a stockholders' meeting urging the corporation to withdraw from South Africa. In spite of the unanimous disagreement of my fellow board members, I supported the resolution. It was the first time in GM history that a Board member had dissented publicly from the Board's view on any issue. In a speech delivered at the meeting, I said:

> My reason for speaking today . . . regards General Motor's involvement in the Union of South Africa. Apartheid is the most ruthless and dehumanizing practice perpetuated in the world today. Blacks in the Union of South Africa are relegated to subhuman treatment without freedom of movement, without economic equality in wages . . ., and without even basic elemental rights. Apartheid must come to an end.

> In great measure, the system of apartheid is being underwritten by American industry, interests, and investments simply by virtue of our operations there.   . . . [O]ver 300 American businesses operate in the Union of South Africa . . ., including the General Motors Corporation. These companies, by their very presence, are helping to sustain the existence of the terrible practice I have alluded to today. Either the leaders of the Union of South Africa will end apartheid, or one day apartheid will mean the end of the Union of South Africa--and everything General Motors has in it.

> But, even more than economic or political considerations, American industry cannot morally continue to do business in a

country that so blatantly, ruthlessly and clearly maintains such dehumanizing practices against such large numbers of its people. . . . [Therefore, I] call on General Motors to leave South Africa.

. . . I will continue to pursue my desire to see that American enterprises, including General Motors, withdraw from the Union of South Africa until clear changes have been made in the practices and . . . policies of that government, as they pertain to the treatment of blacks and other nonwhites. I have no desire to be spectacular. [But] I want to see GM out of the contemporary unparalleled oppressive situation that exists there. . . . And although I know I shall lose today, I shall continue to pursue this interest tomorrow, until black people in the Union of South Africa are free.

Of course, we lost the vote on that day, with less than 2 percent voting for GM's withdrawal, but I determined to go as far as I could to work towards the eradication of apartheid.

II

For four years I held to my view for total withdrawal of all American companies from South Africa. In 1975, however, on a trip to Lesotho, a small, independent kingdom landlocked by the Republic of South Africa, I had the opportunity to meet with black South African leaders, union officials, and company executives. I was told that my call for United States companies to withdraw was a negative one with limited chance of success. Conversely, it was argued that a strong Code of Conduct establishing norms for the treatment of black labor by those companies would have a positive effect, and would bring about meaningful change. Repeatedly, the blacks and union officials urged me to draw up such a code, and made suggestions for its design.

I was ambivalent, but decided to try the route of what were to become the Sullivan Principles, because I was not getting support for my withdrawal efforts. Perhaps such a set of principles could be increasingly strengthened and, along with other thrusts, help change the apartheid system.

The initial Sullivan Principles announced on March 1, 1977 included:

-   nonsegregation of the races in all eating, comfort and work facilities;

-   equal and fair employment practices for all employees;

-   equal pay for all employees doing equal or comparable work for the same period of time;

- initiation and development of training programs that would prepare, in substantial numbers, blacks and other nonwhites for supervisory, administrative, clerical and technical jobs;

- increasing the number of blacks and other nonwhites in management and supervisory positions;

- and improving the quality of employees' lives outside the work environment in such areas as housing, transportation, schooling, recreation and health facilities.

The first twelve American companies in 1977 who signed the Principles were: American Cyanamid Company; IBM Corporation; Burroughs Corporation; International Harvester Company; Citicorp; Minnesota Mining & Manufacturing Company; Ford Motor Company; Mobil Oil Corporation; General Motors Corporation; Union Carbide Corporation; The Chase Manhattan Bank; and The Upjohn Company.

It was never my intention or remotest belief that the Sullivan Principles could be a total solution to the South African problem. But I repeatedly argued that they could be instrumental in effecting change if they were steadily strengthened, and if they were maximally enforced by American and other companies operating in South Africa. Along with other thrusts (moral, educational, economic and political) the Principles could contribute to the peaceful elimination of apartheid. I placed much emphasis on "other thrusts" within and without South Africa. I especially urged the establishment of independent, black, free trade unions, and the growing empowerment of black workers. I envisioned millions of blacks as members of such unions, standing up not only for workers rights in the companies and mines, but also throughout the country, effecting economic, social and political change.

It was clear, however, that if the Principles were to be implemented effectively, monitoring of the situation would be necessary. Thus, from the outset, I insisted on regular reporting by signatory companies. Such reporting provided the basis for public information on the commitment of the companies to social programs. It also required each company to prepare annual reports on its activities, and to submit those reports for an outside independent assessment. In 1978, the Arthur D. Little Company (ADL), one of America's most respected consulting organizations, was retained to make those assessments. The latter were the only basis for evaluating the social behavior of multinational corporations operating in South Africa. Companies that refused to report were dropped as members of the program.

By 1986, there were nearly 200 United States signatories to the Sullivan Principles. As a result of efforts made by these companies, many changes were effected. The significance of these changes is readily apparent when it is recognized that prior to 1977, when the Principles were formulated, blacks were not even legally recognized as workers, and that virtually all company operations in South Africa involved some form of racial segregation. By 1985:

- all United States company facilities were desegregated, in spite of South African laws requiring the separation of races;

- black labor unions had been recognized by the South African Government, and all United States companies had agreed to recognize black and integrated labor unions; this has been one of the great achievements of the Sullivan Principles; in the recent coal miners' strike, we can see coming to fruition the hope for black workers' power; in time, it will become one of the most formidable forces for black liberation in South Africa: social, economic and political;

- all United States companies paid equal wages for equal work to all employees, regardless of race;

- United States companies led the way for improving education for black youth, a unanimous priority of black leaders in South Africa: 10,000 college scholarships were provided for blacks; 300 schools had been "adopted" by signatories; more than 300,000 pupils had received updated equipment; teachers were trained; facilities were improved; literacy training was provided to 250,000 blacks a year; technical centers and schools, training more than 75,000 blacks per year with special technical skills, were established; United States companies supported interracial schools, thereby beginning to break down the barriers of segregated education; they also supported a Teacher Opportunity Program that upgraded the skills of thousands of black teachers;

- for the first time in South Africa's history, blacks began to supervise whites in companies;

- health-care programs developed by United States companies annually served 1 million South Africans;

- United States companies supported more than 1000 black businesses with purchasing contracts and technical services;

- within ten years, $275 million dollars was spent by United States companies for education and social causes, and the wages of black workers were upgraded by millions of Rand;

- United States signatories had begun to attack the pillars of apartheid through an Amplification of the Principles that called on U.S. companies to work for economic, social and political justice.

To institutionalize these developments, I requested that ADL add a seventh principle to its Ninth Report evaluating the implementation of the Sullivan Principles. The new principle called on U.S. companies to: "Work eliminate all laws and customs which impede social, economic, and political justice,"

- including equal education for non-employees (non-employees include family members of employees, as well as others not affiliated with the signatory company);

- provide quality education to black, coloured and Asian non-employees;

- provide increased opportunity for training and advancement of black, coloured and Asian employees, including managerial, supervisory, professional and sales job classifications;

- provide assistance to housing, health and welfare, civic recreation and the development of black, coloured and Asian enterprises;

- and work toward the abolition of all apartheid laws and practices.

Other codes were formulated after the Sullivan Principles were established. However, none of them imposed on companies requirements regarding social, economic and political activities that remotely approached those of the Sullivan Principles. Without question, the latter became the hallmark of corporate social responsibility for companies operating in South Africa.

Indeed, if the Sullivan Principles, as applied in South Africa, were required for foreign multinational companies doing business in all the developing African countries, there would be a renaissance in social and economic benefits for blacks throughout the continent. There would also be a surge of economic revitalization of black education, resulting in advances and benefits not yet seen in all of Africa. In fact, the Sullivan principles, if implemented by companies in America, would result in advancement for blacks and others on a scale never before realized.

Thus, the Sullivan Principles, as they were developed, contained the most stringent standards of measurement for corporate responsibility ever imposed on United States companies operating in any foreign country, or in fact, standards more exacting than those imposed on companies in the United States.

Moreover, the results of the Sullivan Principles have been far from cosmetic, as some would have predicted. The Principles, steadily evolving in accord with the original plan, created a revolution in industrial race relations in South Africa. That revolution has affected millions of black workers there, a number far exceeding the small percentage of the labor force employed by U.S. companies operating in South Africa. The changes resulting from the Principles will affect the way companies treat black workers in that country for centuries to come.

The reporting process was one of the key reasons for the effectiveness of the effort. According to the ADL Report of October 25, 1985, the measurement process has encouraged the signatories to strive constantly for higher goals. Moreover, the process has increased the influence of those companies far beyond what could have been expected from their proportion of the nation's total employment. According to the report, Sullivan code standards have continually risen as a result of negotiation between the signatories and Dr. Sullivan. Today, signatories are satisfying requirements they would not have tolerated when the program was initiated. This, the report concludes, has been made possible by a dynamic, voluntary effort.

III

Notwithstanding the progress described above, and because of growing unrest in South Africa, I decided in November of 1985 to challenge directly the South African Government to bring about political and consitutional change. Therefore, I intensified pressure on corporations conducting business in South Africa. Before an audience of 300 company executives in New York City, I called on corporations for a bold new initiative--"corporate civil disobedience" against the unjust laws of apartheid. I also sent the following letter to the chief executives of signatory companies:

> The purpose of this letter is to inform you of the broadened initiatives I am advocating that Signatory Companies to the Sullivan Principles should take in the light of the unprecedented turmoil in South Africa. My goal since the inception of the Principles has been to assist with the total elimination of South Africa's apartheid system. It is very clear that until the system is actually removed, the crisis in South Africa will worsen. Therefore, this letter is a call for your Company and all other United States Signatory Companies to increase, intensify, and broaden their efforts to maximize their impact in South Africa. I am, therefore, requesting today that each company should individually and collectively work toward the common objectives outlined.

> First, I am stressing that U.S. Signatory Companies continue their present programs in keeping with full adherence to the Sullivan Principles. These programs have demonstrated their value, and the human and financial resources expended on each of these activities should be continued and expanded upon. Special emphasis must be given immediately to increasing the number of blacks in management positions to assure that as quickly as possible there will be appropriate representation of blacks and other nonwhites in the management group of each company at all levels of operations as detailed in Principle Five.

> Second, I am advocating that U.S. Signatory Companies increase their activities in the areas of the Fourth Amplification, which calls for U.S. Signatory Companies individually and collectively to issue public statements opposing the existence of apartheid and calling for its total abolition--including full and equal citizens rights for all blacks, and full

and equal participation of blacks in the political process, and
that you take every possible action to help bring this about.

Third, I am calling upon the Signatory Companies to follow
a stringent course of "corporate civil disobedience," which means
U.S. Signatory Companies should not administer any unjust laws
or discriminatory practices or requirements pertaining to the
apartheid system at any of their company operations.   Also, I
am asking the companies to use their legal and financial
resources to the fullest possible extent, wherever their
companies are located, to assist blacks in the equal use of all
private and public amenities such as parks, beaches, hospitals,
theaters, public transportation, schools, and housing.

I am urging you, as Chief Executive Officer of your
company, which is a Signatory to the Sullivan Principles, to
support these initiatives. The coming year will be a crucial one
for United States' companies and for companies from around the
world that operate in South Africa to do all they can to
contribute to the unequivocal freedom of South Africa's black
population.

Sincerely,

/s/ Leon H. Sullivan

To the amazement of many, several companies immediately began to
take steps in these directions. Some executives of companies had become
"Corporate Freedom Workers."   Indeed, I believe they had become so
emotionally, morally and spiritually involved in the process of justice and
social change that at that time some were prepared, if necessary, to go to
jail for the cause of liberating black South Africans.   Few will ever
believe the depth of commitment of a number of American company
executives who worked assiduously with the Sullivan Principles Movement,
far beyond the expectations of their own corporations.

In the meantime, a black freedom movement was emerging within
South Africa.   At its center were both the African National Congress
(ANC) and the spirit of Nelson Mandela, the most representative and
respected black leader in South Africa. Given continuous pressure by the
ANC, other organizations, and the growing involvement of thousands within
South Africa, both black and white, things were beginning to happen.
Large numbers of teenagers were now actively demonstrating their
willingness to make whatever sacrifices would be necessary for their
freedom.   On one occasion, a fellow member of the Board of General
Motors, now deceased, went to South Africa to observe conditions there.
He had always supported my efforts in general, but had hesitated to
endorse aggressively strong measures, such as "corporate civil disobedience"
and calls for urgent and immediate political change.   Upon his return he
said to me, "Leon, you are right. What black people in South Africa need

is not just fair employment, but 'Freedom.'" And that was what the young people in South Africa were shouting, and singing, and dying for: "Freedom."

That quest is articulated in the Freedom Charter of the ANC, which reads:

> WE, the People of South Africa, declare for all our country and the world to know: that South Africa belongs to all who live in it, Black and White, and that no government can justly claim authority unless it is based on the will of all the people; that our people have been robbed of their birthright to land, liberty and peace by a form of government founded on injustice and inequality; that our country will never be prosperous or free until all our people live in brotherhood, enjoying equal rights and opportunities; that only a democratic state, based on the will of all the people, can secure to all their birthright without distinction of colour, race, sex or belief; And therefore, we, the people of South Africa, Black and White together--equals, countrymen and brothers--adopt this Freedom Charter. And we pledge ourselves to strive together, sparing neither strength nor courage, until the democratic changes here set out have been won.

The freedom movement within the country was joined by many: whites, professors, students and ministers. The struggle had reached a new stage. And I pushed the companies for greater and greater efforts. Also, in the United States the push of such effective efforts as Trans-Africa, which picketed the South African Embassy in Washington, and other anti-apartheid initiatives was taking hold. The pronouncements of courageous black leaders, such as Nobel Laureate Bishop Desmond Tutu, were also enlightening and effective.

However, during the period between January 1983 and January 1985, I had seen the South African government move towards greater recalcitrance, stiffening its opposition to further change. Jailings without trial were increased, thousands of children imprisoned and many dissenters killed. I believed that the time for decisive action was growing short. In my view South Africa was at the crossroads; it could go in the direction either of an independent, free South Africa or violent revolution. Something had to be done to wrench the South African Government out of its intransigence and to bring about full political rights for blacks. I saw that it was time for United States companies to use their ultimate leverage on the South African government for fundamental action.

Therefore, in March 1985 I set a deadline, first published in the Philadelphia Inquirer. I wrote that if in 24 months statutory apartheid had not come to an end, and there was still no clear commitment to the vote for blacks, I would call for two actions: withdrawal of all American companies from South Africa, and a total United States economic embargo against that country. My hope was that other companies and nations would follow.

In the meantime, I worked harder to bring about the changes I espoused, intensifying my efforts worldwide. I invited top leaders of some of the world's largest industrial companies operating in South Africa to secret summit meetings held outside of London. The purpose of the meetings was to discuss initiatives companies could take towards the ending of apartheid. Chairmen and senior officers of companies from the United States, the United Kingdom, Germany, Scandinavia, Canada and France attended. But most important was the presence at all of the meetings of major South African industrial leaders. The discussions were lengthy, enlightening, candid, and stressful.

As a result of these international gatherings, many of the companies agreed to increase their efforts to promote full equality of social and economic opportunity for blacks in South Africa. As of 1986, I could see progress. I received a call from a member of the ruling party in the South African Parliament, asking me to keep the pressure on, because "something is happening." Companies began to move blacks into all-white areas in greater and greater numbers in defiance of apartheid regulations. Companies paid for advertisements calling for total social, economic and political justice and freedom, including equal political participation for blacks in the governmental process. Also, companies called for Nelson Mandela's freedom, and for negotiations between white leaders and acknowledged, representative black leaders. South African business leaders visited ANC representatives in Lusaka, Zambia. There was a small window of hope. Small, yet a glimmer of light. We had hoped the election of May 1987 would be a watershed.

But the South African Government created a climate of fear, danger and panic in the white community; it bombed Mozambique; and it muzzled the press. Trepidation moved through the white community, and this was the environment in which the elections were held. The results were disappointing. The South African Government's campaign of fear had won the day. The moderates and liberals lost seats in the new Parliament, and the reactionaries and supporters of apartheid gained strength.

Still, I remained hopeful. I sought admission to South Africa to learn what black leaders thought about the approaching May 31st deadline and what my next step should be. But my visa was refused.

Nonetheless, even though I was banned from South Africa, the convictions of some of its black leaders were conveyed to me. I was strongly urged to extend my two-year deadline. One such request came from Chief Minister Mangosuthu G. Buthelezi, traditional leader of 5 million Zulus, and a man I greatly respect. In a letter dated May 8th, he wrote, in part:

> We know how long and hard the road has been in our struggle[;] . . . we do not know how long and hard that road will yet be. All we know is that we walk it and that we have no option but to continue walking it. When we meet intransigence, . . . racism[,] and . . . the terrible poverty that we as the dispossessed of South Africa suffer, we can neither

turn left nor right nor can we go backwards. We must . . . forge forward with everything we have got, or die where we stand. I ask you as a Christian brother to continue reaching out your hand of friendship by struggling with us.

. . . . When I think back on some of the things you have said when talking about South Africa, I remember that you . . . oppose violence. . . . [We therefore] appeal to your deep commitments when we ask you to face the challenge of remaining in staunch support with those of us who struggle to establish radical changes in South Africa through non-violen[t] tactics and strategies.

. . . . If you now join in with the international clamor for the punitive isolation of South Africa, you will be joining with others who do not intend standing with the poorest of the poor who are the victims of apartheid. The punitive isolation of South Africa is a punitive isolation of the Black forces of democracy. Isolation severs our lifelines to major influences which should be flowing into the South African situation from abroad. Please hear me when I say that the way forward is not through confrontation. The punitive isolation of South Africa makes the State President, Mr. P.W. Botha, step into the arena where he is . . . the most resilient. Those who want to bring about the downfall through violence attack . . . Botha where he is the strongest. [He] must be attacked where he is the weakest, and he is the weakest in his stated commitment to reform and his actual inability . . . to lead South Africa toward reform.

. . . . I am talking about reforms which are radical and [which ultimately] will . . . [re-write] our constitution to make South Africa an open, just society. . . .

That kind of reform, Chief Buthelezi continued, can only result from the politics of negotiation, and he asked me to continue working towards that end. Violence, he said, will not lead to justice and to an improvement in the standard of living for the poor. He argued that "the punitive isolation of South Africa favors the forces of violence. . . ." In his view, "those forces know that punitive isolation increases the prospect of a bloody revolution . . . dictating the course of events in South Africa." Therefore, he urged me to oppose violence, saying

I am writing to you [just] as the cause of non-violent change in South Africa has . . . received a foul body blow. The election . . . of May 6th produced evidence of a substantial swing to the right by white South Africa. The forces of violence will crow the old refrain: "I told you so." They will cite the election results as evidence that apartheid cannot be reformed. . . . Of course apartheid cannot be reformed. It must be eradicated, but [it] . . . can be eradicated through the politics of negotiation.

There is now more urgent reason than . . . ever . . . for your continued involvement in the South African situation. We are faced with having to scrap the . . . constitution itself and of having to rewrite it. We need the building blocks of a new society, and if the South African economy is destroyed with apartheid, we will have to attempt to build on the quicksands of deepening poverty. Everywhere in the Third World, political victories which have been followed by deepening poverty have not led to decent democracies. We are striving to take our rightful place in the government of our own country.   . . . [W]hen we do so, I would not like to have to build a new South Africa on the quicksands of poverty.

In addition to Chief Buthelezi's appeal, I also received petitions signed by 20,000 black South African workers, urging me to continue the Sullivan program. I pondered the situation, but after much prayer and thought I decided the time had come for the maximum utilization of social, political and corporate force against the evils of apartheid. A line had to be drawn. Statutory apartheid had to be ended. Something decisive had to be done--something with the greatest economic implications.

To my mind, America had to take the lead. Therefore, on June 3rd, I returned full circle to June 1, 1971. After having met first with the leaders of the 200 American companies who comprised the Sullivan Principles corporation, I publicly announced my new position on South Africa. I said:

I have assessed, to the best of my ability, the situation as it now exists in the Republic of South Africa, and have decided that the time has come for American companies, and the United States of America, to take a definitive stand against the evils of apartheid. [The conditions of my May deadline have not been remotely met.]

Therefore, today, I am calling for the withdrawal of all United States companies from the Republic of South Africa, and for a total United States embargo against that country, until statutory apartheid is ended, and blacks have a clear commitment from the South African Government for equal political rights. I am also calling on the President of the United States to end diplomatic relations with South Africa until the atrocities against black people end, and apartheid is dismantled. . . .

This action of mine comes after years of effort, through the Sullivan Principles . . . and other thrusts, to help bring about fundamental change in South Africa. I am proud of the effect of those Principles, and proud of the efforts of the companies that have followed them. The Principles . . . broke new ground for black rights that had not existed in South Africa for 300 years, bringing about a revolution in industrial race relations.

In recent years, as the Principles have evolved, some United States companies have begun to challenge the apartheid system itself, and have begun to practice "corporate civil disobedience" against apartheid practices, regulations and laws. Many United States companies engaging in this effort have left a notable record in corporate social responsibility in South Africa. Whatever happens in the future, the work of those companies to change conditions for blacks has been outstanding.

Yet in spite of these and other efforts, the main pillars of apartheid remain. Blacks are still denied simple basic human rights in their own country, and are still deprived of the right to vote. Regardless of appeals, protests and cries for change and justice within South Africa, repression grows. Dissent is ruthlessly suppressed. Thousands are jailed without trial, including little children; people are beaten, brutalized and killed; and the press is muzzled. Intransigence against fundamental change continues, and, today, the government pushes back even minimal progress and reform. South Africa has become a police state.

There is no greater moral issue in the world today than apartheid! Somewhere, somehow, it must be said as loudly, as clearly, and as firmly as possible that what is happening in South Africa to black people is immoral. It must be brought to an end. Not ten years from now, or five years from now, or three years from now, but now.

The winds of change have reached South Africa, and they will not be subdued until the people have no less than their full economic, social, and political freedom. And violently or nonviolently black people in South Africa are going to have it. And nothing but the elimination of apartheid, which is the root cause of the nation's problems, will end the rising surge of the people's aspirations for their freedom and for justice in South Africa.

IV

The ethical and moral influence of multinational companies is being tested in South Africa. That test will have broad implications regarding the role that the companies of America and other nations should play in helping to ameliorate the deep social problems facing the poor and disadvantaged of the countries within which the companies operate. I believe the latter's role is critical, not only for the sake of justice, but also for the survival of free enterprise. On September 4, 1980, I delivered the Hoernle Memorial Lecture at the University of Witwatersrand in Johannesburg, and said:

Recent developments have demonstrated to all that rising tides of discontent among the disadvantaged can change the course and the character of economic, social and political systems. Historically, we know the revolutions that have shaken the world have come from lack of economic and political equality for the masses, and lack of justice for the disadvantaged.

The free enterprise system and multinational corporations historically have been unresponsive to the needs of the poor, and, for the most part, they are still so today. They have disregarded human and social needs in the communities and environments where their plants and businesses exist. In fact, many companies have added to the pain and inequities . . . [endured by] the workers and the people. The great majority of the companies have been more interested in the bottom line than in helping people out of bread lines.

Within third world nations, the free enterprise system and multinational companies are regarded as enemies of the people, and obstacles to social and economic progress. This need not be the case. The multinationals have the resources and capabilities to improve the quality of life for millions of people, and to play a vital role in upgrading the social and economic lives of individuals. This is what western multinational companies, and American companies in particular, must quickly learn. This view is not generally accepted. A number of years ago, the following editorial appeared in one of the great American financial journals:

It seems to us that the policy of American businesses makes little difference in South Africa, one way or another. . . . Most United States businesses in South Africa are expounding the sensible view that we provide goods and services to our customers, and profits to our investors; we obey the local laws and try not to do anything beastly. . . . Politics is the politician's business.

I believe that many American companies operating in South Africa now have a different view. Nonetheless, in most parts of the world the belief prevails that business is in business for business' sake. That belief must be dispelled everywhere. While it once might have been considered sensible policy to provide "goods and services to customers and profits to investors" without any consideration for the societies within which those goods and services are produced, that is no longer so. Observing local laws and trying not to do anything beastly is for a day long gone. Today, morals and ethics had better be the concern of the companies if they expect free enterprise to survive.

We must not continue, as many do, to blame the Communists for unstable conditions and social unrest in the world. The greatest enemy of capitalism is not communism, but the selfishness and the lack of humanity of capitalism itself. Western enterprise must go on the ethical offensive.

Companies must learn to leave something in the countries where they operate, rather than taking everything out of them.

South Africa itself is at the crossroads. It can follow the path of a unified, free country; or it can take the route of chaotic revolution, which would result in the killing of millions of people, the destruction of the country, and the devastation of the entire southern region of Africa. This, in turn, could lead to a confrontation between the world's great nuclear powers, as a race war at that strategic point of the world would certainly become an ideological war. If the United States were to become involved in such a war, race riots far worse than anything ever seen in the history of America would break out in every major city in our own country.

Thus, it is in the interest of peace in South Africa, in the world and in America that apartheid be ended. Its evils go beyond South Africa. Apartheid is against the will of God and the humanity of man; like Nazism and Fascism, it must be stopped. America and the world must draw a line, and speak out, and act against it. If the world had stopped Hitler in time, we might not have had World War II.

It is clear the South African Government does not intend to end apartheid on its own. Since the recent elections, that Government has become more defiant to further change. Therefore, something must be done now to dramatize the issue before America and the world. Every moral, economic, and political force must be brought to bear to help influence the South African Government to move towards dismantling the apartheid system, while there is still time. In this regard, America, including our companies and our government, as the leader of the free world, should set the example for others.

Therefore, I again call on all American companies to withdraw from the Republic of South Africa, until statutory apartheid has been abolished, and there is a clear commitment to the vote for blacks, in accordance with agreements reached with authentically representative black South African leaders.

Also, I call on the United States Government to enact, with urgency, a total United States economic embargo against South Africa. We should seek vitally needed materials elsewhere; or seek alternatives; or stockpile; or recycle; or do without.

I further call on the Congress to consider stringent penalties against trading partners of the United States who assume markets left by departing companies, and who continue to do business in South Africa, such as the Japanese. I also call on the President of the United States to break diplomatic relations with South Africa, until atrocities against black people end and apartheid is dismantled. The only exceptions to this call for withdrawal are philanthropic and educational initiatives and the media.

Should, at anytime, the South African government abolish statutory apartheid and commit full political rights to blacks, restrictions against

American companies operating in South Africa should be lifted; American companies should be free to return to that country; and unlimited United States investments in a unitary, free South Africa should be permitted.

V

This is my message to the companies of America, to the Congress and the President of the United States, and to the Government of South Africa. Now, I await the results of my actions. Already several companies have made their decision to leave South Africa, albeit many with inadequate methods to meet the guidelines appearing as an appendix to this article. Nevertheless, the withdrawal of American companies has begun, and by March of 1988, that movement could become a flood.

The Sullivan Principles have already had a powerful effect in South Africa, particularly on the lives of black workers, and I believe my call for withdrawal of companies will be even a greater force for change in years to come. I also believe that one day the equal rights principles will be adopted and utilized to promote equity and better opportunities for workers, especially in developing nations around the earth. Indeed, something like this is needed, and must be done if Free Enterprise is to survive in the Third World.

APPENDIX I

SOME GUIDELINES FOR COMPANY WITHDRAWAL
FROM SOUTH AFRICA

- Companies should begin the process of withdrawal immediately.

- Withdrawal should be completed within a nine-month period.

- Companies should sell their businesses only to buyers who agree to promote: equal rights for blacks, black labor representation, and company ownership plans making possible road black participation.

- Companies should end all business relationships with buyers of South African products and services including: logo, trademarks, components, materials, consulting services, and other supporting contracts. Excluded from the foregoing are products and services of undeniably black-owned and initiated businesses.

- Emergency medical supply needs should be dispensed through recognized world humanitarian organizations.

- Companies should favorably consider relocating in neighboring nations (such as: Botswana, Lesotho, Mozambique, Swaziland, Zambia, or Zimbabwe) thereby helping strengthen regional and local economies with industrial development, growth and jobs.

- Individual and institutional stockholders, including pension funds, unions, churches, universities, and other fiduciaries, are asked to support this call for withdrawal by selling their holdings in non-cooperating companies, or by voting for disinvestment stockholder resolutions.

- Government bodies at all levels are asked to support this call through disapproval of purchase agreements or contracts for goods or services with companies choosing to remain in South Africa, as well as through the sale of investments or securities held in those companies.

APPENDIX II

After the Statement on June 4, the reactions from South Africa were immediate.

(From) DIE BURGER Newspaper

American Contradictions

The latest pleas by the Reverend Leon Sullivan, pioneer of the anti-apartheid code for American businessmen in South Africa, is symptomatic of American contradictions, arrogance and naivety concerning South Africa generally.

After stipulating a strict code to which American businessmen in South Africa had to adhere to ensure their black workers were treated well, he now demands that all American business be withdrawn from South Africa within the following nine months.

He intends chastising South Africa with this step because the Government did not heed his ultimatum to eliminate "apartheid" within a period of two years. It does not seem to bother him that bread can be taken from the mouths of the very same Black workers and their families whom he ostensibly wants to help if his plan is implemented successfully.

This counter-productive approach is also characteristic of American foreign policy generally but against South Africa specifically.

One of the reasons for this is that the USA does not have a strong government which can lay down policy and implement it. Many parties play a role in the determination of foreign policy and hence undermine the authority of the strongest Western power.

Although President Ronald Reagan was re-elected with a very large majority, he could not stop completely the economic sanctions imposed by the American Congress on South Africa. He has been discredited further by the Irangate affair and the Tower Commission's findings concerning him and his administration's handling of the scandal.

South Africa has in many respects become an extension of American domestic politics. Foreign policy is, therefore, also influenced by all kinds of pressure groups and civil rights activists.

The Reverend Sullivan's warning should be seen in the light that the USA will be ravaged by unprecedented disorder if a racial war were to break out in South Africa and America were to find itself on the "wrong side."

If Americans continue in this vein their influence in Southern Africa will diminish continuously. The recipe they are now following is how to make enemies and antagonise everybody.

Cape Town   A - June 5

THE STAR Newspaper

Pressure Burst

The philosophy behind the Sullivan Code must continue to influence business practice in South Africa, even though its author, the Rev. Leon Sullivan, has lost hope. He has now abandoned the code as a tool in favour of more extreme pressure-economic withdrawal.

Mr. Sullivan's withdrawal call has received a mixed reception. Though sanctions supporters will welcome his weight, there is also disenchantment with the sanctions campaign - especially since the recent white elections served to prove sanctions helped strengthen the white backlash against reform.

The Sullivan Code has meant a great deal to South Africa in the years it has operated, by promoting fair employment practices. It has undoubtedly set standards for American firms, influenced the attitudes of European trading partners who have similar standards, and has been an example for local firms.

It would be a bitter irony if, after raising the living standards of black workers significantly through his code, Mr. Sullivan should in any way now be instrumental in causing their unemployment.

Johannesburg   E - June 5

THE ARGUS Newspaper

The American Crusade Gathers Steam Again

America's enormous power, coupled with a high indignation factor and a looming Presidential election campaign, spells a rough ride for South Africa over the coming year and more.

The US decision to revoke the double tax agreement with South Africa and the Rev. Leon Sullivan's call on American business to pull out from here altogether (Mr. Sullivan is clearly finely tuned to the way the political winds blow in Washington) are powerful early warnings.

"The Lord is with me on this one," says Mr. Sullivan referring to his call for sanctions against South Africa - which would put South Africa in the same situation vis-a-vis Washington as Vietnam, Libya, Cuba and Kampuchea. The quote strikes to the core of the problem with the Americans. Thanks to apartheid, denouncing South Africa is safe for any politician. Actions against this country take on the warm glow of a crusade. Anti-South African activists in the United States occupy the high moral ground and it is more than any politician's reputation is worth to gainsay that.

None of this, of course, takes much cognisance of the realities inside South Africa - a fundamental one being that purposeful reform has more of a chance of flowing from a healthy economy than a struggling one. Punitive action such as that advocated by Mr. Sullivan and others leave[s] workers with little influence - not to mention fewer jobs and domestic security - in a struggling economy.

Cape Town   E - June 5

BIBLIOGRAPHY

"The African Homelands of South Africa." Johannesburg: Institute of Race Relations, 1973.

Davidson, Basil. Africa. New York: MacMillan, 1972.

Cross Currents 28 (1978-79): 385-402.

DeGrunchy, John W. The Church Struggle in South Africa. Grand Rapids, MI: Eerdman's Publishing, April 1979.

Freedomways. First Quarter (1980): 5-6.

Hoagland, Jim. South Africa Civilizations in Conflict. Boston: Houghton Mifflin, 1972.

Kahn, E. J., Jr. The Separated People. New York: W. W. Norton, 1968.

Sullivan, Leon.   Report of the Special Committee Against Apartheid. General Assembly 42nd Session Supplement No. 22, United Nations, New York, 1987, pp. 18-45.

_____.   Ninth Report, Signatory Companies, Sullivan Principles. Cambridge, MA: Arthur D. Little Co., October 25, 1985.

_____.   Eighth Report, Signatory Companies, Sullivan Principles. Cambridge, MA: Arthur D. Little Co., October 25, 1984.

_____.   Third Report, Signatory Companies, Sullivan Principles. Cambridge, MA: Arthur D. Little Co., October 15, 1979.

_____.   Second Report, Signatory Companies, Sullivan Principles. Cambridge, MA: Arthur D. Little Co., April 2, 1979.

_____.   South African Institute of Race Relations: Full Report. 1978-1979.

_____.   First Report, Signatory Companies, Sullivan Principles. Cambridge, MA: Arthur D. Little Co., November 17, 1978.

_____. Alternatives to Despair. Valley Forge, PA: Judson Press, 1972.

_____. "Legislation and Race Relations." Johannesburg: South African Institute of Race Relations, 1971.

_____. Build Brother Build. Philadelphia: Macrae Smith, 1969.

West, Martin, and Jean Morris.   Abantu.   London and Capetown, South Africa: C. Struik, 1976.

U.S. NATIONAL INTERESTS AND NATIONAL STRATEGY: ARE THERE PARALLELS WITH U.S. INTERNATIONAL CORPORATE INTERESTS?

by Donald E. Nuechterlein

The term "national interest" is as old as the nation-state, and the concept has conditioned the way governments have formulated foreign policies for more than three hundred years. For an even longer span of time, international commerce and business interests have been a driving force in international relations--since trading ships and caravans set out from Europe and Asia in search of markets and foreign goods. The degree of interrelationship between national interests and business interests in the conduct of a state's foreign policy has varied over time and from state to state, depending on the extent to which governments of sovereign states were willing to use military power to support the overseas commercial interests of their citizens. Of the major free-enterprise countries today, the United States probably exhibits less cooperation between government and home-based international corporations than does Britain, France, West Germany, Japan, or Canada. A question thus posed is whether it is desirable for American corporations and the U.S. Government to seek greater cooperation in the 1990s in pursuing their international interests.

This paper outlines a conceptual framework for defining United States national interests in the current and future international environment, including U.S. international economic interests. This framework suggests that U.S. policymakers should, before they decide on a particular course of action in foreign policy, consider the importance of four basic national interests of the United States--those which undergird all of its foreign and national security policies--and then assess the intensity of these basic interests in a specific foreign policy issue or crisis. A parallel framework is proposed to assist major American corporations in defining their international business interests, including a calculation of U.S. government objectives and policies. To demonstrate how these concepts of national and corporate interests complement each other, the People's Republic of China is used as an example to show where U.S. corporations and the U.S. Government probably have parallel interests. China is but the most recent case, however, of how government and business may significantly advance their respective interests through consultation and active cooperation.

I

HISTORICAL INTERESTS OF THE UNITED STATES

Throughout its history, the United States has had four enduring national interests which condition the way our government views the external world and this country's place in it. They are: (1) defense of the U.S. homeland, including our consitutional system of government; (2) enhancement of the U.S. economic well-being; (3) creation of a favorable international environment, or world order; and (4) promotion abroad of a set of core values which reflect this country's political heritage.[1] It should be noted that most defense pacts concluded by the United States since World War II were a part of its world-order interest and that most military interventions initiated by various presidents since 1945 were done in the name of international security. Throughout our history, these four basic interests have competed for primacy in U.S. foreign policy, although the defense-of-homeland interest has not been seriously tested since the War of 1812. The U.S. economic well-being interest was the most important one during the 19th century and has largely been taken for granted since World War II. Creation of a new world order, one that is favorable to the United States, has dominated U.S. foreign policy since 1945. Promotion of American values abroad was largely neglected for much of the postwar period until Congress mandated in the 1970s that human rights be accorded a higher priority in the formulation and conduct of foreign policy.

From the War of 1812 until the Second World War, the United States was never threatened in its homeland by any outside power. Therefore, it was able to concentrate its energies during the 19th century on building an industrial and commercial base at home and enhancing its economic interests abroad.[2] During this 125-year period, U.S. policy also reflected the fourth basic interest--promotion of the American concept of democracy, with its emphasis on individual rights and limited government. For most of the 19th century, U.S. business interests abroad were enhanced by the international policeman's role exercised by Great Britain through the presence of the Royal Navy.

At the close of the 19th century, Britain suggested to the McKinley Administration that it was time for the rich United States to accept a more active role in maintaining international order, one that would also be congenial to the promotion of U.S. business interests abroad. Britain's world dominance was being challenged by Imperial Germany and Japan-- particularly in East Asia, and by 1898 London sought to reduce the cost of its worldwide commitments. This coincided with the American business community's desire to encourage the United States to play a larger political role in the Caribbean and the Pacific. The first power thrust in this direction followed the short war with Spain in 1898 during which U.S. forces seized Cuba and Puerto Rico in the Caribbean and the Philippines and Guam in the Pacific. Within a year, the United States had become a major Pacific power and it also dominated the Caribbean Basin area. The next step was to build a canal across Central America to facilitate international commerce.

After being rebuffed by Colombia in 1903 over his plan to build a canal running through Panama, President Theodore Roosevelt assisted Panama to gain its independence from Colombia and then concluded a treaty with the new state giving the United States authority to build and run a canal there "in perpetuity." These actions served both U.S. strategic interests and the objectives of U.S. business which desired U.S. government political support for its growing investments in Central America, the Caribbean area and in the Philippines. American business also showed an interest in expanding its commercial relations with China, and Secretary of State John Hay then issued his "Open Door" policy of permitting all nations to trade in China during that country's political disintegration at the turn of the century. In sum, by 1905 the United States was a world power with expanding investments and commercial interests in Asia as well as in Latin America. It also appeared that this country was on the way to replacing Britain as the preeminent power in the Western Pacific.

By 1909, a strong anti-imperialist and isolationist public reaction had set in. Except for the period 1917-19, an introspective outlook then dominated U.S. foreign policy--until the outbreak of war with Japan in 1941. This narrow view of U.S. national interests reflected the sentiments of millions of recent European immigrants who wished to escape Europe's power struggles and frequent wars. It also reflected general concern that the country might jeopardize its booming economic expansion if it engaged in great power politics.[3]

The test came in 1914 when war engulfed Europe. The internationalists, led by former President Theodore Roosevelt, asserted that the United States had a vital interest in seeing that Britain and France did not lose the war to Germany and thereby upset the European and world balance of power. American big business sided with the Allied Powers when it became apparent that its interests and the world economy might be adversely affected by a German victory. The isolationists had powerful representation in Congress as well as in Secretary of State, William Jennings Bryan. However, Bryan resigned in 1915 because he believed President Woodrow Wilson was moving away from strict neutrality in the war. After the resumption of German submarine attacks on American ships in 1917, the internationalists finally persuaded President Wilson that the only way to prevent a German victory over the exhausted Allies was for the United States to enter the war. Although the conflict ended in an Allied victory, it became clear by 1919 that American internationalists had won only a temporary victory over the isolationists in defining U.S. national interests in the postwar period.

The Senate's defeat of President Wilson's cherished League of Nations and the disillusionment felt in the country over the cost of the war resulted in another twenty years of isolationism. It was a period during which economic nationalism reigned in the United States; defense-of-homeland interests were taken for granted; the promotion of American values abroad was neglected; and concern for the balance of power in Europe and Asia was nearly non-existent. Only in Central America and parts of South America did the American people see vital interests at stake, and U.S. forces intervened there and in the Caribbean to insure that U.S. economic and world-order interests were protected. During the 1930s, few members of Congress showed any concern over the rise of totalitarianism in Germany, Italy and Japan, and President Franklin Roosevelt could not arouse the public until France fell to German armies in June 1940. Even then the President had great difficulty persuading Congress that the United States had a vital interest in helping Great Britain to resist the expected German invasion, even though the U.S. business community by then strongly supported the Lend-Lease program.

The Japanese attack on Pearl Harbor shocked Americans out of their complacency and fundamentally changed the way we looked at U.S. national interests. After 1945 it was no longer believed to be sufficient that the country's security interests stopped at the Atlantic and Pacific shores. Total war in Europe and Asia and the rise of postwar Soviet power convinced the public that the United States had vital world-order interests in Western Europe and the Mediterranean, the islands off the East Asian mainland, and in the whole of South America. The inheritors of Theodore Roosevelt's view of America's world-order interests, however, went even beyond this: they argued that U.S. military power and economic supremacy mandated that the United States take up the world policeman's role being relinquished by Great Britain and become involved in any part of the world where the Soviet Union was challenging Western interests, including Western colonial interests in East Asia, the Middle East and Africa. Consequently, during the late 1940s and early 1950s alliances were made with more than forty countries in every part of the world in the name of "containment" of Soviet and Chinese communism.[4] American military power was greatly expanded after the Korean War began in 1950 in order to support this global view of U.S. interests, and American private investment and trade expanded into many new areas. On the other hand, promotion of American values in foreign policy was all but ignored in the 1950s as anti-communism became the new American ideology. Defense alliances and executive agreements were made with many countries that were headed by anti-communist dictatorships because containment was seen as being more important then promoting democracy and individual freedom in allied countries.

The Vietnam War marked the zenith of American globalism in foreign policy, as the public and Congress came to understand the costs that are entailed in exercising a world policeman's role. Since 1969, four presidents (Nixon, Ford, Carter and Reagan) have been cautious about introducing combat forces into world trouble areas in defense of U.S. world-order interests or anti-communism. In 1981, the Reagan Administration heralded its determination to restore American prestige in the world, following the humiliating Iran hostage crisis and Soviet encroachments in Central America, southern Africa and its invasion of Afghanistan. Nevertheless, during seven years in office, Mr. Reagan has shown considerable caution about the actual use of American combat forces in foreign conflicts. The invasion of Grenada in 1983 was an exception and lasted a few months. Withdrawal of 1,500 Marines from Lebanon in 1984, signalled the President's unwillingness to send a much larger force into that divided country without having a clear notion about what the end result would be. Reinforcement of U.S. naval forces in the Persian Gulf during 1987 and their limited confrontation with Iranian ships demonstrated restraint rather than belligerence on Washington's part. In sum, the legacy of Vietnam remains strong in the United States, and the struggle between the globalist viewpoint and the more restricted view of U.S. national interests persists into the late 1980s.

II

A NATIONAL INTEREST APPROACH TO FOREIGN POLICY
DECISION MAKING

When assessing the degree of national interest or stake that the
United States has in a specific international issue or crisis, a U.S.
policymaker may employ the interest matrix shown in Figure 1 as a guide
in making wise policy choices in a systematic manner. It does not, of
course, insure that the "right" answer will be found because key foreign
policy decisions result from subjective judgments made by political leaders
on the basis of differing perceptions of reality. Nevertheless, the value of
the national interest approach to decision making is that it forces
policymakers to think through carefully the criteria which should be taken
into account before an interest is determined to be "vital"--one that is so
important that it may require the use of armed force to defend it. The
four basic national interests described above are shown in Figure 1 on the
vertical plane, and the four degrees or intensities of interest (stake) are
shown on the horizontal plane.[5]

Figure 1

NATIONAL INTEREST MATRIX

Basic National Interests	Intensity of Interests			
	Survival (critical)	Vital (dangerous)	Major (serious)	Peripheral (bothersome)
Defense of Homeland				
Economic Well-being				
Favorable World Order				
Promotion of Values				

The task of the policymaker is to decide which basic interests are at stake
in a specific international dispute or crisis and then assess their intensity,
ranging from "survival" to "peripheral" as shown above. Although the four
basic interests--defense, economic, world order and promotion of values--
are not listed in any priority order, the defense-of-homeland interest is
the most fundamental one. This is so because a country's inability to
defend its territory and political system, either through its own strength
or in alliance with other powers, will likely result in its loss of
independence and render the other three basic interests unachievable. In
the classical sense, therefore, defense of national sovereignty is the
overriding national interest of a state.

In terms of intensities of interest, one at the "survival" level would be an immediate, credible threat of massive destruction on the territory of the United States, or a civil war supported by external forces. For strategic reasons, Canadian territory is part of the U.S. defense-of-homeland interest, and an attack on Canada would be viewed by the United States as a survival (critical) threat. Many strategic planners believe that Mexico's territory is a survival U.S. interest because that country is critical to the defense of the western United States. Survival interests usually apply only to the defense-of-homeland category because they pose immediate, credible military threats to the United States and urgently require decisions by the President. The Cuban Missile Crisis in 1962 is the only recent example of a crisis in which the United states approached this level of interest.

Vital interests involve dangerous (not critical) issues affecting not only defense of U.S. territory but other basic interests as well. These include dangerous trends or threats to allies of the United States (world order), international threats to U.S. economic stability (economic well-being), and a threat to the overthrow of a democratic allied government (promotion of values). Vital interests also include considerations of strategic balance of power between the United States and the Soviet Union because serious changes in this military equation may adversely affect the United States' ability to protect itself and its allies. Vital interests differ from survival ones in the degree of danger posed to U.S. territory, and they usually provide policymakers more time than do survival threats to work out appropriate policy responses. Vital interests differ from "major" ones primarily in terms of whether the issue lends itself to negotiations, or whether the stake is so high that it cannot be negotiated. If an international dispute becomes intolerable and officials conclude that U.S. policy should not be compromised further, the issue is at the vital level and may require strong action--including the limited use of economic and/or military force--to persuade the adversary to change an unacceptable policy. U.S. air strikes against Libyan cities in 1986 and the U.S. naval buildup in the Persian Gulf in 1987 are examples of the President's determining that vital U.S. world-order interests were at stake and his decision to use force to deal with the threat. The double line shown in Figure 1 between "vital" and "major" interests suggests that most of the difficult decisions in U.S. foreign policy and national security affairs are about whether the United States should negotiate further or risk the use of force.

Major interests involve either threats to basic U.S. interests or opportunities to enhance them. They differ from vital ones in that they usually are subject to lengthy negotiations and produce compromise solutions rather than armed confrontations. They involve serious matters relating to defense-of-homeland, economic well-being, world order and promotion of core values; but they do not generally lead to economic and military confrontations because the parties either see important mutual advantages to be gained through bargaining or they are not prepared to let issues escalate to the vital level and risk a break in relations or the use of force. Major interests clearly do justify the use of economic and political pressures, however, and occasionally even a show of military force. Examples of major U.S. interests are trade disputes with Japan, ideological issues with South Africa over its apartheid system, and security issues with New Zealand involving visits of U.S. Navy ships. Nicaragua's internal and external policies are on the borderline between a major and vital world-order interest because a majority in Congress believes negotiation with the Sandinista regime is preferable to an armed confrontation.

Peripheral interests generally are associated with private U.S. citizens and institutions operating or residing outside the United States. American tourists are in this category. American businesses operating abroad usually are a peripheral interest except when there is infringement on or expropriation of U.S. private property. Other exceptions are the detention of U.S. citizens without legal charges and significant discrimination against U.S. products by another country. These issues are treated as major level interests. Detention of a U.S. citizen abroad on drug charges would be a peripheral interest, but hostage-taking is clearly a major interest and can escalate to the vital level, as Washington's reaction to the terrorist attack on the cruise ship Achille Lauro in 1985 illustrated.

Most national security issues debated by a president and his National Security Council entail decisions on whether a threat is a major or vital national interest, particularly if a potential crisis may become intolerable and open the possibility of using military force. To make that judgment, policy planners in the White House, the State and Defense Departments, the Central Intelligence Agency, and occasionally the Treasury Department, need to take account of both the values and the cost/risk considerations which would apply if there is a possibility that strong action may be required. Figure 2 suggests sixteen criteria that should be assessed, eight

Figure 2

CRITERIA FOR DETERMINING VITAL INTERESTS

Value Factors	Cost/Risk Factors
Proximity of the Danger	Economic Costs of Hostilities
Nature of the Threat	Estimated Casualties
Economic Stake for the US	Risk of Enlarged Conflict
Sentimental Attachment	Cost of Protracted Conflict
Type of Government	Cost of Defeat or Stalemate
Effect on Balance of Power	Risk of US Public Opposition
National Prestige at Stake	Risk of Congressional Opposition
Support of Allies	Risk of International Opposition

of them being key value factors and eight others dealing with the costs and risks that will be involved if military forces are employed.

If a planner calculates the value side to be high and potential costs to be medium or low, the issue at hand is likely to be put into the vital category. On the other hand, if costs/risks are considered to be high and the values to be achieved are moderate, it is likely that the issue in question is at the major interest level. In that case, negotiations rather than confrontation will be seen as a wise policy. Presidents and cabinet members may not consider all of these factors or assess them in a systematic manner, but a policy planner should never recommend the potential use of force to influence the outcome of an international dispute without carefully calculating whether this action is likely to achieve the desired result and at reasonable cost. What is suggested here is that much discussion should be given to the cost and risk criteria so that miscalculations, such as the U.S. intervention in Vietnam in 1965 and in Lebanon in 1982 will not recur and bring humiliation to the United States due to costs turning out to be much higher than anticipated. If policymakers calculate the values/costs equation with reasonable accuracy, more international issues affecting the United States are likely to be assessed as major rather than vital interests, and diplomacy rather than military force will more often be used to attempt to achieve a solution.

After a calculation is made that an important interest is major, vital, or bordering on the survival level, a policymaker should then consider the question of which instruments of foreign and national security policy are appropriate in dealing with the specific case. Figure 3 lists twenty U.S. policy instruments which are available to influence the outcome of an international dispute. The first eleven are political/economic tools, and the last nine are political/military ones. They are listed here in ascending order of influence and/or pressure that a president may bring to bear on another country to persuade it to accept the U.S. position.[6]

The use of any of these twenty policy tools should be proportionate to the level of interest the United States has in a specific international issue. It is not appropriate, for example, to threaten to use military force to settle an economic dispute, such as Cuba's expropriation of U.S. private property in 1959-60. On the other hand, it was clearly appropriate for President John Kennedy to threaten an invasion of Cuba, even the use of nuclear weapons, during the Cuban Missile Crisis in 1962 because a survival defense-of-homeland interest was perceived to be at stake. If an issue is determined to be a vital national interest, conventional military forces may be used if political, economic and covert pressures are unsuccessful in bringing about a desired solution. Strategic forces--those employing massive destruction weapons--should not be employed unless the level of interest is at or near the survival level, involving an imminent attack on the United States, because use of these weapons would likely lead to nuclear retaliation. Such a threat should never be made except to deter an enemy from launching an invasion or nuclear attack.

Figure 3

INSTRUMENTS OF FOREIGN AND NATIONAL SECURITY POLICY

POLITICAL/ECONOMIC ACTIONS

1. Diplomatic Relations

2. Scientific and Cultural Exchanges

3. Humanitarian Assistance

4. Technical Assistance

5. Information and Propaganda

6. Economic and Financial Assistance

7. Economic and Trade Policy

8. Military Assistance

9. Covert Actions

10. United Nations Security Council Debate

11. Trade Embargo and Economic Sanctions

POLITICAL/MILITARY ACTIONS

12. Military Show of Force

13. Increased Military Surveillance

14. Suspension of/Break in Diplomatic Relations

15. Quarantine/Blockade/Mining of Ports

16. Local Use of Conventional Forces

17. Mobilization/Evacuation

18. Local Use of Tactical Nuclear Weapons

19. Threatened Use of Massive Destruction Weapons

20. Limited Use of Massive Destruction Weapons

III

CASES TO ILLUSTRATE USE OF THE INTEREST MATRIX

The national interest matrix may be employed in foreign policy decision making to assess the intensity of U.S. interests in any international issue or crisis. In addition, it may be used to calculate the national interests of other principal countries involved in the crisis and thus help the policymaker to judge whether any other country is likely to go to war rather than negotiate a settlement. If two principal parties to a dispute have vital national interests at stake, the likelihood of armed conflict will be present because neither side is willing to negotiate beyond a tolerable level for itself and may use force to achieve its goals if other measures fail. Figure 4 employs the interest matrix to assess the stakes of four countries which had important interests in the Falkland Islands (Malvinas) conflict. When Great Britain and Argentina were unable to resolve their differences through negotiations, Argentina decided in March 1982 to use force to achieve its objectives and Britain then went to war to retake the Falklands.

Figure 4

THE FALKLAND ISLANDS WAR - 1982

Basic National Interests   Intensity of Interests

Basic National Interests	Survival (critical)	Vital (dangerous)	Major (serious)	Peripheral (bothersome)
Defense of Homeland		Argentina	Gr. Britain	US Venezuela
Economic Well-being			Gr. Britain US	Argentina Venezuela
Favorable World Order		Gr. Britain US	Argentina Venezuela	
Promotion of Values		Gr. Britain Argentina	US Venezuela	

This analysis of the interests of Argentina, Great Britain, the United States and Venezuela (a strong Latin American supporter of Argentina in the dispute) reflects the deep intensity of national interests of the two principal antagonists, Britain and Argentina. The British government viewed the Falkland Islands as having been its sovereign territory for 150 years, and Prime Minister Margaret Thatcher was not prepared to accept Argentina's decision to take the islands by force. The Argentine government argued that the Malvinas had been seized by Britain in the

19th Century, and it therefore was able to arouse nationalist sentiment at home to take the islands by force after Britain refused to negotiate a peaceful transfer of sovereignty. The United States tried earnestly to avoid having to choose sides in this struggle between two of its allies; but when it became clear that Britain would fight to retake the territory, Washington decided that it had a vital U.S. interest in supporting Britain and it therefore gave London material as well as diplomatic support. The result of this short war was that British forces retook the Falkland Islands, the military regime in Argentina was ousted, and a consitutional government then came to power in Buenos Aires.   Some Argentine observers believe that their country owes its democracy to Margaret Thatcher who stood up to Argentina's military junta and won.

Another example was the U.S. decision to bomb Libyan cities in April 1986, following a series of Libyan-sponsored terrorist attacks on U.S. citizens. Figure 5 assesses the national interests of five key participants in this episode, which involved the selective use of U.S. air power.

Figure 5

U.S. BOMBING OF LIBYA - 1986

Basic National Interests	Intensity of Interests			
	Survival (critical)	Vital (dangerous)	Major (serious)	Peripheral (bothersome)
Defense of Homeland	Libya		US France Gr. Britain	USSR
Economic Well-being			Libya France	US USSR Gr. Britain
Favorable World Order		US Libya Gr. Britain	USSR France	
Promotion of Values		Libya	US Gr. Britain	USSR France

In this case, Libya and the United States professed to have vital world-order interests at stake in the Gulf of Sidra, which Libya claims as territorial waters, and in the Eastern Mediterranean where the United States exerts a dominant great power role. The immediate cause of the U.S. decision to bomb the Libyan cities was evidence of Libyan complicity in the highjacking of a U.S. airliner and the bombing of a nightclub in Berlin where several U.S. servicemen were injured. When Washington decided to retaliate by bombing Libyan territory, Britain and France were asked to permit U.S. Air Force bombers stationed in Britain to fly a direct route to Libya. France objected but Britain reluctantly approved. This indicated that France did not perceive a vital French interest to be at stake. On the other hand, Britain decided--in part because of U.S. support during the Falkland Islands War--to authorize Washington to use F-111 bombers based in Britain to attack Libya. The Soviet Union, by withdrawing its ships from Libyan harbors, showed that its interest was at best at the major level. Libya had a survival defense-of-homeland interest at stake because U.S. bombers hit its capital city and tried to depose its leader, Col. Muammar Kadaffy. As a result, Libyan-sponsored terrorism declined markedly. The significance of the Libyan case is that the United States shifted its view of world-order interests from the major to vital level because of Libyan terrorism and used limited military force in an effort to bring a solution to a vexing issue. The United States also wished to use the attack on Libya as an example to other states which sponsored terrorist acts against Americans.

The issue of trade sanctions against South Africa has been an interesting test case in terms of conflict over the perception of U.S. interests in southern Africa. Although defense-of-homeland is not at issue, economic well-being, maintenance of a favorable world order in southern Africa, and the promotion of U.S. values abroad were key issues in 1986. Figure 6 shows how the Reagan Administration assessed U.S.

Figure 6

U.S. TRADE SANCTIONS AGAINST SOUTH AFRICA - 1986

Basic National   Intensity of Interests
   Interests

	Survival (critical)	Vital (dangerous)	Major (serious)	Peripheral (bothersome)
Defense of Homeland			S. Africa	US Gr. Britain
Economic Well-being		S. Africa	US Gr. Britain	
Favorable World Order		US Gr. Britain	S. Africa	
Promotion of Values		US S. Africa	Gr. Britain	

interests in South Africa at the beginning of 1987, following Congress' pressure on the President to convince him to impose economic sanctions on South Africa because of its apartheid racial system. After Congress threatened to override a presidential veto of trade embargo legislation, the President agreed, reluctantly, to impose sanctions on his own authority while keeping up diplomatic pressure on the Pretoria regime to change its system.

Whether U.S. sanctions will produce the desired effect on South Africa's racial policies is doubtful because of the white government's power and determination. Yet this episode shows the intensity of the promotion-of-values interest on the U.S. government when strong domestic constituencies bring the full weight of their political influence to bear on an important foreign policy issue. Clearly, the United States has strong economic and world-order interests in this strategically located country, but the racial policies of the South African regime are so repugnant to Americans' sense of justice that this factor assumed overriding importance in determining U.S. policy in 1986. The British government views its interests in South Africa differently, and British firms have not been pressured into divesting their South African holdings. This results from Britain's historical interest in South Africa and lack of strong domestic pressures for tough sanctions.

IV

U.S. CORPORATION INTERESTS IN THE INTERNATIONAL ENVIRONMENT

We turn now to a discussion of what parallels exist between the way the U.S. Government views national interests and the way American-based corporations with large investments abroad see their interests.[7] An assumption made here is that large U.S.-based corporations are no less concerned than is the federal government in making correct assessments about which foreign countries are important to their long-range security and well-being. Corporate planning executives with major responsibility for deciding where and under what conditions their companies should invest large sums of capital abroad use various methods in making these judgments, but the bottom line is whether the proposed investment will add to the growth and profitability of the firm.

Harvard Business School Professor Michael Porter observed in an article in the Economist (May 23, 1987), that all successful corporations employ strategic thinking to guide their investment decisions and operating objectives. Entitled "Corporate Strategy: The State of Strategic Thinking," Porter's review describes six analytical techniques that corporate boards should take into account when developing a strategy on investments:

- An analysis of the industry in which the firm competes

- Sources of competitive advantage

- An analysis of existing and potential competitors

- An assessment of the company's competitive position

- Selection or ratification of a strategy

- Concrete actions to support the strategy, including the need for capital spending and staff training and development

In Porter's view, the key to strategic planning is creating a sustainable competitive advantage. This is not possible, he argues, if a company simply imitates its competition: "Sustainable competitive advantage arises from altering the basis of competition--new product attributes, new types of services, new production methods, new delivery systems."[8] In sum, the most successful corporations are those which take calculated risks while being creative and innovative.

What relevance is there in applying Porter's criteria to U.S. corporations operating in the international sphere? Additionally, how useful is it to compare the criteria used in business planning with factors used by government to assess priorities in foreign and national security policy? One answer is that both business and government executives must think through systematically the values and costs/risks of allocating substantial economic and human resources to certain foreign countries where important opportunities and/or interests are at stake. In assessing a corporation's international strategy, however, one important factor should be added to Porter's list, namely: U.S. government policy. Many U.S. corporations deny that they are influenced by what the State and Commerce Departments think about trade and investment opportunities, or political assessments, in specific countries. Nevertheless, most American companies operating abroad have to be mindful of Washington's foreign policy priorities even though they may deny being influenced by them.

I suggest that the national interest matrix described earlier in Figure 1 and also the list of values and cost/risk factors contained in Figure 2 can readily be adapted to the strategic planning done by major U.S. international corporations. This may be accomplished by altering the wording of the four basic interests and by modifying the description of the four levels of intensity, as seen in Figure 7. What is suggested here is that U.S. international and transnational corporations have basic business interests and objectives that are comparable, even complementary to the national interests of the U.S. government. A corporation executive will have as his bottom line the question of whether a large investment in country "X" will add to the company's growth and profitability and enhance its market share. For a U.S. foreign policy planner, the principal consideration is whether a proposed policy will promote a favorable world environment in which U.S. security, enterprise, and U.S. constitutional values are enhanced. Both the government and business executive are interested in enhancing the prestige or image of their organizations. It may be asked, however, whether a corporation ever has a survival interest at stake in its international operations--an investment which could bring it to financial ruin. Although such instances are rare for corporations, as they are for a great power, survival issues do nevertheless occur, particularly among financial institutions operating in foreign countries. Several major American banks recently have been forced to merge or face bankruptcy because of loans made in the 1970s to Third World countries, particularly in Latin America. Normally, however, international firms are able to absorb substantial losses in overseas investments without declaring bankruptcy or being absorbed by other corporations.

Figure 7

U.S. CORPORATION INTERNATIONAL INTERESTS

Basic Corporation Interests	Intensity of International Interests			
	Survival (critical)	Vital (essential)	Major (desirable)	Peripheral (marginal)
Protect Shareholders' Equity				
Profitability of Investment				
Enhance Market Share				
Advance Corporate Core Values				

The sixteen values and cost/risk criteria (Figure 2) used to decide whether a vital national interest is at stake may also be adapted to a corporation's assessment for determining whether it should make a large capital investment in a foreign country. Figure 8 contains eight values which a corporate executive might take into account when looking for investment opportunities abroad, and eight cost/risk factors which are important in making that assessment.

For most major American corporations, a driving force in decisions about investing in foreign countries is whether expansion will enhance the corporation's market share for its products, whether in manufactured goods, loans or services.   Like the U.S. Government, which tends to measure its reputation in terms of economic and military power on a worldwide scale, international corporations place a high value on size, profitability, and market share. Prestige among other large corporations is enhanced by being one of the top U.S. or global business enterprises, and very often these are the firms which are willing to expand operations abroad even when these decisions entail calculated risks to the firm's financial standing.   Because sales and profits are the key measures in a corporation's view of success, a company which ceases to expand is likely to decline relative to others in its league.   In short, the world of international business is not so different from the world of international

Figure 8

CRITERIA FOR DETERMINING VITAL CORPORATE
INTERESTS ABROAD

Value Factors	Cost/Risk Factors
Opportunities for Regional Business Growth	Size/Nature of Investment
Effect on Market Share	Risk of Prolonged Losses
Prospects for Sales/Profits	Risk of Poor Relationship with Local Government
Entrepreneurial Instinct	Risk of Unstable Work Force
Local Government Policy	Risk of Loss of Market
Exploitation of Existing Research and Technology	Prospect of U.S. Public Opposition
Corporate Image/Prestige	Prospect of International Opposition
Interest of Other Corporations	Risk of U.S. Government Opposition

politics: important countries and important corporations need to expand in order to remain in the front ranks. Stability often equates with stagnation, and U.S. corporate executives no less than U.S. government officials put a high premium on the dynamic quality of their leadership in the international environment.

Applying the corporate interest matrix shown in Figure 7 and the value and cost/risk criteria listed in Figure 8 to the specific issue of major investment in South Africa, a corporation executive might reasonably have calculated in 1982 that his company had a strong interest in investing there. By 1987, however, the same executive would have had to conclude that business prospects in South Africa had diminished significantly because of political considerations. Figure 9 indicates with "X" the calculations that probably would have been made in 1982, and with an "O" the changed assessment that would have been required in 1987.

This breakdown of corporate interest suggests that a corporation executive in 1982 would have found South Africa to be a good investment opportunity, where the risks listed in Figure 8 appeared to be small compared to the values expected to be achieved. By 1987, however, after the U.S. Government imposed economic sanctions on the Pretoria government, South Africa's desirability as an investment opportunity declined significantly, and many U.S. corporations decided to divest.

Figure 9

U.S. CORPORATION INTEREST IN SOUTH AFRICA: 1982 (X) AND 1987 (O)

Basic Corporation   Intensity of International Interests
      Interests

	Survival (critical)	Vital (essential)	Major (desirable)	Peripheral (marginal)
Protect Shareholders' Equity			X	O
Profitability of Investment			X	O
Enhance Market Share		X	O	
Advance Corporate Core Values		X	O	

South Africa thus serves as an important case in highlighting the relationship between government policy and corporation decisions in international relations.   Clearly, U.S. corporation interests in this instance were heavily influenced by a change in America public opinion and by the consequent change in the U.S. government's policy toward South Africa. Other, less dramatic, recent examples of government policy influencing corporate decisions are Iran, Libya and Angola, where local governments wanted U.S. investment and trade but Washington was opposed for political reasons.   Although many U.S. corporations may not seek U.S. government guidance or advice when making overseas investment decisions, it is nevertheless true that when the President and Congress place political and economic sanctions on a foreign government because of foreign policy considerations, U.S. businesses will comply.

V

NATIONAL INTERESTS AND CORPORATION INTERESTS IN CHINA[9]

From 1949 to 1972 the United States and the People's Republic of China (PRC) had no diplomatic relations and no legitimate trade and business ties.   In 1971,   President Nixon's national, security adviser, Dr. Henry Kissinger, traveled secretly to Beijing and held talks with China's Premier, Zhou Enlai, to see whether the basis for detente existed between their hostile countries.   This meeting opened the way for President Nixon's official visit to China in March 1972 and the opening of informal relations. After China's paramount leader, Mao Zedong, died in 1976, China's new leaders, led by Deng Xiaoping, indicated that they desired to normalize diplomatic and trade relations with Washington. President Jimmy Carter formally established relations with Beijing in 1979 and encouraged U.S. trade and investment in China. Since then, China's economy has undergone a mild transformation as Deng Xiaoping and his allies vigorously pressed ahead with reforms designed to stimulate productivity and attract foreign investment. However, reform of the Communist Party and the entrenched bureaucracy has gone slower. The Politburo's leadership continues to wrestle with the dilemma of how fast the movement toward free-market enterprise should go and whether political control of that vast country will be endangered. Student disturbances in Chinese universities in December 1986 were a reminder to China's leaders that economic liberalization leads to pressure for relaxation of political controls and greater individual freedom. The Communist Party's 13th Congress in October 1987 showed that Deng had succeeded in moving a younger group of loyal pragmatists into key positions of power and that the old conservatives were gradually being retired. Nevertheless, China remains a highly regimented society, and Deng's liberalizing movement will need more time, perhaps five to ten years, and strong leadership to sink deep roots into Chinese communist psychology.

An underlying reason for the change in U.S. and Chinese policies over the past fifteen years has been a recognition in both Washington and Beijing that the countries' national interests had been altered significantly during the 1960s and, consequently, that a convergence of interests had emerged in the 1970s despite continuing ideological differences. The Vietnam War caused the U.S. Government to accept the reality that a friendly China was the key to a peaceful withdrawal from its untenable military involvement in Vietnam. Nixon and Kissinger believed that improving relations with China would have a beneficial effect on U.S.-Soviet relations, particularly in the field of arms control. Following conclusion of the Vietnam War in 1975, the Soviet navy and airforce were given bases in South Vietnam astride the shipping lanes of the South China Sea. This increased the pressure on the United States and China to cooperate in curbing the growing Soviet political influence in Southeast Asia and the Western Pacific.

As for China, two main factors pushed it toward opening relations with the United States. The first was a fear of increased Soviet intimidation following a clash between Soviet and Chinese forces in Manchuria in 1968. This caused China's leadership to fear that Moscow might use force to bring China's Communist Party under its influence, in accordance with the Brezhnev Doctrine. The second factor was China's desperate need for Western technology and economic assistance to modernize the economy and provide improved living conditions for the country's one billion people. Concern about growing Soviet ambitions in Asia therefore led Washington and Beijing to recognize that their interests in this regard were parallel. Even the difficult issue of Taiwan was not allowed to inhibit the growing relationship, although strong political pressures in each country encouraged divergence over this issue.

The Assistant Secretary of State for East Asian Affairs, Dr. Gaston Sigur, summarized U.S. interests in China during a speech to the National Issues Forum at the Brookings Institution in April 1987. Under the title "U.S. Policy Priorities for Relations With China," Sigur first described the political side of the relationship: "In the broadest sense, our chief priority is to continue building a friendly and cooperative relationship with China that will be a stabilizing factor in East Asia and the world."[10]   He referred to a broad consensus on this national interest (what I call the world-order interest) among the Reagan Administration, the Congress and the public.   This consensus rests, Sigur said, on "certain central beliefs" which he enumerated as follows:

- U.S. long-range foreign policy goals in East Asia require it to meet the Soviet strategic and geopolitical challenge in the area;

- To do so the United States must preserve a communality of interests with major Asian states such as China, with our allies, and with other key East Asian nations;

- U.S. interests must be pursued within the context of a one China policy; and

- Taiwan's future should be determined by the Chinese on both sides of the strait.   The United States' sole interest is that the issue should be resolved peacefully.

Sigur suggested that a second key element in the U.S. interest in China is economic, namely "the conviction that U.S. interests are served by the P.R.C.'s continued commitment to economic modernization, internal reform, and expanded relations with foreign countries--the so-called open door policy." He recalled that once China had emerged from the chaos of the Cultural Revolution, it became preoccupied with achieving rapid modernization under the leadership of Deng Xiaoping.   China had undertaken major initiatives on many fronts, he said, "raising agricultural production, improving living standards, economically developing the less advanced interior regions, reforming industry, expanding foreign trade and investment, and playing a more active role in the global economy."

The State Department's East Asia policy chief then asked why the United States should be interested in China's modernization; in effect, what is the U.S. national interest in helping to build a strong China.   He answered his question: "The flow of goods, people and ideas not only contributes to China's modernization but also yields opportunities for American business. It enriches the cultural life of both nations and builds American and Chinese constituencies supportive of the overall relationships. . . .   In sum, it is in our own self-interest to cooperate with China in its modernization efforts."[11]

Sigur thus affirmed both the U.S. economic interest and the promotion of values interest.   Yet, the fundamental basis of the rapprochement with China is the change in Washington's view of its world-order interests in Asia since 1968. The Johnson Administration's decision to negotiate an end to the Vietnam War necessitated a change in U.S. policy toward the People's Republic, which was then ready for detente with the United States.

U.S. national interests in China today may therefore be described on the matrix as shown in Figure 10.

Figure 10

U.S. NATIONAL INTERESTS IN CHINA - 1988

Basic National   Intensity of Interests
Interests

Basic National Interests	Survival (critical)	Vital (dangerous)	Major (serious)	Peripheral (bothersome)
Defense of Homeland			X	
Economic Well-being				X
Favorable World Order			X	
Promotion of Values				X

The defense-of-homeland interest is at the "major" level of intensity because of China's strategic importance in the global balance of power with the Soviet Union. The U.S. economic well-being interest currently is at the peripheral level, although some analysts may give it a higher priority because of China's economic potential. It is the U.S. world-order interest which is the driving force in U.S. policy on China because a friendly China serves as a stabilizing political factor in Asia. An unfriendly China, on the other hand, had helped to bring on the Korean and Vietnam Wars. Finally, in the promotion-of-values category, the U.S. interest is peripheral because changing China's communist system is not a high priority in Washington today. This was not true when Ronald Reagan became president in 1981 and reiterated his support for Taiwan. But his state visit to China in 1984 confirmed a new view that Taiwan is part of China and that his Administration would not insist on political reforms in China as the price of closer relations with the United States.

Some political analysts argue that China is a vital U.S. world-order interest, for balance of power reasons, and that the United States therefore should go further in helping Beijing to strengthen its military

capability vis-a-vis the USSR.   However, so long as China remains a
totalitarian system, it is unwise to view it as a vital interest and thereby
obligate the United States to defend China in case of attack, even if
Beijing should want such an implicit arrangement with Washington.

When considering the subject of U.S. corporation interests in China,
we find a somewhat different perception of the value of strong links with
China.   The American business community's attitude in 1987 could be
described as "skeptical," with some corporations being somewhat more
optimistic than others about the economic and political prospects in China
over the next few years.

Two American lawyers with intimate experience in China, Jerome Alan
Cohen and Stuart J. Valentine, prepared a report in April 1987 on progress
and problems encountered by American corporations doing business in
China.   They concluded that foreign direct investment in China has been
considerably less than either China or many U.S. observers had anticipated
in 1979 when the People's Republic of China (PRC) promulgated the
landmark Chinese-Foreign Joint Venture Law.   Most of the reasons result
from difficulty in dealing with changing internal Chinese attitudes and
regulations that discourage foreign venture capital from investing major
resources there.   Despite the many difficulties encountered, however, the
authors found that the record of these first eight years of the FDI
(foreign direct investment) process was in many respects "quite
impressive."   On the other hand, they acknowledged that statistics "suggest
that the PRC has hardly begun to take advantage of the opportunity to
attract investors from North America and Western Europe."[12]   They
pointed out that Hong Kong and Macao companies provided 66.5 percent of
the foreign direct investment in China, Japanese companies had 11.5
percent and the United States was third with only 9.5 percent.   It should
be noted, they cautioned, that much of the Hong Kong investment lies in
the corridor between Kowloon and Canton.

Although Cohen and Valentine were optimistic about the Chinese
government's willingness to make additional changes in China's legal and
administrative practices in order to attract western investment, they were
candid in discussing the major concerns of American investors about
entering joint ventures in China.   These concerns are: (1) political
stability in China; (2) repatriation of earnings, in light of foreign exchange
controls; (3) the escalation of costs of doing business in China, as
compared with doing business elsewhere in Asia; (4) protracted negotiations
and enforcement of contracts; and (5) lack of consistency in taxation
policy.

The writers conclude their appraisal on an optimistic note.   They are
convinced that current economic liberalization in China will continue, and
that the Chinese political situation will not deteriorate and make joint
ventures more risky.   Their advice to foreign corporations contemplating
significant investment in China is to channel their investment into those
sectors that are of interest to China as well as to themselves, i.e., to look
carefully at China's priorities as well as their own.   They recommend that
corporations allocate managerial and technical personnel to China who are

"both professionally competent and culturally sensitive, be able and willing teachers, and at the same time be fair and equal partners in what is surely one of the most significant and hopeful efforts at international business corporation the world has seen."[13]

On the basis of this and other reports on the scale of American investment in China in 1987, we may generalize about U.S. corporations' interests there on the interest matrix, as shown in Figure 11.

Figure 11

U.S. CORPORATION INTERESTS IN CHINA

Basic Corporation Interests   Intensity of International Interests

	Survival (critical)	Vital (essential)	Major (desirable)	Peripheral (marginal)
Protect Shareholders' Equity				X
Profitability of Investment				X
Enhance Market Share			X	
Advance Corporate Core Values				X

In sum, the American corporation's interest in making large investments in China at present is low on the priority list of most U.S. business enterprises because the investment climate there is only slowly improving, while the political outlook remains uncertain as China continues to undergo a significant political transition from Deng Xiaoping to a new party leadership group headed by Zhao Ziyang. Concern about the extent to which new political leaders will look with favor on business ties with Western capitalists is probably the single most important factor militating against significant increases in American private investment in the PRC today.

CONCLUSION

As the United States prepares for the international challenges and opportunities of the 1990s, it seems clear that it will need to pay far greater attention to its economic interests than it has since World War II.

This will require increasing the productivity and competitiveness of American business, and it will also require government to be tougher in persuading other countries to open up their markets to U.S. goods and services. For the United States to remain a great power into the 21st century, it needs to have sufficient military and economic power to support its worldwide interests. Although American-based corporations with large international investments do not have as large a stake as government does in sustaining the United States as a preeminent world power, most corporation executives understand that U.S. international political influence sets an environment in which business investment and trade can flourish. Consequently, it would seem to be in the self-interest of both government officials and business leaders to consult frequently and try to influence one another's thinking on how best to improve U.S. government and U.S. corporation objectives abroad. This paper proposes a conceptual framework in which each side may employ a similar methodology to analyze its interests in specific countries and geographic reasons. China is a prime example of where cooperative arrangements may pay rich dividends in terms of corporation profits and market share, and to the U.S. government in terms of its world-order interests and promotion of U.S. values abroad. Together, the two sides can promote their parallel interests to a far greater extent then either can accomplish on its own.

NOTES

1. These basic national interests, as well as their intensity in specific international issues and crises, are discussed in detail in Donald E. Nuechterlein, <u>America Overcommitted: United States National Interests in the 1980s</u> (Lexington, Kentucky: University Press of Kentucky, 1985), pp. 8-14.

2. For a fuller discussion of U.S. national interests in the 19th and early 20th centuries, see Charles A. Beard, <u>The Idea of National Interest</u> (New York: Macmillan Company, 1934); Hans J. Morgenthau, <u>In Defense of the National Interest</u> (New York: Knopf, 1952); Walter Lippmann, <u>U.S. Foreign Policy: Shield of the Republic</u> (Boston: Little Brown, 1943); and George F. Kennan, <u>America Diplomacy: 1900-1950</u> (Chicago: University of Chicago Press, 1951).

3. An analysis of the tension between internationalists and isolationists during the early 20th century is contained in Robert Osgood, <u>Ideals and Self-interest in America's Foreign Relations</u> (Chicago: University of Chicago Press, 1953), chap. 1.

4. The "containment policy" of the United States is usually associated with the name of George F. Kennan, a Soviet expert in the State Department who formulated his ideas for containing Soviet expansionist policies while studying at the National War College in 1946-47. However, the large expansion of U.S. alliances during the 1950s in support of the containment policy is generally attributed to

the vision of two Secretaries of State, Dean Acheson and John Foster Dulles.

5. Use of the national interest matrix is discussed in Nuechterlein, op. cit., pp. 14-17.

6. See Nuechterlein, chap. 2.

7. In this analysis of U.S. corporation interests abroad, I am indebted to Professor Leslie F. Grayson of the Darden Graduate School of Business Administration, University of Virginia, for his valuable insights and suggestions. I also consulted with Mr. Roger Bohrband, former director of corporate planning, The Dow Chemical Company, Midland, Michigan.

8. "Corporate Strategy: The State of Strategic Thinking," The Economist, May 23, 1987, p. 23.

9. During May 1987, I had occasion to visit China for three weeks and to talk with American business executives and to observe several Chinese business enterprises.   My impressions are incorporated into this discussion.

10. U.S. Department of State, Current Policy, no. 948, "U.S. Policy Priorities for Relations with China," p. 2.

11. Ibid.

12. "Foreign Direct Investment in the People's Republic of China: Progress, Problems and Proposals," a paper prepared for the United Nations Centre on Transnational Corporations Roundtable, conducted in Beijing on May 25-26, 1987, p. 24.

13. Ibid., p. 73.

CONCLUSION

The introduction to this collection underscored the centrality of the business corporation in capitalist societies. It also emphasized the role of reciprocal influences between corporations and other institutions and forces in bringing about significant societal change. In addition, it drew attention to the need for analyses of these phenomena from different perspectives and for integrating the results of these analyses.

As a way of integrating this material, it is useful to summarize the issues and problems considered by our authors, as well as the solutions proposed by them, so as to get a picture--or rather, a collage--of what they perceive to be at stake. Perhaps with such a collage before us, we will be able to gain, in some measure, a better appreciation for obstacles confronting us and complex interconnections between them. The issues, their nature, the level at which they occur, and the actors involved appear in Table 1.

The business corporation, it is important to note, figures prominently in all of the issues sketched out in Table 1. The corporation is, as well, part of all the solutions proposed. Regarding those solutions, cooperation is common to all of them.

Kanter describes a degree of management-labor cooperation at the level of the individual firm. Riesman urges corporate support for liberal arts colleges, which he sees as a national resource. Korb calls for the elimination of stereotypical misperceptions of each other held by some DOD and defense industry officials, as well as greater commitment on their part to constitutional principles and procedures. Wenk wants the business-government partnership to be made open, accepted as legitimate and controlled, for when covert it is dangerous to our democratic system and values. Anderson, Ferguson, Nuechterlein and Sullivan urge business-government cooperation on the United States in its conduct of foreign affairs, but for different reasons (economic, economic-national security, ideological). Wood suggests a combination of national and international business-government cooperation in the interests of containing the political-military threat of the Soviet Union. And Inkeles alludes to the desirability of global (universal) cooperation.

Cooperation at any level, however, requires consensus, the forging of which is frustrated by the complexities so characteristic of the contemporary world. However hackneyed the term "complexities" has become, it does, nonetheless, point one in the correct, albeit very general, direction for exploring the current period.

It might be protested that every generation has been faced with complexities greater than those of its predecessor, and that therefore complexity itself does not distinguish the current situation from previous ones. Such a view, though, would be a dangerous oversimplification.

221

Table 1

ISSUES*

management-labor relations	Kanter
the American constitutional system, democratic values and their projection abroad	Korb, Wenk, Sullivan
competitiveness of a particular U.S. industry	Ferguson
U.S. global competitiveness	Anderson, Nuechterlein
U.S. national security and foreign policy	Korb, Nuechterlein, Sullivan, Wood
combined U.S. commercial and national security interests	Nuechterlein and Wood
an emerging worldwide social system	Inkeles
technology	Anderson, Ferguson, Inkeles,
leadership	Riesman

NATURE

social, economic, military, political, ideological

LEVEL

universal, international (but not universal), international (focus on a single industry), national, single firm

ACTORS

management, labor, business corporation, business/government, business/educational institutions, business/media, general public, foreign corporations, foreign governments

*Actually, all authors, directly or by implication, are concerned with all of the issues noted above. The listing of an author by a particular issue merely indicates her or his focus on that issue.

Complexities are to a significant extent cumulative; those of later generations are often additions to, rather than substitutes for, earlier ones. Moreover, change, which tends to increase complexity, is accelerating at geometric rates. To ignore these realities would be to forfeit whatever chance we might have to be aware of, to understand and to influence (however marginally) powerful, multidimensional and intricately connected forces shaping the human condition.

In addition to the need for cooperation and consensus amid complexity, another key, not surprising, fact emerges from these essays. As we shift our analysis from lower to higher levels of organization, and therefore to greater comprehensiveness, the complexities challenging us themselves increase markedly in number and nature. Given their increased numbers and the interconnections between them--interconnections that cut across both functional lines and geographic boundaries--the aggregate of these complexities takes on qualities of ever greater intricacy and seeming impenetrability.

Still another important reality to focus on is what Kanter has called the "fragility" of the new alliances between industrial firms and local labor unions. If alliances at that level are fragile, then it is no exaggeration to describe cooperative efforts (especially new ones) at the international level as extremely brittle. The terms "fragile" and "brittle" have been chosen advisedly. Fragility suggests the need to handle any given object (be it material or organizational) with great care, otherwise it might be destroyed. Brittleness is unequivocal; in the absence of such care, destruction is certain.

Thus, the overriding theme that thrusts itself upon us from all of the foregoing is suggested by the image of a "continuum of cooperation" angling upwards from left to right, with the individual firm at the lower left and Inkeles' worldwide social system at the upper right. As one moves left to right up the continuum, there is a geometric increase in the number of issues and problems; the number of actors; the number of proposed solutions; and the number of complexities, many of which, given the growing degree of global interdependence, are becoming increasingly entangled with each other at all levels, thereby creating still further complexities. All of the foregoing, moreover, is occurring in a rapidly changing, fragile, even brittle, environment. Hence, as we probe upward along the continuum in search of cooperative arrangements for resolving interconnected problems, we encounter an ever-greater turbulence that threatens to shatter the entire enterprise. It might be well, then, to have our continuum in mind as we discuss, at least in some detail, the problems addressed in this volume, the solutions proposed, and some obstacles to implementing the latter.

One of the most instructive, but disquieting, facts that emerges from this collection is that several problems are common to all (or, in a few cases, almost all) of the issues explored. The disquiet stems from the ubiquity and nature of the problems. The latter involve: attitudes; real conflicts of interest; the potential negative side effects of technology; the rapidity of change; complexities and fragmentation within the nation state;

and, even more so, complexities and fragmentation, as well as vulnerabilities, at the international level.

Included in attitudinal problems are: (1) mistrust, fear and hostility; (2) concerns about constitutional procedures, democratic values and conflicting ideologies; and (3) the dominance of short-run orientations. Mistrust is at least implied in Riesman's lament that loyalty, for many individuals, extends no further than narrow, personal interests. At the level of the firm, Kanter makes clear that considerable effort was required to overcome mistrust, fear and hostility in order to establish strategic alliances between management and labor. Moreover, it has thus far been possible to do so only in a relatively few cases. At the national level, mistrust and hostility also figure in the relationship between the Pentagon and defense industries analyzed by Korb, and the same feelings are harbored, at least to some degree, by the general public about both DOD and its suppliers. Certainly, mistrust is inherent in Wenk's insistence that the "hidden partnership" between business and government be made open. And most assuredly, mistrust, fear and hostility (mitigated only slightly by cooperative efforts here and there) abound at the international level. Otherwise, there would be no need for Wood to propose the combining of national industrial policies to cope with the potential threat posed by the Soviet Union. Inkeles also points to fear and hostility elicited by the growing vulnerabilities we all share, given increasing global interdependence.

As for threats to constitutional procedures and democratic values, Korb has reported the disregard for Congress and the media on the part of some officials in both DOD and the defense industry regarding their responsibility to be publicly accountable for their actions. We have had demonstrated to us, all too often, the dangers to the Republic inherent in "the arrogance of power," a phrase used by William Fulbright two decades ago in another context. Although Wenk does not use this particular phrase, that arrogance is among his concerns when he warns us about the hidden nature of business-government relations and the potential emergence of a corporate state. Sullivan, too, focuses attention on democratic values and conflicting ideologies, but he wants us vigorously to project the former abroad. And although Wood and Nuechterlein do not directly speak of democratic values and conflicting ideologies, it is concern over both (and in Nuechterlein's case, economic interests, as well) that have prompted their proposals regarding the conduct of American foreign policy.

Also in the realm of attitudinal problems, there is the curse of the short-run orientation. As examples of this orientation, Riesman points to consultants with no institutional loyalty even "to the firm for which they are currently working." He also refers to business executives who, because of their own inner drives and the quarterly profit statement, are "prompted . . . toward undermaintenance of people and plants and underfunding of research and development." Ferguson, too, identifies the short-run orientation as a problem. The environment in the American semiconductor industry, he says, encouraged "short-term calculations . . . and consumption relative to investment . . . ." Wenk discusses at length "pathologies of the short run" that permeate American society. And Anderson tells us that in 1986 "Americans consumed 4 percent more than they produced, and financed this deficit by borrowing" from abroad.

In addition to attitudinal problems, there are concrete conflicts of interest in every arena. Kanter analyzes conflicting interests within firms, within labor unions, and between the two kinds of organizations. Korb points to the conflict of interest inherent in the DOD-defense industry relationship, wherein the former wants to minimize costs and the latter wants to maximize profits. With regard to corporations in general, their narrow, short-run goals can frequently clash with the long-term public interest, and these are among the kinds of goals that worry Wenk.

Conflicts of interest at the international level include the economic ones that have prompted Ferguson and Anderson to turn their attention to the competitiveness issue. The conflict of ideologies (democracy versus apartheid) has engaged Sullivan's energies, and has led him to urge diplomatic and economic sanctions against South Africa. That conflict has also led him to warn about the certainty of increasing violence in that country, and the possibility of international military conflict into which the superpowers, he asserts, would be drawn. The same confluence of conflicting political-ideological, military and economic factors (with a somewhat different cast of actors) has shaped the proposals of Wood and Nuechterlein. And, at the universal level, the world can be viewed as being divided between the have- and have-not nations, with the gap being increased, Inkeles tells us, by rapidly developing technology.

All of these problems, attitudinal and concrete, have to be addressed in an environment, the already considerable turbulence of which well might be exacerbated by the technology just referred to. Inkeles provides statistics of a truly phenomenal rate of change. It is not at all clear whether, let alone how, we are going to channel that change along constructive paths in our fragmented world. But we have no rational option other than to attempt to devise solutions for the problems confronting us.

To begin at the lowest level of organization considered here--the individual firm and its interactions with local labor unions--we find, encouragingly, that indeed cooperation is possible between heretofore largely antagonistic groups. Kanter tells us that new strategic alliances may change profoundly how American business operates. However, she warns us, these partnerships "still represent, by any measure, only a small proportion of all American corporate activity." This is possibly because of the management difficulties they involve. The challenge, Kanter tells us, is three-fold: "managing the inherently fragile relationship between partners, and then managing the changes in each of the partners' own organizations." Thus, even at this level the obstacles to consensus and cooperation are formidable.

Moreover, the difficulties in any given relationship tend to increase as the number of participants increase. We are reminded powerfully of this axiom when we move from management-labor relations at the level of the firm to national affairs. The number of corporations that do business with DOD is very large indeed, and the DOD-defense industry relationship is characterized by the stereotypical "fatal misperceptions" described by Korb.

His approach to eroding these misperceptions involves having more leaders include in their careers both government service and employment in the defense industry. The rotation of individuals between the two sectors would be conducive to a more sympathetic understanding by persons in one sector of the needs, problems and viewpoints of their counterparts in the other sector. While such understanding would not automatically eliminate conflicting interests and other problems, it would make their resolution easier. Regarding the requirement of public accountability currently denigrated by some officials in both the defense industry and DOD, Korb contends that more emphasis on the liberal arts in the education of future leaders would help to inculcate an appropriate sense of responsibility. Such an emphasis would also result in a deeper understanding of, and commitment to, the procedures of our constitutional system by those leaders. Korb is somewhat pessimistic, though, about the prospects for positive change.

That pessimism is warranted. There is a tradeoff inherent in Korb's proposal for ameliorating the misperception problem by rotation. That tradeoff concerns the degree to which such rotation strengthens the parochial ties between a given industry and a particular government agency. Korb certainly knows that industries often "capture" the very government agencies that are supposed to regulate them. And that phenomenon is not unlike the issue under discussion here. But he evidently sees such "capturing" as less dangerous to the nation than the stereotypical myths he has described. Whether his judgment is right or wrong, Korb's article underscores for us the need to make difficult choices in a complex world. As for his observation that more exposure to the liberal arts would inculcate in future leaders a greater commitment to constitutional procedures, Korb is almost certainly correct. The problem is the absence, in recent decades, of business, governmental and academic leaders who want to, and are capable of, transforming this goal, with which no one can argue in the abstract, into a priority vigorously pursued by society.

Wenk, after describing a greater range of concerns than those addressed by Korb, identifies several steps designed to cope with the problems. The "hidden partnership" between business and government must become open and accepted by the nation as a whole. Business must abandon its paradoxical, but traditional, characterization of government as the enemy, act in accord with ethical principles, and accept its responsibility to account publicly for its actions. Organized labor must contribute to increased productivity. Educational institutions will have to develop in their students a commitment to protect democratic values and the ability to analyze complex relationships. "Investigative reporting unfettered by any pernicious influence from business and government must be depended upon . . . to alert the public to the social repercussions [of advancing technology.]" And business, government and the American people in general must develop foresight about "the way ahead" in order to exorcise the demon of the short run.

There are three problematic aspects to Wenk's solution. First, there is the call for what amounts to a massive attitudinal change, a transformation not easily accomplished. Second, Wenk's approach is comprehensive, and therefore would require broad and deep support difficult to marshall. And third, his reliance on our educational system, the mass media and the general public might prove to be excessive. Indeed, there is a good chance that those ultimately responsible in a democracy for exercising control--currently, a public fixated on the short run and "consumed by consumerism"--are either unaware of, indifferent to, or overwhelmed by staggeringly swift technological change and its potential for good or evil. If there is any validity to the foregoing, then the citizenry in Walter Lippmann's day had an easy time of things by comparison. It follows, then, that the mass media are destined to be at best only marginally successful in their role of keeping the American people aware of the growing dangers to democratic values, unless our educational institutions improve dramatically their performance in the preparation of the citizenry for its responsibilities.

None of the foregoing is to say that Wenk is wrong. Alas, he is right! His multifaceted solution to our problems is the correct one. The question is: Where and how do we begin? The answer is not apparent.

One of the most intractable problems in U.S. society is that of achieving and sustaining consensus over the long term. That inability is due to, among other factors, the country's size, its regional differences (political, social and economic), the short-run orientation characteristic of the entire society, and the fragmented nature of our political system. In that government is the primary institution to which the task of forging national consensus falls, it is in the governmental sphere that the difficulties of agreeing upon and pursuing common goals are most visible.

Some of those difficulties confront us when we begin to think about how to pursue Anderson's goal of having the government play a major role in developing the social infrastructure he views as essential to American competitiveness in international markets. It would not be easy to achieve even a temporary national consensus on his proposal, but let us assume, for the moment, that it were possible to do so. Certainly, Ferguson's call for cooperation between U.S. semiconductor firms combined with supportive public policies is consistent with Anderson's program. Also compatible with that program is Nuechterlein's proposal for closer collaboration between the U.S. Government and American business firms operating abroad in the pursuit of complementary goals.

However, even assuming such a national consensus, we are still left with the perennial problem in a democracy of how to sustain the nation's commitment to any given set of priorities over the long run. Political leaderships in democracies change, with the new leaders often bringing new priorities to the agenda. But essential to Anderson's approach is a long, sustained effort resulting in the creation of a general consensus on overriding priorities so that <u>whatever</u> president takes office he or she will adopt those priorities as a matter of course. Ferguson's goal of making the U.S. semiconductor industry again competitive in international markets, although much more focused than Anderson's broad, general program, faces the same kind of problems that confront the latter--consensus and long-term commitment.

Further complicating the task of sorting things out and establishing priorities are: the nature of the international environment within which we find ourselves, its multiplicity of problems, and the entanglement with each other of foreign and domestic issues to the extent that the distinction between the two categories is becoming less and less meaningful. Although, or perhaps because, there is more frequent and more intense interaction between a growing number of actors in the world arena (one cause of which is the growing economic importance of some heretofore peripheral players--for example, Taiwan, South Korea, Singapore and Hong Kong), we <u>still</u> have an arena, not a cohesive community.

A salient characteristic of that arena is an unpredictability exacerbated by rapid, often basic, change. That change, in turn, is elicited by phenomena such as technological breakthroughs; volatility in globally connected currency markets, which itself was intensified by the new technological development of computerized program trading; third-world debt, which potentially could undermine the international financial system; regional military conflicts into which the superpowers might be drawn; conflicting ideologies; domestic upheavals, such as the South African situation described by Leon Sullivan, which, he asserts, also could lead to superpower confrontation; and a host of other intertwined, frequently conflicting political, diplomatic, economic, financial, commercial and military phenomena.

Perhaps the most important conclusion to be drawn from the foregoing is the vulnerability of <u>all</u> players, major and minor, stemming from the heightened unpredictability brought on by this turbulence, only a few examples of which have been noted. As Inkeles says, "There is no way to erect barriers which can prevent a crash in the New York stock market from having almost instantaneous repercussions in all the other markets of the world. . . ." Indeed, there are many other forces indifferent to national boundaries whose negative effects can be severe. Stark examples of such forces include the AIDS virus and the combination of technology and human error that produced Chernobyl.

Concomitants of the resulting uncertainty are fear and hostility. Part of the hostility derives from the age-old problem of uneven distribution of the benefits and costs associated with new developments. Most modern communications, for example, is a high-tech endeavor. This fact limits active participation in the adventure largely to the advanced industrialized countries, which then reap the rewards. Technology, hence, tends to concentrate wealth and power, as Wenk has pointed out in the U.S. domestic context. Economically-less-developed countries and, perhaps more demonstrably to the point, newly industrializing ones are unlikely to accept with their previous passivity such a concentration of the world's wealth. Recent suspension of debt payments by some third-world countries shows that they have the capacity to disrupt the international financial system. Thus, the environment within which all of us, including business corporations, are functioning has a brittle quality previously unwitnessed by the nation-state system.

Apartheid is only one example, however important, of the kind of issue that brings about an intersecting of commercial, political, military and ideological interests. That confluence of interests requires choices between differing perceptions of the national interest. For example, would a major effort by Washington to pressure the South African Government to abolish apartheid endanger American geostrategic interests, or would such an effort enhance those interests in the long run? What would be the impact on American commercial interests? Is there a need to choose between the desire to project democracy abroad and the risk of alienating an ally against communism? Or does the failure to pressure vigorously the South African Government increase the prospects of gains for communism in the long term? Would, indeed, as Sullivan argues, the superpowers be drawn into a race war, if one were to be ignited? Will the free enterprise system be destroyed if apartheid is not abolished? The answers to these questions are not unequivocal. However, all observers would agree that in South Africa many conflicting forces are at work with commercial, political and military ramifications that frustrate consensus and cooperation.

When Nuechterlein broadens our orientation to the conduct of American foreign policy and commercial affairs in general, and proposes closer coordination between American business and government in the identification and pursuit of complementary interests, he is issuing a more substantial challenge, in terms of complexity, than the one posed by Sullivan's focus on a single country. Nuechterlein, though, does provide us with a system that could be helpful in evaluating the importance and intensity of multiple interests. Nonetheless, the task is formidable. There is also the issue of how to utilize Nuechterlein's system. That is, would it be used by business and government leaders in an informal way on an ad hoc basis? Or would it be more regularized, with a representative public/private body established? It would appear self evident that a group meeting regularly would be able to maximize the benefits of the system. But who would serve? How would they be chosen? What issues would they address? And so on.

If Nuechterlein's proposal stretches the possibilities of cooperation within the American context, Wood's suggestion of combining national and international industrial policies might be pushing those possibilities to their outer limits, given the greater complexities involved. That suggestion, it will be recalled, was elicited, by America's dependence on Japan for components of many military items used by NATO. The dependence was created both by decisions of private businesses to increase their reliance on foreign manufacturers (because of production costs) and by public policies (antitrust laws, and so forth).

One result is that Europe now relies for its defense upon two major partners (the United States and Japan) rather than one. Moreover, the relationship between those two partners is undergoing considerable change and stress because of economic developments. The resulting potential for instability threatens European security. In addition, the new situation has political ramifications that spread through much of international affairs. The evolving nature of the U.S.-Japanese alliance will change the tone, and possibly even the substance, of other relationships, including those involving: the U.S. and Europe; the U.S. and the Soviet Union; Japan and Europe; Japan and the Soviet Union; Europe and the Soviet Union; and a similar series of relationships involving China.

Wood's response to these increasing complexities includes   elements of a U.S. industrial policy, designed to lessen dependence on foreign sources.   Simultaneously, Wood approves of the notion of American-Japanese cooperation "in basic research, engineering and commercialization" in the interest of coping with the threat of communist political-military pressure.   That suggestion, he recognizes, would appear "to counter the drive to moderate U.S. dependency.   But U.S. security ties and the depth of interdependency," he says, "dictate intergovernmental as well as national policies."

However, even assuming the feasibility of forging an American industrial policy, there is the prior question of deciding what its major thrust would be: "making America competitive again" or containing communism. One would tend to assign priority to the former after reading Ferguson's article on U.S.-Japanese competition in the semiconductor industry or the more general essays by Anderson and Nuechterlein.

Establishing American competitiveness as the key priority, however, could downgrade, if not ignore, Wood's concern with the threat of Soviet political influence and military power, because such a policy might increase Japanese-American tensions.   Indeed, as of this writing, a trade bill containing significant anti-Japanese provisions is being debated in the U.S. Congress. If Wood is correct that Europe's defense is dependent upon Japan, even if only in the short run, then the United States is faced with the difficult task of mitigating multiple, conflicting forces in its relations with Japan and Europe: the courting of Japan in the interests of European defense, while simultaneously addressing the concerns articulated by Anderson and Ferguson regarding U.S.-Japanese economic competition, an issue of great, immediate (here again, the short run) importance to the American business community.

Some observers would argue that it is impossible, in any event, to establish an American industrial policy, to say nothing of the far more complex task of combining, at the international level, national industrial policies that conflict with each other in substantial ways. Their argument would be that the fragmentation inherent in the U.S. political system (which, due to Watergate, has increased since the mid-1970s) plus the conflicting interests between Japan and the United States, would foredoom such an undertaking.

Coping with these conflicting economic, political and military forces will require greater wisdom and vision than thus far have been in evidence in any quarter.   In the meantime, this Japanese-American-European quandary gives a concreteness to the oft-used term, "interdependence."

In any rational scheme of things, interdependence, by definition, demands cooperation. In that interdependence is global, the implication is clear--global   cooperation.   Logically,   the   explosion   in   global communications should facilitate such cooperation.   The communications revolution, along with expanding world trade, has led Inkeles to speak of an emerging "single worldwide social system." From statistics he cites, one senses the magnitude of that revolution, the rapidity with which it is developing and the reciprocal ways in which business and technology influence each other.

In spite of these staggering developments, Inkeles' "worldwide social system," as he himself points out, is still far from being a "global village." Unfortunately, the amount of international cooperation that can be brought to bear on the world's problems is dependent upon the degree to which we move away from the familiar orientations of the "international arena" towards the sense of community implied by the notion of "global village."

However, even to speak of global cooperation is, in some quarters, to be dismissed as naive.   While this is an excessively harsh assessment, it is certainly true that we have barely undertaken the journey.

Also, although we are generally aware, as we move up our "continuum of cooperation," that complexities increase and cooperation becomes more difficult, such general awareness is insufficient. It is important to have a realistic understanding of just how difficult the challenge is. To approach that understanding, we should return for a moment to our point of departure.   It will be recalled that Kanter described cooperation at the level of the individual firm as "inherently fragile."   To realize that collaborative arrangements are fragile even at the lowest level is to be keenly aware of the increasing brittleness of such arrangements at higher levels, and thus to have a sober appreciation of the magnitude of the challenge confronting us as we attempt our journey up the continuum, striving to overcome the increasing potential for failure along the way.

In spite of that potential, we are compelled, by a growing awareness and understanding of the dangers and promises of interdependence, to accept the challenge. Inevitably, interdependence will grow. The dangers cannot be wished away.   The promises beckon. Thus, we will need business, academic, governmental and other leaders with the kind of broad vision and commitment Riesman has written about to inspire and manage the collaborative efforts required to ameliorate problems and to move us from conflict towards cooperation.

ABOUT THE EDITOR

HERBERT L. SAWYER is professor of government at Bentley College and a fellow of the Russian Research Center, Harvard University. His Ph.D. is from The Fletcher School Of Law And Diplomacy. Among his works is Soviet Perceptions of the Oil Factor in U.S. Foreign Policy: The Middle East-Gulf Region.